D1233658

# Transfer
# of Learning

# Transfer
# of
# Learning
## Cognition, Instruction, and Reasoning

### Robert E. Haskell
Department of Psychology
University of New England
Biddeford, Maine

## ACADEMIC PRESS

A Harcourt Science and Technology Company

San Diego    San Francisco    New York    Boston    London    Sydney    Tokyo

PROPERTY OF
BAKER COLLEGE OF OWOSSO

*The sponsoring editor for this book was Nikki Levy, the editorial coordinator was Barbara Makinster, the production editor was Eileen Favorite. The cover was designed by Cathy Reynolds. Composition was done by The Composing Room Kalamazoo, MI and the book was printed and bound by Edwards Brothers in Ann Arbor, MI.*

This book is printed on acid-free paper. ∞

Academic Press
*A Harcourt Science and Technology Company*
525 B Street, Suite 1900, San Diego, California 92101-4495, USA
http://www.academicpress.com

Academic Press
Harcourt Place, 32 Jamestown Road, London NW1 7BY, UK
http://www.academicpress.com

Library of Congress Catalog Card Number: 00-102889

International Standard Book Number: 0-12-330595-0

PRINTED IN THE UNITED STATES OF AMERICA
00   01   02   03   04   05   EB   9   8   7   6   5   4   3   2   1

# Contents

# What Transfer of Learning Is

## 1. THE STATE OF EDUCATION AND THE DOUBLE TRANSFER OF LEARNING PARADOX

## 2. TRANSFER OF LEARNING: WHAT IT IS AND WHY IT'S IMPORTANT

## 3. TO TEACH OR NOT TO TEACH FOR TRANSFER: THAT IS THE QUESTION

## 4. TRANSFER AND EVERYDAY REASONING: PERSONAL DEVELOPMENT, CULTURAL DIVERSITY, AND DECISION MAKING

## 5. A BRIEF HISTORY OF TRANSFER AND TRANSFER AS HISTORY

# What Makes Transfer of Learning Work

## 6. KNOWLEDGE BASE AND TRANSFER: ON THE USEFULNESS OF USELESS KNOWLEDGE

## 7. THE SPIRIT OF TRANSFER AND PERSONALITY: MOTIVATION, MEANING, AND EMOTION

## 8. CULTURES AND CONTEXTS OF TRANSFER: SOCIAL ORIGINS AND SUPPORT SYSTEMS

## 9. WHEN THEORY FAILS: THE IMPORTANCE OF A LEARNER'S THEORETICAL KNOWLEDGE FOR TRANSFER

# Foreword

The Educational Psychology Series is adding a new dimension to its collection of edited volumes. Robert Haskell has authored an exciting new book that will appeal to the educator, to the researcher, and to anyone concerned with how we as human beings cope and adjust to our world. *Transfer of Learning: Cognition, Instruction, and Reasoning* is a creative work with unlimited potential for impacting the way we view the learning process. Through a unique combination of academic scholarship and an engaging writing style, Robert has written a book that not only challenges current learning theory, but is intuitively appealing to the casual observer of human behavior.

Within psychology and education, transfer of learning has been one of the most enduring issues for scholars, researchers, and teachers. Though some academicians have suggested that "transfer is dead," Haskell has provided a frame of reference for a reconstruction of our view of transfer. This exciting new perspective of the transfer process will have an impact, similar to that of Howard Gardner's book *Multiple Intelligences*, on educational practices in the classroom.

*Gary D. Phye*
Series Editor

# Introduction

*When we have lived any time, and have been accustomed to the uniformity of nature, we acquire a general habit, by which we always transfer the known to the unknown, and conceive the latter to resemble the former.*

—DAVID HUME, *An Essay Concerning Human Understanding*[1]

*Psychology's first general law should, I suggest, be a law of generalization.*

—ROGER N. SHEPARD[2]

Transfer of learning is our use of past learning when learning something new and the application of that learning to both similar and new situations. At first glance, it's very simple. Transfer of learning, however, is the very foundation of learning, thinking, and problem solving. Despite the importance of transfer of learning, research findings over the past nine decades clearly show that as individuals, and as educational institutions, we have failed to achieve transfer of learning on any significant level.

Time and again in the literature, beginning with the work of Edward Thorndike (1874–1949) in 1901 to the present, the verdict has been as Douglas Detterman observes: "If there is a general conclusion to be drawn from the research on transfer, it is that the lack of general transfer is pervasive and surprisingly consistent."[3] In the preface to their edited book, *Teaching for Transfer*,[4] Ann McKeough, Judy Lupart, and Anthony Marini lament

> Transfer of learning is universally accepted as the ultimate aim of teaching. However, achieving this goal is one of teaching's most formidable problems. Researchers have been more successful in showing how people fail to transfer learning than they have been in producing it, and teachers and employers alike bemoan students' inability to use what they have learned.[5]

The implications of this general failure are serious not only for a society increasingly dependent on what is called "knowledge workers," as opposed to skilled workers, but for the democratic process as well. The Founding Fathers of the U.S. Constitution understood that for a democracy to work well an informed populace is required; the term *informed* includes the ability to think and reason well. Transfer of learning underlies the ability to think, reason, plan, and to make good decisions. So if this is the case, why write a book on transfer of learning? Is this book going to lament past failures, cry about our bleak future, or just offer a postgame motivational pep talk? The answer is no to all of these.

In the foreword to a 1987 book, Edwin Fleishman states, "Given the centrality of the topic in so many areas of basic research and application, it is indeed surprising that there has been no comprehensive book on the subject."[6] I think we now know more than enough to offer workable solutions to the transfer of learning problem. As two psychologists of a recent research-based and technical book on transfer of learning note, "It is especially timely to revive interest in transfer now because detailed, comprehensive theories of skill acquisition now exist."[7] Research data on transfer are now available and have awaited an appropriate compilation.

Since the classic work of psychologist Edward Thorndike in 1901, interest in the subject has waned within the fields of psychology and education. However, there is now considerable rigorous psychological research on transfer, with most of the research coming from the fields of instructional and cognitive psychology, the latter a subfield of psychology concerned with investigating how we think, reason, and process information. Though it's generally agreed that transfer of learning is most elusive to demonstrate, it is, nevertheless, the key to all effective instruction and learning. For education to be effective, then, curricula must be designed with our eyes focused on transfer of learning, particularly for poorer students. For as Carl Bereiter observes "transfer is usually poorest with students who need it most."[8] And I should add, they need it most because they are poorest at transfer.

Although I do not intend to rediscover the transfer of learning wheel, I do intend to reinvent transfer of learning and revise what it means to think. I will show that the very structure of thinking and learning *is* transfer of learning by presenting a prescriptive theory of learning and instruction that opposes what many colleagues and the popular educational zeitgeist believe to be true. By and large, the instructional zeitgeist is to instill skills, techniques, and strategies. This approach to transfer of learning has not worked; indeed, it cannot work. There are no quick fixes.

Although this is a how-to book for increasing transfer of learning, it is not a how-to book in the traditional sense. The book explains why the prevailing educational view of instruction emphasizing specific learning strategies and teaching techniques does not result in significant transfer. The book is a prescriptive how-to book in providing eleven principles with their research-based justification. These principles must be fostered in the learner at least concurrently with the application of strategies and instructional techniques. Finally, this book is a necessary introduction to all instructional approaches and methods.

In brief, then, this book suggests that in order to achieve significant transfer of learning, much more than the current approach to education, which emphasizes techniques and algorithmic-like learning strategies, is required. For significant learning and transfer to occur the following 11 principles are required:

1. Acquire a large primary knowledge base in the area in which transfer is required (see Chapter 7).
2. Acquire some level of knowledge base in subjects outside the primary area (see Chapter 7).
3. Understand what transfer of learning is and how it works.
4. Understand the history in the area(s) that transfer is wanted (see Chapter 5).
5. Acquire motivation, or more specifically, a "spirit of transfer" (see Chapter 8).
6. Develop an orientation to think and encode learning in transfer terms (see Chapters 7 and 8).
7. Create cultures of transfer or support systems (see Chapter 9).
8. Understand the theory underlying the area(s) in which we want to transfer (see Chapter 10).
9. Engage in hours of practice and drill (see Chapter 11).
10. Allow time for the learning to incubate.
11. Observe and read the works of people who are exemplars and masters of transfer thinking.

At first glance, these 11 requirements for transfer of learning may not seem to say anything new, but the following chapters will show otherwise. These requirements constitute a general theory of transfer. Learning strategies alone will not suffice to ensure transfer. Strategies are, however, often important in augmenting transfer of learning. Learning strategies and heuristics constitute what I consider a special theory of transfer.

The problem of achieving transfer of learning is both simple and complex. I don't intend to rail against the schools, teachers, and teaching methods. They are only a portion of a much larger and more fundamental set of problems. Other problems lie in our social values about the importance of education and learning and what we expect and think is necessary for students to learn. As many have pointed out over the years, the United States has an ambivalent relationship with education and learning.[9] We are an overly pragmatic society requiring instant success: not a useful prescription for transfer of learning.

The material in this book has been framed in terms of the classic label "transfer of learning," instead of other labels often used or related to it. Transfer of learning cuts across all educational domains and methodologies. Although many educational approaches, for example, constructivism, imply some of the ideas and principles presented in this book, they don't address transfer of learning directly. As Manfred Prenzel and Heinz Mandl note in their excellent review, "When dealing with the question under which circumstances knowledge is flexibly applicable, constructivists approach a typical problem of transfer without, however, referring systematically to the concept of 'transfer'."[10]

This book will not revisit material that most other books on learning have covered. It will be confined to learning as it directly pertains to transfer of learning, for it's through transfer of learning that we reach the very foundations of learning itself. Only those studies considered to be seminal and/or representative of the relevant areas will be documented as part of this discussion.

In order to lay a foundation for this approach to transfer, voluminous, complex, and technical research findings had to be reviewed. Accordingly, specialized and technical findings have been translated into everyday terms. Integrative scholarship carries a cost, however. Just as there are dangers in translating a poem into a different language, something is always lost in the translation.

In addition, I should note that individual studies can no doubt be found that may not support some details of this approach to transfer. The conclusions presented here, however, are derived from a broad array of research in multiple contexts over a number of years and should be judged in this light. Theories are not disproven on the basis of contradictory finding of a few studies conducted in specific situations.

This translation of research into everyday terms should not be seen as rejecting experimental, technical, and other statistical research. This book helps to lay out the key issues in the field in a way that reflects these complex findings. It also investigates some new problems and issues that need further review.

The building materials for the transfer of learning theory constructed here have been around for years; indeed, some of the material has been used in the construction of other small transfer theories. But no general transfer of learning edifice has been designed from these materials that integrates what we know about transfer into a useful prescriptive theory of learning and instruction. This book is meant to be a practical and general theory of transfer of learning and instruction and thinking as it applies to both classroom and everyday activities.

I speak not only from an academic research perspective, but from personal experience on the use and importance of transfer of learning, which must be accessible to everyone. I began my career with a poor educational background and history. My early interest in transfer of learning was a spontaneous survival strategy. I was interested in thinking and teaching with analogies and metaphors at a time when both were generally considered "literary" devices. I have developed transfer of learning exercises for both my lecture courses and small, experiential group classes, where students learn about groups by actually functioning as a group. Since my early interest in analogical reasoning, cognitive psychology researchers have recognized the importance of what has become known as analogical transfer. Considerable work has been done in this area. I should also note that I'm not an education theorist. My professional training and experience is in social and cognitive psychology.

From my 25 years of creating instructional design and teaching college and university psychology courses to all ages, including many ethnic groups, and from my ongoing review of the research findings on the transfer of learning, there are three things I've learned: (a) there are no quick fixes or shortcuts to learning, (b) learning is hard work—which doesn't mean it can't be enjoyable, and (c) what is learned in everyday, instructional, and workplace settings tends to stay welded to those settings. The point is that transfer of learning is crucial for all those who would be learners, teachers, and designers of instructional problems at any level.

The failures in transfer of learning and the lack of development in the field are in large measure due to a lack of an adequate theoretical base. If the transfer of learning in educational and instructional psychology is to continue to play its historically significant role, researchers need theoretical development based squarely in empirical and experimental data. As one early researcher has stated, "There has probably never been an attempt to make a theoretical construct of transfer." With one historical exception, this statement remains valid. That exception was an early attempt to use stimulus generalization as a lower order explanatory principle for transfer of learning.

There are those, however, who see neither the requirement nor the justification for a general theory of transfer. At the risk of responding ad hominem, it seems that this view itself is the consequence of a failed transfer of learning, where an array of transfer phenomena are seen as separate entities instead of a general class of phenomena. Moreover, because of its complexity, some investigators are understandably pessimistic about developing a general theory of transfer, lamenting that "It's not clear that a single theory could exist to cover the range of phenomena to which the term might be and has been, applied."[11]

For years researchers have needed a more useful approach to the study of transfer of learning. As Lee Sechrest, an early psychological researcher and practitioner, said, it's been clear for some time that "a major difficulty in the design of studies related to conditions affecting generalization of training stems from the lack of any particularly useful theory."[12] He also recognized that a productive approach to the problem of transfer "depends on a more adequate theory than has heretofore been provided."[13]

Yet another researcher has emphasized that because transfer is at the core of the instructional process, "educational research and theory should have as a primary focus the understanding of the nature of transfer as well as an understanding of how to teach students to maximize transfer."[14] What Henry Ellis pointed out over 35 years ago remains valid today: perhaps, he says, "the most stressing impression that one receives from an examination of the current status of transfer is that it is relatively strong on empirical findings and somewhat weaker in the development of theory."[15] He goes on to point out that, with few exceptions, theory has tended to be of the functionalist type, characterized by a close adherence to data and an avoidance of extensive theory. Continuing the approaches of Edward Thorndike and Charles Osgood, Ellis himself stuck close to data and to experimental procedures in his 1965 book, suggesting that transfer of learning is based on similarity relations, and that the development of transfer of learning models will only occur after the development of better ways of measuring stimulus and response similarity.

In fact, the entire history of transfer of learning in terms of the identical elements model should be seen as the consequence of a lack of adequate theory development (see Chapters 5 and 10). However, in the 99 years of experimentation, based almost exclusively on identical elements models, better measuring of stimulus and response similarity has not yielded a theoretical base. Even now, in cognitive psychology and artificial intelligence, theoretical development is so closely tied to the individual datum that it isn't generally useful.

Theory development should be of primary (not secondary or tertiary) concern in the design of instructional methods and curriculum. In the field of artificial intelligence, which has been largely restricted to concrete operationalizing, Christopher Longuet-Higgins suggested that "the time has come, it seems, when the task of theory construction is altogether too intricate to be consigned to spare moments away from the laboratory; it is at least as much a discipline as good experimentation."[16] Developing a useful theory of transfer of learning instruction is imperative. This book is a response to the continuing failure of educational and cognitive theory to be useful to educators.

Psychology in the United States is well known for being quite different from psychology in Europe. American psychology considers itself closely tied to the "facts," whereas European psychology sees the merit of general theory development. Moreover, all theories need not be quantitative. In 1955, renowned physicist J. Robert Oppenheimer (1904–1967) addressed the American Psychological Association and warned that "it is not always tactful to try to quantify; it is not always clear that by measuring one has found something worth measuring." And that "as scientists," he said, "we are always faced with the problem of keeping the purity of academic and abstract research intact, while at the same time to nourish and be nourished by practice."[17] More recently, an artificial intelligence researcher argued that theoretical rigor is obtained by operationalizing one's definitions and by sticking as close to the data as possible. Or, he says, "One can be rigorous by taking measures to be sure that one's theoretical ideas are complete, consistent, and logically sound, and by bringing everyday knowledge to bear on the development of theoretical ideas."[18]

The great social psychologist Kurt Lewin (1890–1947) had a famous dictum: there's nothing so practical as good theory. Research on the transfer of learning needs not only a general theoretical conceptualization of the construct of transfer, but a sufficiently robust taxonomical system that generates development of phenomena, is capable of concrete verification procedures, and extends applied instructional research. Enough said.

This book is unique in many respects. First, the book is presented in an informal style for the general reader and teachers. Anyone interested in learning or who teaches in any situation could utilize this book.

Second, my research for this book included the transfer of learning over the past 99 years in the field of education, cognitive psychology, business, industrial training, and from other related fields, including applied and theoretical research on analogical transfer.

Third, the theory presented here unifies many terms and labels currently used in various fields that refer to the transfer of learning (e.g., generalization, analogical reasoning, isomorphic relations, etc.).

Fourth, by using a varied set of examples and illustrations, this book integrates transfer of learning as it's used in education, business, and industry. This aspect reflects the renewed emphasis on schools and the goal of teaching that transfers to the workplace.

Fifth, this book is not only about transfer of learning, but also about cognition—how the human mind reasons. Transfer of learning provides the most useful vehicle for explaining how we think.

Sixth, this book may be considered the missing link in the transfer of learning, educational, and training literatures on how to promote learning and thinking.

Seventh, this book presents a practical and integrative (but research-based) framework and theory of transfer of learning that shows how it can be promoted by educators and students in the classroom as well as increased in everyday life.

Eighth, this transfer approach to learning and instruction is an overarching theory. With certain exceptions relating to strictly technological subject matter, the theory of transfer presented here doesn't necessarily supersede or invalidate any current educational theory, technique, or instructional methods, though it may call for some revisions to them.

Ninth, this book presents a novel theory of transfer based on the evolution and structure of the brain. Any theory of transfer, any explanation of how and why transfer works, should be compatible with what we know about the brain. A theory of transfer that's based on neurological findings not only lends support to the importance of transfer and explanations of it, but may even help us to develop instructional methods for transfer. Currently, there exists no neurological theory of transfer (see chapters 11 and 12).

Last, a prominent feature of this book is the extensive use of short quotes by respected practitioners and researchers from many fields—both past and present. Quotations bring a contextual meaning and flavor to findings that are frequently lost in paraphrasing. In addition, quotations emphasize that the material isn't just the opinion of a single author but is solidly based on the works of many other researchers. In addition, these citations are important for this book, which owes so much to the dedication and often tedious pursuit of many scientific researchers. Accordingly, the chapters are designed to demonstrate the complexity of the subject matter. It's not enough to simply accept, for example, that knowledge base is important to transfer. As the theory presented here will demonstrate, it's necessary to understand why knowledge base is important to transfer and how it works. Thus the quotations also act as a kind of shorthand documentation and everyday database for the reader.

Finally, this book is consistent with what I have found to be fundamentally crucial for achieving general transfer of learning. Consequently, it involves covering a lot of material. This book is not meant to be just another supplement to what a reader may already know. The goal of this book is nothing less than to transform how a reader thinks about significant learning, instruction, and cognition.

# Notes

[1]Hume, D. (1961). *An essay concerning human understanding*. Oxford: Clarendon Press.

[2]Shepard, R. (1987). Toward a universal law of generalization for psychological science. *Science*, 237, 1273–1388. p. 1317.

[3]Detterman, D. K. (1993). The case for the prosecution: Transfer as an epiphenomenon. In D. K. Detterman & R. J. Sternberg (Eds.), *Transfer on trial: Intelligence, cognition, and instruction* (pp. 1–24). Norwood, NJ: Ablex, p. 18.

[4]McKeough, A., Lupart, J., & Marini, A. (Eds.) (1995). *Teaching for transfer: Fostering generalization in learning*. Mahwah, NJ: Lawrence Erlbaum.

[5]Ibid, p. vii.

[6]Fleishman, E. A. (1987). Foreword. In S. M. Cormier & J. D. Hagman (Eds.), *Transfer of learning contemporary research and application* (pp. xi–xvii). New York: Academic Press, p. xi.

[7]Singley, M. K., & Anderson, J. R. (1989). *The transfer of cognitive skill*. Cambridge, MA: Harvard University Press, p. 30.

[8]Bereiter, C. (1995). A dispositional view of transfer. In A. McKeough, J. Lupart, & A. Marini (Eds.), *Teaching for transfer: Fostering generalization in learning* (pp. 21–34). Mahwah, NJ: Lawrence Erlbaum Associates, p. 28.

[9]Emberley, P. C. (1995). *Values education and technology: The ideology of dispossession*. Toronto: University of Toronto Press; Trilling, L. (1948). *The liberal imagination*. New York: The Viking Press.

[10]Prenzel, M., & Mandl, H. (1992). Transfer of learning from a constructivist perspective. In D. H. Jonassen, T. M. Duffy, & J. Lowyck (Eds.), *Designing environments for constructive learning*. Heidelberg: Springer Verlag.

[11]Campione, J. C., A. M. Shapiro, & A. L. Brown (Eds.) (1995). Forms of transfer in community of learners: Flexible learning and understanding. In A. McKeough, J. Lupart, & A. Marini (Eds.), *Teaching for transfer: Fostering generalization in learning* (pp. 35–68). Mahwah, NJ: Lawrence Erlbaum Associates, p. 35.

[12]Sechrest, L. B. (1966). Transfer of therapeutic learning. In A. P. Goldstein, K. H. Heller, & L. B. Sechrest (Eds.), *Psychotherapy and the psychology of behavior change* (pp. 212–259). New York: John Wiley and Sons, p. 214.

[13]Ibid, p. 214.

[14]Haslerud, G. M. (1972). *Transfer, memory and creativity*. Minneapolis: University of Minnesota Press, p. vii.

[15]Ellis, H. C. (1965). *The transfer of learning*. New York: MacMillan Company.

[16]Longuet-Higgins, H. C. (1981). Artificial intelligence—A new theoretical psychology? *Cognition*, 10, 197–200, p. 198.

[17]Oppenheimer, R. (1956). Analogy in science. *American Psychologist*, 11, 127–135, p. 128, 135.

[18]Pylyshyn, Z. W. (1979). Metaphorical imprecision and the "top-down" research strategy, in A. Ortony (Ed.), *Metaphor and thought* (pp. 420–436). London: Cambridge University Press, p. 429.

PART

**I**

# What Transfer of Learning Is

# The State of Education and the Double Transfer of Learning Paradox

*There is no more important topic in the whole psychology of learning than transfer of learning . . . practically all educational and training programs are built upon the fundamental premise that human beings have the ability to transfer what they have learned from one situation to another.*

—JAMES DESSE, 1958, *The Psychology of Learning*[1]

For some years now, many students who have arrived in my classes with A and B averages from high school college-preparatory programs are unable to read a college introductory psychology text written on a high school level or lower. When asked to write an analytical paper, they say they have never been asked to think. When given different forms of the *same* question on an exam, they fail to transfer their answers to virtually identical questions, even after having been constantly reinforced throughout the entire course with multiple examples. My experience isn't unique; it's been reported by faculty from third-rate universities to the Gothic classrooms of Harvard. In addition, businesses have lamented that both high school and college graduates are not able to adequately read, write, and think, let alone engage in productive transfer of learning. And this is just for openers. Something is profoundly wrong.

The aim of all education, from elementary, secondary, vocational, and industrial training, to higher education, is to apply what we learn in different contexts, and to recognize and extend that learning to completely new situations. Collectively, this is called *transfer of learning*. Indeed, it's the very meaning of learning itself. Although some disagree,[2] most researchers and educational practitioners, whether "liberal" or "conservative," agree—a rare event, indeed—that meaningful transfer of learning is among the most—if not *the* most—fundamental issue in all of education.[3] They also agree that transfer of learning seldom occurs. The "liberal" psychologist, Howard Gardner of Harvard's Project Zero, author of numerous well-received books for the general public, including *The Unschooled Mind: How Children Think and How Schools Should Teach,*[4] and the "conservative" Columbia University philosopher, Allan Bloom, in his *The Closing of the American Mind,*[5] not to mention William Bennett's, *The Book of Virtues,*[6] and E. D. Hirsch's *Cultural Literacy,*[7] all lament the poor state of education in the United States. Where these authors part company is on the issue of how to best achieve transfer of learning. An extreme approach in the liberal education camp has been typically to give students unstructured free reign for self-discovery; a corresponding conservative approach has been typically to demand very structured drill in the basics. Neither approach has worked very well. Whatever educational fads come and go, the transfer of learning problem remains with us like an antibiotic-resistant bacterium. No matter what we attack it with, it just won't go away.

## A WORLD AT RISK: NATIONAL REPORTS

Concern about mismanagement and misinstruction in the U.S. educational system isn't new. The popular press has always been on top of this perennial issue. In a long line of such articles, *Time Magazine,*[8] in a special report, "The Costly Crisis in Our Schools," noted that the crisis continues almost 12 years after the landmark federal study "A Nation At Risk: The Imperative for Educational Reform" warned as follows:

> We report to the American people that while we can take justifiable pride in what our schools and colleges have historically accomplished and contributed to the United States and the well-being of its people, the educational foundations of our society are presently being eroded by a rising tide of mediocrity that threatens our very future as a Nation and a people. What was unimaginable a generation ago has begun to occur—others are matching and surpassing our educational attainments.[9]

The report revealed that on 19 academic tests, U.S. students were never first or even second, and, compared with other industrialized nations, U.S. students scored lowest seven times. Twenty-three million U.S. adults are functionally illiterate as measured by simple tests of everyday reading, writing, and comprehension, with a functional illiteracy among our minority youth that may be as high as 40%. Many 17-year-olds do not possess the "higher order" intellectual skills that they need, with nearly 40% unable to draw inferences from written material; only one-fifth can write a persuasive essay, and only one-third are able to solve a mathematics problem requiring multiple steps.

An increasing number of professors (myself included) complain that before teaching their college-level subject matter, they have to teach students to read and write. Consequently, there's an increasing number of remedial (not-for-credit) writing and mathematics courses on college and university campuses. Achievement scores of students graduating from college are also lower, and business leaders complain that they have to spend millions of dollars on remedial education and training programs on reading, writing, spelling, and computation. These deficiencies come at a time when the demand is increasing for highly skilled and flexible workers who have the ability to process large amounts of information. We continue to remain a nation at risk.

Evidence from a number of recent studies clearly suggests that students complete 12 or 13 years of public schooling and can demonstrate only a superficial understanding of the concepts, relationships, and procedural strategies fundamental to the subjects they have studied. They can graduate from college without ever developing competence in thinking.[10] We expect that there will be transfer of learning, for example, from a high school course in introductory psychology to a college-level introduction to psychology course. It has been known for years, however, that students who enter college having taken a high school psychology course do no better than students who didn't take psychology in high school[11] Some students who have taken a psychology course in high school do even worse in the college course. All this, in spite of the fact that the education budget is the biggest line item in most state budgets, and despite the fact that the total U.S. spending on education for 1992–1993 was $458 billion, and in 1994–1995 it was an estimated $509 billion.[12]

On any day, approximately 200,000 individuals in the military are involved in some form of training. According to a survey published in *Training* magazine, American companies spend over $4 billion on training hardware, materials, seminars, conferences, and consultants. As sizable as this figure may be, it doesn't consider expenditures associated with in-house staff and equipment. When these costs are added, the total annual expenditure for training in the United States lies somewhere around $70 billion.[13] These expenditures are supposed to produce a learner who can transfer his or her learning, to produce a mentally adaptable learner. An adaptable employee, says one early report on occupational adaptability and transferable skills, is "one who can generalize, transfer, or form associations so that the skills, attitudes, knowledge, and personal characteristics that have been learned or developed in one context can be readily used in a different context."[14] Unfortunately, most of the research on employee training clearly shows that although "millions of dollars are spent on training in the public sector . . . there is little empirical evidence linking training to improved job behavior or employee attitude."[15] Something is wrong somewhere.

The issue of transfer, then, is an extremely serious one for the public schools, for business, and for society. It's especially important given findings that the average person will change vocations (not merely job locations) five times in the span of his or her life. The particular information and concrete strategies learned to navigate one's chosen profession quickly become outmoded, not once but many times. We need to teach information and thinking that will transfer. Writing in the *Journal of Vocational and Technical Education*, Jean Bryan and her colleagues observe that "as the number of coordinated training programs between corporations and school increase, accountability and transfer to the work environment becomes increasingly important."[16] Thus, the concern about transfer of learning becomes increasingly salient in a world where rapid scientific and technological change often penalizes those who are narrowly skilled and mentally inflexible. Most of these failures are not found only in the United States. They can be found in Canada, and elsewhere, as Peter Emberley and Waller Newell have so vividly described and documented in their book, *Bankrupt Education*.[17]

The United Kingdom funded the Pegasus Program, a program specifically directed at transferring skills learned in the schools to the workplace. The initial funding level was 20 million pounds. The U.S. government, too, launched a similar school-based transfer program. British researcher, Carol Myers, writing in "Research Core Skills and Transfer in the Youth Training Schemes: A Field study of Trainee Motor Mechanics," observes that "the growing popularity of broad-based approaches to training has raised important new practical and theoretical questions about how to train for transfer" but she concludes that "it is not clear how these aims can be achieved."[18] Citing field research findings,[19] she suggests that there is "little directly relevant evidence on the core skills approach." The core skills approach to transfer of learning, while intuitively appealing, she says

> is inadequate in promoting occupational flexibility. Although its aim to promote the recognition of similarities across skills is admirable, it is by no means obvious which aspects of tasks need to be similar for transfer of learning to take place. While the core skills list uses common descriptions for tasks and jobs these are not based on any coherent theory of the relationships of skills and jobs and are of unknown validity.[20]

In England transferable skills is the subject of increasing numbers of articles and books.[21]

Nor is the problem simply not enough money. The philosopher, Anthony Flew, maintains,

> In Britain we have to scratch around for the evidence showing only that a huge increase in resource input has quite certainly not been rewarded with any corresponding improvements in educational output, in the U.S. it is possible, from compellingly clear and hard evidence, to know that a similarly vast increase in expenditure *has yielded not just no improvement at all but a quite disastrous decline* [italics added].[22]

This is serious business.

At a time when we are becoming increasingly concerned with teaching science at all levels of schooling, one educational researcher has noted that "although transfer of learning is recognized as a major teaching goal, only rarely has science education research taken a direct look at transfer, i.e., how it comes about, or what blocks it, or how to teach for it."[23] Since these words were written, however, there has been renewed interest for transfer of learning in science instruction. But another researcher has recently observed that science courses still seldom show "transfer much beyond the problems presented"[24] to students in the classroom. In other words, at best, what's learned in the classroom, stays in the classroom.

Moreover, technology in education is increasing at a rapid rate, especially the use of computers. In an attempt to achieve transfer of learning, technological methods claiming to have a payoff, in fact offer only a promissory note, a note that's unlikely to be redeemable in the near future. It comes as no surprise that in a technological society, we turn to technology to solve all our ills. The most pervasive of these methods is the increasing trend toward modeling the brain and instruction on computer programming (computational) methods. Many believe that computers will be centrally involved in the salvation of education. But computers are not the educational equivalent of the second coming. Transfer of learning is. As I will show in chapter 3, computational methods not only don't work, they can't work. I say this not being a humanistic technophobe, but an enthusiastic fan of computer technology. (I love my computer—and just about every other electronic gadget on the market).

Earl Butterfield and Gregory Nelson, writing in the journal *Educational Technology, Research & Development*, also warn that "solid research to test the uniqueness of particular technologies as aids to education *will capitalize on basic understandings of transfer* [italics in original]."[25] The authors further warn that "unless we use available theories of learning and transfer in concert with sound research methods, we will not discover the educational potential of technology, or indeed of schooling itself."[26] They further note that "past comparisons between technologically innovative and prosaic education usually have not reflected favorably on the technological. The raw comparisons that have favored technology confounded it with teaching method, thereby making it impossible to attribute findings uniquely to technology."[27] Furthermore, other research shows that the early hopes that teaching computer programming languages, like Logo, would transfer to better thinking by students have been clearly shown to not work. The reverse, however, *is* true: ability for transfer of learning does facilitate the learning of Logo.[28] In short, it's not technology that will promote transfer of learning, but transfer of learning that will promote the effective application of technology to education.

Writing in *The Chronicle of Higher Education* on the curriculum assessment movement in the United States Harley Sacks and Jon Westling observe that it

> is based on a fundamental misdiagnosis of the malaise of American higher education. Does anyone really believe that the failure of colleges and universities to produce adequately educated young people is the consequence of our failure to develop precise instruments to measure what we are doing? Or that true education requires elaborate technical criteria to evaluate its effectiveness?[29]

Unfortunately, some educators do believe that the problem is a methodological one. It's not. It's a human one based in evolution.

The human brain has evolved over millions of years. During most of this time, the environment has not demanded of our brain what our modern Information Age demands. At no time in history have we been required to process the amount of new information that we do today. We process this information with a brain that has not yet sufficiently evolved to cope with the modern demands of the Information Age. The brain is an old and wise organ that has its own evolutionary reasons for functioning the way it does. The last evolutionary update was probably over a hundred thousand years ago. There's thus an evolutionary lag between the development of our brain and our current need to process large amounts of information. For the most part we have an ancient brain trying to function in a Space Age. Transfer of learning is a way to shorten this evolutionary lag.

Again, beyond a minimal level, the literature clearly shows that we've failed to achieve significant transfer of learning, historically or currently, on any level of education. Over 20 years ago, one author observed, "Common is the lament that graduate schools are turning out specialists rather than the broadly educated teachers needed for the development of the next generation. At the root of this problem may be the neglect of transfer."[30] Of course things have changed in the last twenty years—they've gotten worse. In psychology, for example, Robyn Dawes recently noted that "the quality of the training of clinical psychologists . . . has deteriorated rapidly in the past several years."[31] I should note here that there's every reason to suspect that psychology isn't unique in this regard.

Our future depends on our ability to transfer what we learn, for it's the transfer of our learning that creates our understanding of peoples, that creates technological innovation, that creates scientific discovery, that creates our competitive and cooperative edge in a global market, and understanding in an ethnically diverse culture. As Lauren Resnick, a well-known educational researcher, has observed,

> The search for teachable, general learning abilities is as old as the history of education. The issues of what such abilities are and how they are acquired have occupied the attention of psychologists in every phase of the discipline's history. Educational research has long addressed this question under the rubric of transfer. In a sense, transfer is the Holy Grail of educators—something we are ever in search of, that hope pretends lies just beyond the next experiment or reform program.[32]

We haven't found the Holy Grail, of course. I might add that our failure to find it in more recent times is because we've been too busy searching for the golden fleece: Simple learning strategies, which, of course, we also have failed to find. Perhaps a better analogy is that transfer is not education's equivalent to the Holy Grail, but to the Ark of the Covenant. It's transfer of learning that not only creates the learning of any content material, and its extended application, but it's the essence of poetry, and it goes to the very core of who we are. (See chapters 4 and 7.)*

---

*For economy of expression, from this point on I will use the single word *transfer* instead of the phrase *transfer of learning*, except when it seems more appropriate to use the complete phrase.

## CORPORATE BUSINESS TRAINING AND TRANSFER

In their book, *Transfer of Training*, two well-known corporate trainers, Mary Broad and John Newstrom, emphasize that "For . . . organizations to remain competitive in the global marketplace, and to develop the highly skilled workforce that can contribute to solutions for the world's pressing problems, improving transfer of training must become . . . top priority."[33] As Frank Pratzner concluded years ago, occupational adaptability is based upon individuals "who can *generalize, transfer,* [italics added] or form associations so that the skills, attitudes, knowledge and personal characteristics that have been learned or developed in one context can be readily used in a different context."[34] I concur. But as I have documented in the first chapter of my book, *Reengineering Corporate Training: Intellectual Capital and Transfer of Learning,*[35] beyond a—and this is, at best—very concrete technical level of training, most business training programs have failed to demonstrate transfer of learning.[36]

For a number of years there has been a shift in the instructional needs of the corporate sector. In 1989 Peter Drucker presaged a shift in the workforce. He saw the emergence of what he called "the post-business society, with a work force dominated by knowledge workers."[37] In 1962, Warren Bennis, one of the academic-based gurus of organizational and business management training, prophesied that "the organization of tomorrow, heavily influenced by the growth of science and technology and manned by an increasing number of professionals, appears to have the necessary requirements for constructing organizations based on inquiry."[38] When these words were written, they sounded to many as just so much ivory tower theorizing. But such organizations are now realities. An organization based on inquiry *is* currently called a learning organization. Peter Senge, perhaps the current leading business management consultant, in his seminal book *The Fifth Discipline: The Art and Practice of the Learning Organization,*[39] outlines the shift from an Industrial Age model of a business organization to one based on the necessity of surviving in the Information Age. This new organization is the learning organization. Transfer ability is a necessity for such organizations. There's a missing piece, however, in the learning organization literature: the transfer of learning.

## THE DOUBLE TRANSFER OF LEARNING
## PARADOX: IMPORTANCE

The concept of transfer of learning has been wrapped in a kind of double paradox. The first paradox[1] is this: Although transfer has been almost universally recognized as fundamental to all learning and must therefore occur all of the time, the history of research findings on transfer suggests it seldom occurs in instructional settings. The history of transfer of learning, says Wilbert McKeachie, is that it "is paradoxical . . . of when we want it, we do not get it.

Yet it occurs all of the time."[40] Part of the problem of transfer is that our learning tends to be welded to a place (e.g., learning in a classroom or a particular everyday context) or to a subject matter (e.g., when learning mathematics doesn't transfer to physics). Most teachers, however, would settle for students learning how to calculate the area of a square in their classroom and then being able to transfer this to figure how much carpet is needed at home to cover the student's bedroom floor.

But when I say that transfer seldom occurs, I am telling a half truth (the most important half, however). The other half is that transfer takes place every day in most situations. Yet, general transfer from instructional settings and "significant" transfer in everyday settings, as well as transfer leading to invention and discovery, seldom seem to occur.

It is important at this point to instantiate the significance and scope of transfer of learning. To do this, I will present a series of summarizing quotes gathered throughout the transfer literature by historically recognized educators and researchers as well as current researchers and educators. The quotes, which span nearly the entire history of transfer, will serve as an index of the transfer paradox: Given the importance of transfer and the prevalence of everyday transfer—we have failed to significantly achieve it. Since the beginning of research on transfer, virtually every educational and cognitive researcher has repeatedly pointed out that

> there is no more important topic in the whole of psychology of learning than transfer of learning.... Practically all educational and training programs are built upon the fundamental premise that human beings have the ability to transfer what they have learned from one situation to another.... The basic psychological problem in the transfer of learning pervades the whole of the psychology of human training.... There is no point to education apart from transfer.[41]

All learning involves transfer from prior learning to a greater or lesser degree.[42] One early researcher noted "there is no complex psychological function or event which is not in some way a function of transfer of training."[43] Another early researcher asserted, "The concept of transfer occupies a critical position in any theory attempting to relate learning to human ability"[44]; indeed, "After small amounts of learning ... every instance of learning is a function of the already learned organization of the subject; that is, all learning is influenced by transfer."[45] "A theory of instruction," says Harvard's Jerome Bruner, "is principally concerned with how to arrange environments to optimize learning according to various criteria—to optimize transfer."[46]

Ann Brown and Richard Campione observe that "transfer is one of the enduring issues in the history of psychology, assumed to be central to learning and development, but surprisingly little understood."[47] Says James Royer, "There are few topics more central to the education process than the transfer of learning. ... despite the importance of transfer, the topic has been neglected in recent years."[48] Transfer is involved in just about every cognitive and intellectual function. Yet another researcher notes "reasoning ability, intellectual power, mastery of the great disciplines, functional skills in problem solving—whatever the name, the aim is transfer."[49] Still yet another observes, "Transfer is also integral to the concepts of "learning how to learn" and "learning sets."[50] J. Mcgeoch asserts:

> The learning of complex abstract, meaningful material and the solution of problems by means of ideas (reasoning) are to a great extent functions of transfer. Where the subject 'sees into' the fundamental relations of a problem or has insight, transfer seems to be a major contributing condition.[51]

Gick and Holyoak believe that "understanding the mechanism of transfer is inextricably linked to our knowledge of human memory, learning, categorization, reasoning and problem solving."[52] Similarly, Wilbert McKeachie, well known for his research and educational leadership, states, "Transfer is involved in all learning, remembering, problem solving and cognitive activities."[53]

Moreover, transfer figures prominently in the "new wave" of interest in instruction of critical thinking. Early in the critical thinking movement in education, it was noted that "transfer is integrally involved in teaching critical thinking and problem solving."[54] Says Wilbert McKeachie, "When faculty members talk about teaching critical thinking, problem solving, or reasoning, they typically are referring to teaching students to use their learning in new situations to solve problems."[55] In language learning, because nearly every rule or principle has the potential to produce both positive and negative transfer, much of the concern over the different methods of teaching language involves transfer. Even the logical concept of inference is based on the "carrying over" or the transfer of meaning. "A theory of transfer is of necessity a theory of learning and inference,"[56] observe Mary Gick and Keith Holyoak. In recent years, what are called metacognitive learning strategies (i.e., strategies involving a learner's decision whether to use a previously learned rule or strategy, and how to adapt it to a new situation) have also been thought to promote transfer. But one researcher has suggested the reverse; that such metacognitive methods "might be more likely discovered in the context of transfer paradigms."[57] Psychotherapeutic processes are also heavily dependent on transfer of learning, sufficiently so to lead one well-known therapist, thirty years ago, to note, "it is strange that so little systematic attention has been paid to transfer of learning research as it might bear on psychotherapy."[58] Thus many practitioners recognize that transfer of learning continues to be an "issue of practicality."[59]

In a recent issue of the *National Association of Secondary School Principles*, David Lohman recognizes that "transfer is part of the hidden agenda for enrichment activities when we hope that, through participation, the student will develop an interest in music, or art, or sport that will enrich future life as well. Thus, in one way or another, transfer is an important, if not the most important goal of education."[60] Finally, two prominent cognitive psychologists note that the significance of transfer goes beyond its importance as an instructional process; rather "the study of transfer is a stringent but necessary test for all comprehensive theories of cognition."[61] Transfer, then, cuts across all educational domains and methodologies.

Transfer is not just simply a teaching or learning strategy: I am talking about serious implications here for mental functioning. The succinct words of one contemporary researcher perhaps sums up this section the best: "Everyone believes in transfer."[62] But there are serious glitches in its workings.

## THE DOUBLE TRANSFER OF LEARNING
## PARADOX: FAILURE

Having now established the importance of transfer, it's equally important to look at our failure to achieve it. Because the failures are so profound, and lest readers think I am exaggerating and overstating the case, I will again let researchers and practitioners speak for themselves. Critics may undoubtedly find a few studies (of varying degrees of methodological rigor) that appear to contradict the following corpus of failures, but the general validity and consistency of the findings, which span multiple disciplines using different methodological designs, from varied learning settings—including laboratory and classroom—and which span over nine decades, remain valid. I should note, however, that despite these dismal conclusions, I'm not pessimistic. On the contrary, I am in principle—note that I stress *in principle*—optimistic.

The years of transfer failures, note Richard Clark and Alexander Voogel, are "a curiosity since the literature on transfer is one of the oldest in education. . . . The evidence that our newest instructional technologies typically result in only near transfer of learning is disturbing."[63] Indeed, there remains an enormous "gap between our technical knowledge about transfer and our aspirations about enhancing and promoting it en masse in general education and vocational education and training."[64] Equal to the recognition of it's importance, from Thorndike's classic research on transfer in 1901,[65] to current findings, virtually every educational and cognitive researcher has repeatedly pointed out that "The hopes for the use of transfer as a means of applying old learning in new situations have been repeatedly dashed on the rocks of critical experiments."[66] Again, Douglas Detterman, whom I quoted in the Introduction, concludes his review of findings on transfer by saying, "If there is a general conclusion to be drawn from the research on transfer, it is that the lack of general transfer is pervasive and surprisingly consistent. . . . Significant transfer is probably rare and accounts for very little human behavior."[67] Two authors writing in the *Encyclopedia of Educational Research* observe that "with some notable exceptions, most investigators have ceased to look or hope for global theories of transfer."[68] Strong words. But only the tip of the iceberg. Other researchers and practitioners conclude similarly.

Two prominent cognitive scientists, Mark Singley and John Anderson, have observed that "there has as yet been no strong demonstration of the existence of general transfer. . . . [A] long line of research (starting with the work of Thorndike and James) casts a gloomy pall on the prospect of general transfer. . . . The problem faced by the architect of general transfer is a difficult one."[69] In a more recent edited book on transfer, Anthony Marin and Randy Genereux note: "Unfortunately, achieving significant transfer of learning has proven to be a difficult chore. Dating back to the beginning of this century, the research literature on transfer is replete with reports of failure."[70] These transfer failures span the entire educational spectrum.

In teaching problem solving, one recent report entitled, "On the Limited Evidence for the Effectiveness of Teaching General Problem-Solving Strategies," the author concludes, "There is very little evidence of successfully teaching general problem-solving techniques in mathematics education."[71] Another researcher concludes, "There is relatively little empirical evidence concerning transfer of formal problem-solving procedures."[72] Yet another observes that the effectiveness of problem-solving programs appears to be "limited to near transfer situations where the test problems are similar to those encountered during training. Evidence for far transfer is generally lacking."[73] Still another finds from her review of such academic and popular programs that "there are no outstanding documented cases where general problem-solving instruction has produced obviously noticeable gains in learning."[74]

As the teaching of problem solving goes, so goes the teaching of learning strategies. As one researcher notes, "Many of the learning strategies programs have nonempirical foundations, provide relatively superficial strategy training (usually only a subset of the essential learning concepts), are evaluated against nonspecific criteria (such as grade-point average), and consequently, lack specific evidence on which to base modifications."[75] Michael Pressley, Barbara Snyder, and Teresa Carigilia-Bull note, "The main problem is that we know very little about whether these programs work or how they work. . . . All the studies have methodological difficulties that make it impossible to accept the evidence uncritically."[76]

After reviewing numerous programs purporting to successfully teach learning strategies that transfer, the authors conclude that

> there is no convincing evidence that any of the six approaches to strategy instruction outlined here produce generally competent strategy users, although some are certainly more promising than others. There are many strategies, much metacognition, and a massive declarative knowledge base that must be mastered. The development of good strategy use takes years.[77]

And Laura Resnick's research suggests that "most programs . . . report successes only in terms of improvements in the particular skills that students practiced. . . . This leaves us without evidence as to the extent to which such programs can produce transfer to the kinds of performances that are actually valued either in school or in practical life."[78] Somewhat the optimist, Mc-Keachie concludes,

> Unfortunately, many of the programs for developing intellectual abilities have demonstrated effectiveness so far as student's achievement on tests very similar to those upon which training occurred, but it is less common to find convincing examples of "far-transfer," particularly far-transfer extending over longer periods of time following the training.[79]

In the area of learning disabilities, the transfer findings are no different.

Lynn Gelzheiser's research, one of the most extensive strategy-training studies with learning-disabled students, is consistent with other findings, and indicates that transfer of strategies and skills isn't readily achieved.[80] And the currently popular educational programs attempting to foster writing across the curriculum "Are based on the unexamined assumption that whatever skills are being practiced will simply transfer to new content situations."[81] There is virtually no good evidence that learning to write well in one content area will transfer to other content areas. The reason is that to write well requires not just the rhetorical and compositional skill involved in writing, but a considerable knowledge base in each of the areas the student is to write about.

In the cottage industry of teaching students to transfer their (hopefully) newly acquired "critical thinking," skills, the evidence is no better. This failure occurs because "many critical thinking programs simply assume that the skills taught in these courses will be readily applicable in diverse problem areas."[82] "Conspicuously missing from all of the critical-thinking literature are empirical data on the nature of reasoning (either valid or faulty) that children and adults in fact engage in, in the course of their own thinking."[83] Failure also occurs because "the critical thinking courses that teach logic, both formal and informal, frequently have made the boldest transfer claims. However . . . the transfer of logical skills is just as problematic as it is for many other skills. Logic is not exempt from the transfer problem."[84] Norman Frederiksen concludes, "There appears to be little if any transfer from one domain to another; being an expert in chess apparently does not transfer. . . . Skill in solving physics problems does not transfer to politics or economics."[85] Worse yet, transfer doesn't even occur within the domain of economics for many students.

A study by James Voss and his colleagues is instructive. In a chapter entitled, "Informal Reasoning and Subject Matter Knowledge in the Solving of Economics Problems by Naïve and Novice Individuals," non-college graduates, college graduates who had not taken an economics course, and college graduates who had taken an economics course were asked questions about everyday economic issues. What they clearly found was that there were general reasoning differences between the college graduates and those with no college degree. "For college-educated individuals, however, little performance difference was obtained between those individuals having and those not having formal training in economics and/or economics-related experience."[86] In short, no transfer from having taken an economics course occurred. Perhaps never before have so many agreed on so much. But there's more.

If there's one instructional method in the transfer literature that's agreed upon by just about every practitioner and researchers to promote transfer, it's the use of numerous examples. Study after study clearly shows that students who are provided the opportunities to study examples of a problem do better than students who are merely given the opportunities to work out a given problem. Research by Michelene Chi shows that when students study examples there is a reduction in errors and increased speed in solving problems. Students who are provided examples excel on subsequent test problems when these test problems are similar to the example problems. On dissimilar problems, however, we seldom find significant differences. These data suggest, says Chi, "that example solutions tend to provide an algorithm for students to use and follow on similar problems, but they really have not acquired any deep understanding of the example."[87] Students tend to use examples as very concrete models. This is just one step above rote-memorizing problem solutions. Chi concludes from her research that "in almost all the empirical work to date, on the role of example solutions, a student who has studied examples often cannot solve problems that deviate slightly from the example solution."[88] And these findings are not just from low-ability students.

Although the evidence shows differences in transfer depending on ability level of the learner, the general problem of the failure to transfer learning isn't restricted to lower-ability learners. As Howard Gardner points out in his book, *The Unschooled Mind*, even when schools appear to be teaching successfully, students fail to transfer. Gardner says, "Evidence for this startling claim comes from a by now overwhelming body of educational research . . . that students who receive *honor grades* [italics added] in college-level physics courses are frequently unable to solve basic problems and questions encountered in a form slightly different from that on which they have been formally instructed and tested."[89] And in math, college students frequently fail to solve simple algebra problems when the *same* problems are worded in a slightly different form.

Even in corporate training (as opposed to education), the failure of transfer is widespread. John H. Zenger, chairman of the Times Mirror Training Group, begins his 1996 address in the 50th anniversary issue of *Training and Development Magazine* (perhaps the premier practitioner journal, published by the American Society for Training and Development) by talking about an article he wrote in 1980, lamenting how

> Researchers who rigorously evaluate training have said that demonstrable changes following training are hard to find. Kenneth Andrews in his study of the efficacy of ex-

ecutive-development programs, concluded that companies should expect no dra-
matic change in the behavior of people sent to such programs.[90]

Zenger goes on to quote two other training specialists who maintain that "our research adds additional confirmation to what most practitioners and academicians have long suspected: For management as a whole, training produces only minor changes."[91] He then says that "management training, with such high-potential, has missed something and fallen short of its task. Why? . . . The failure of management and supervisory training can be traced to the fact that it has been operating on shaky assumptions, using inappropriate methodology, relying on untested theories, following fads, ignoring evaluation research, and not defining the behavior changes we seek."[92]

Continuing his assessment of corporate training, Zenger says, "We followed fads that affected both content and methodology, including such content fads as human relations, motivation, assertiveness, negotiation, group dynamics, and power. Methodology fads include case study, programmed instruction, buzz groups, structured exercises, role play, sensitivity training, and simulation."[93] Finally, he concludes, "We ignored evaluation research. We haven't sought assessment studies or real measurements of behavior change. Instead, we've relied on participant reactions and anecdotes."[94] Certainly a telling indictment of corporate training.

An immediate and typical response to Zenger's article may be that the findings are 19 years old and that a lot has been learned since then. Printed beside his 1980 article, however, Zenger wrote an update to his earlier piece, saying "Its eerie to reread an article one wrote 16 years ago. You wonder whether you'll be embarrassed by silly predictions or by points of view that have turned out to be totally incorrect. Fortunately, that isn't the case," he says, "I *still agree with all of it*" [italics added].[95] But it gets still worse.

Based on the transfer research, in the next chapter I present a scheme describing six levels of transfer from least difficult to most difficult. I point out that the first three levels are essentially what I consider to be simple learning, not transfer proper. Now, the striking thing to point out from here is that most of the instructional research that has shown a failure to achieve transfer of learning in fact refers to these first three very basic levels. Conversely, the research that does show success at transfer also refers largely to these first three levels. I will also point out in the next chapter that some researchers clearly suggest that even most of the transfer studies that do manage to demonstrate some low level of transfer don't deserve to be called transfer of learning. These findings thus cast an even more dismal shadow on the problem of transfer of learning. In effect, what the majority of studies show isn't a failure of students to achieve transfer of learning but something worse: a failure of learning itself. I can't stress enough the evidence demonstrating the wholesale failure of transfer in most instructional situations. Without exaggeration, it's an educational scandal.

# CONCLUSION

I close this chapter on the same note it began. Gary Phye, a professor of educational psychology and educational consultant asks,

Can higher thinking skills be taught? Yes! Can higher-order thinking skills be learned? Yes. Will students then demonstrate the ability to use higher-order thinking skills in the classroom? Maybe. . . . In the best of all possible classrooms, where all students are equally prepared, highly motivated, have made an effort to learn and remember, and are interested in the task at hand, this assumption may be accurate. However, after spending 25 years in the classroom, I am still in search of this classroom for even one week.[95]

Yes, the situation is serious. Very serious.

# Notes

[1]Deese, J. (1958). *Transfer of training: The psychology of learning.* New York: McGraw-Hill, p. 213.

[2]See, for example, Bracey, G. W. (1992). The second Bracey report on the condition of public education. *Phi Delta Kappan,* October, 107–117; Jaeger, Richard. (1992). World class standards, choice, and privatization: Weak measurement serving presumptive policy. *Phi Delta Kappan,* October, 118–128.

[3]I place the terms *liberal* and *conservative* in quotation marks to connote simply that these authors are typically labeled with these terms in the public marketplace. By using these terms I do not intend any personal view. Throughout this book, to the extent that it's humanly possible, I intend to stay out of the political fray. Such labels simply enable the opposing camp to dismiss everything an author writes.

[4]Gardner, H. (1991). *The unschooled mind: How children think and how schools should teach.* New York: Basic Books.

[5]Bloom, A. (1987). *The closing of the American mind.* New York: Simon & Schuster.

[6]Bennet, W. (1993). *The book of virtues.* New York: Simon & Schuster.

[7]Hirsch, E. D. (1987). *Cultural literacy.* Boston: Houghton Mifflin.

[8]*Time Magazine* (1995). January 30, 145, No. 5.

[9]National Commission on Excellence in Education (1983, April). *A nation at risk: The imperative for educational reform.* Washington, DC: U.S. Department of Education.

[10]Wideman, H. H., & Owston, R. D. (1993). Knowledge base construction as a pedagogical activity. *Journal of Educational Computing Research, 9,* 165–196, p. 165.

[11]See Federici, L., & Schuerger, J. (1976). High school psychology students versus non-high school psychology students in a college introductory class. *Teaching of Psychology, 3*(4), 172–175.

[12]*Digest of Education Statistics 1995.* Available: *http://www.ed.gov/NCES/pubs/D95/dhlite.html*

[13]Smither, R. D. (1988). *The psychology of work and human performance.* New York: Harper & Row.

[14]Pratzner, F. C. (1978). *Occupational adaptability and transferable skills.* (Information Series No. 129) Columbus, OH: National Center for Research in Vocational Education, p. 13.

[15]Cited in Faerman, S. R., & Ban, C. (1939). Trainee satisfaction and training impact: Issues in training evaluation. *Public Productivity & Management Review, 16,* 299–314, p. 299.

[16]Bryan, J. M., Beaudin, B. P., & Greene, D. S. (1993). Increasing self-efficacy expectations and outcome expectations: A model to facilitate transfer of training. *Journal of Vocational and Technical Education, 9,* 24–30, p. 24.

[17]Emberley, P. C., & Newell, W. R. (1994). *Bankrupt education: The decline of education in Canada.* Toron-

to: University of Toronto Press; Emberley, P. C. (1995). *Values education and technology: The ideology of dispossession*. Toronto: University of Toronto Press.

[18]Myers, C. (1992). Research Core skills and transfer in the youth training schemes: A field study of trainee motor mechanics. *Journal of Organizational Behavior*, 13, 625–632, p. 625.

[19]See, for example, Fotheringhame, J. (1984). Transfer of training: A field investigation of youth training. *Journal of Occupational Psychology*, 57, 239–248; Fotheringhame, J. (1986). Transfer of training: A field study of some training methods. *Journal of Occupational Psychology*, 59, 59–71.

[20]Myers, C. (1992). Research Core skills and transfer in the youth training schemes: A field study of trainee motor mechanics. *Journal of Organizational Behavior*, 13, 625–632, p. 632.

[21]Assiter A. (Ed.). (1995). *Transferable skills in higher education*. London: Kogan page.

[22]Flew, A. (1995). High education, the individual, and the humane sciences. In J. W. Sommer (Ed.), (1995). *The academy in crisis: The political economy of higher education*. (pp. 95–126). London: Transactions Publishers, p. 104.

[23]Wollman, W. (1984). Models and procedures: Teaching for transfer of pendulum knowledge. *Journal of Research in Science Teaching*, 21(4), 399–415, p. 399.

[24]Niedelman, M. (1991). Problem solving and transfer. *Journal of Learning Disabilities*, 24(6), 322–329, p. 326.

[25]Butterfield, E. C., & Nelson, G. D. (1989). Theory and practice of teaching for transfer. *Educational Technology Research & Development*, 37, 5–38, p. 6.

[26]Butterfield, E. C., & Nelson, G. D. (1989). Theory and practice of teaching for transfer. *Educational Technology Research & Development*, 37, 5–38, p. 6.

[27]Butterfield, E. C., & Nelson, G. D. (1989). Theory and practice of teaching for transfer. *Educational Technology Research & Development*, 37, 5–38, p. 6.

[28]Lehrer, R., & Littlefield, J. (1993). Relationships among cognitive components in logo learning and transfer. *Journal of Educational Psychology*, 85(2), 317–330; De Corte, E. (1987). Acquisition and transfer of knowledge and cognitive skills. *International Journal of Educational Research*, 11, 603–606.

[29]Sacks, H. L., & Westling, J. (1988). The assessment movement is based on a misdiagnosis of the malaise afflicting American higher education. *The Chronicle of Higher Education*, October 19, B3.

[30]Haslerud, G. M. (1972). *Transfer, memory and creativity*. Minneapolis: University of Minnesota Press, p. 9.

[31]Dawes, R. M. (1994). *House of cards: Psychology and psychotherapy built on myth*. New York: Free Press, p. 74.

[32]Resnick, L. B. (1989). Introduction. In L. B. Resnick (Ed.), *Knowing, learning and instruction: Essays in honor of Robert Glaser*. Hillsdale, NJ: Lawrence Erlbaum, p. 8.

[33]Broad, M. L., & Newstrom, J. (1992). Transfer of training: Action-packed strategies to ensure high payoff from training investments. New York: Addison-Wesley.

[34]Pratzner, F. C. (1978). Occupational adaptability and transferable skills. (Information Series No. 129) Columbus, OH: National Center for Research in Vocational Education.

[35]Haskell, R. E. (1998). *Reengineering corporate training: Intellectual capital and transfer of learning*. New York: Quorum Book.

[36]See Haskell, R. E. (1997). *Reengineering corporate training: Intellectual capital and transfer of learning*. New York: Quorum Books.

[37]See interview in *Fortune* (1989). Stars of the 1980's cast their light. July 3, p. 66.

[38]Bennis, W. (1962). Towards a 'truly' scientific management: The concept of organization health. In L. Bertalanffy & A. Rapoport (Eds.), *General systems: Year book of the society for general systems theory* (Vol. VII, pp. 269–282). Ann Arbor, MI: Society for General Systems Research, p. 279.

[39]Senge, P. M. (1990). *The fifth discipline: The art and practice of the learning organization*. New York: Doubleday.

[40]McKeachie, W. J. (1987). Cognitive skills and their transfer: Discussion. *International Journal of Educational Research*, 11, 707–712, p. 707.

[41]Deese, J. (1958). *Transfer of training, The psychology of learning*. New York: McGraw-Hill, pp. 213–217.

[42]In Winkles, J. (1986). Achievement, understanding, and transfer in a learning hierarchy. *American Educational Research Journal*, 23(2), 275–288, p. 276.

[43]McGeoch, J. A. (1942). *The psychology of human learning: An introduction.* New York: Longmans, p. 347.

[44]Ferguson, G. A. (1963). On transfer and the abilities of man. In R. G. Grose & R. C. Birney (Eds.), *Transfer of learning: An enduring problem in psychology* (181–194). New York: Van Nostrand, p. 185.

[45]McGeoch, J. A. (1942). *The psychology of human learning: An introduction.* New York: Longmans, p. 347.

[46]Bruner, S. J. (1966). Education as social invention. In J. M. Anglin (Ed.), *Beyond the information given: Studies in the psychology of knowing* (468–479). New York: W. W. Norton, p. 478.

[47]Brown, A. L., & Campione, J. C. (1984). Three faces of transfer: Implications to early competence, individual differences, and instruction. *Advances in Developmental Psychology, 3,* 143.

[48]Royer, J. M. (1979). Theories of the transfer of learning. *Educational Psychologist, 14,* 53–69, p. 53.

[49]Cronback, L. J. (1963). Intellectual development as transfer of learning. *Educational psychology.* New York: Harcourt, Brace and World, p. 314.

[50]Sechrest, L. B. (1966). Transfer of therapeutic learning. In A. P. Goldstein, K. Heller, & L. B. Sechrest (Eds.), *Psychotherapy and the psychology of behavior change* (212–259). New York: John Wiley, p. 222.

[51]McGeoch, J. A. (1942). *The psychology of human learning: An introduction.* New York: Longmans, p. 446.

[52]Gick, M. L., & Holyoak, K. J. (1987). The cognitive basis of knowledge transfer. In S. M. Cormier & J. D. Hagman (Eds.), *Transfer of learning contemporary research and application* (pp. 9–45). New York: Academic Press, p. 41.

[53]McKeachie, W. J. (1987). Cognitive skills and their transfer: Discussion. *International Journal of Educational Research, 11,* 707–712, p. 707.

[54]Ellis, H. A. (1965). *The transfer of learning,* New York: Macmillan, p. 67.

[55]McKeachie, W. J., Pintrich, P. R., Lin, Y. G., & Smith, D. A. F. (1986). *Teaching and learning in the college classroom: A review of the research literature.* National Center for Research to Improve Postsecondary Teaching and Learning, p. 33.

[56]Gick, M. L., & Holyoak, K. J. (1987). The cognitive basis of knowledge transfer. In S. M. Cormier & J. D. Hagman (Eds.), *Transfer of learning contemporary research and application* (pp. 9–45). New York: Academic Press, p. 13.

[57]Borkowski, J. G. (1985). Signs of intelligence: Strategy generalization and metacognition. In S. R. Yussen (Ed.), *The growth of reflection in children* (Vol. 7, pp. 105–144). New York: Academic Press, p. 127.

[58]Sechrest, L. B. (1966). Transfer of therapeutic learning. In A. P. Goldstein, K. Heller, & L. B. Sechrest (Eds.), *Psychotherapy and the psychology of behavior change* (212–259). New York: John Wiley, p. 213.

[59]Goldstein, A. P., Heller, K., & Sechrest, L. B. (1966). Transfer of therapeutic learning. In A. P. Goldstein, K. Heller, & L. B. Sechrest (Eds.), *Psychotherapy and the psychology of behavior change* (pp. 212–259). New York: John Wiley, p. 221.

[60]Lohman, D. (1993). Learning and the nature of educational measurement. *National Association of Secondary School Principles, 77,* 41–53, p. 48.

[61]Singley, M. K., & Anderson, J. R. (1989). *The transfer of cognitive skill.* Cambridge, MA: Harvard University Press, p. 1.

[62]Larkin, J. (1989). What kind of knowledge transfers? In L. B. Resnick (Ed.), *Knowing, learning, and instruction: Essays in honor of Robert Glaser.* Hillsdale, NJ: Lawrence Erlbaum, p. 283.

[63]Clark, R. E., & Voogel, A. (1985). Transfer of training principles for instructional design. *Education communication and technology, 33,* 113–123, p. 113, 121.

[64]Oates, T. (1992). Core skills and transfer: Aiming high. *Education, Training, and Technology International, 29,* 227–239, p. 228.

[65]Thorndike, E. L., & Woodworth, R. R. (1901). The influence of improvement in one mental function upon the efficiency of other functions. *Psychological Review, 8,* 247–261.

[66]Haslerud, G. M. (1972). *Transfer, memory and creativity.* Minneapolis, MN: University of Minnesota Press, p. 56.

[67]Detterman, D. K. (1993). The case for the prosecution: Transfer as an epiphenomenon. In D. K. Detterman & R. J. Sternberg (Eds.), Transfer on trial: Intelligence, cognition, and instruction (pp. 1–24). Norwood, NJ: Ablex, p. 21.

[68]Ripple, R. E., & Drinkwater, D. J. (1982). Transfer of learning. In Encyclopedia of educational research (5th ed.). New York: Free Press, p. 1948.

[69]Singley, M. K., & Anderson, J. R. (1989). The transfer of cognitive skill. Cambridge, MA: Harvard University Press, pp. 26, 28, 230.

[70]Marini, A., & Genereux, R. (1995). The challenge of teaching for transfer. In A. McKeough, J. Lupart, & A. Marini (Eds.), Teaching for transfer: Fostering generalization in learning (pp. 1–20). Mahwah, NJ: Lawrence Erlbaum Associates, Inc.

[71]Sweller, J. (1990). On the limited evidence for the effectiveness of teaching general problem-solving strategies. Journal for Research in Mathematics Education, 21, 411–415, p. 414.

[72]Bassok, M., & Holyoak, K. J. (1989). Interdomain transfer between isomorphic topics in algebra and physics. Journal of Experimental Psychology: Learning, Memory, and Cognition, 15, 153–166, p. 154.

[73]Brooks, L. W., & Dansereau, D. F. (1987). Transfer of information: An instructional perspective. In S. M. Cormier (Ed.), Transfer of learning: Contemporary research and applications (pp. 121–149). New York: Academic Press, p. 132.

[74]Larkin, J. (1989). What kind of knowledge transfers? In L. B. Resnick (Ed.), Knowing, learning and instruction: Essays in honor of Robert Glaser. Hillsdale, NJ: Lawrence Erlbaum, p. 288.

[75]Ibid, p. 139.

[76]Pressley, M., Snyder, B., & Carigilia-Bull, T. (1987). How can good strategy use be taught to children? Evaluation of six alternative approaches. In S. M. Cormier & J. D. Hagman (Eds.), Transfer of learning: Contemporary research and application (pp. 81–119). San Diego, CA: Academic Press, p. 96.

[77]Ibid.

[78]Resnick, L. B. (1987). Instruction and the cultivation of thinking. In E. De Corte, H. Lodewijks, R. Parmentier, & P. Span (Eds.), Learning and instruction (Vol. I, pp. 415–441). Oxford: Pergamon Press, p. 436.

[79]McKeachie, W. J. (1987). The new look in instructional psychology: Teaching strategies for learning and thinking. In E. De Corte, H. Lodewijks, R. Parmentier, & P. Span (Eds.), Learning and instruction (Vol. I, pp. 443–456). Oxford: Pergamon Press, p. 447.

[80]Gelzheiser, L. M., Shepherd, M. J., & Wozniak, R. H. (1986). The development of instruction to induce skill transfer. Exceptional Children, 53, 125–129; Gelzheiser, L. M. (1984). Generalization from categorical memory tasks to prose by learning disabled adolescents. Journal of Educational Psychology, 76(6), 1128–1138.

[81]Teich, N. (1987). Transfer of writing skills: Implications of the theory of lateral and vertical transfer. Written Communication, 4(2), 193–208, p. 194.

[82]McPeck, J. E. (1992). Thoughts on subject specificity. In S. P. Norris (Ed.), The generalizability of critical thinking: Multiple perspectives on an educational ideal (pp. 198–205). New York: Columbia University, p. 200.

[83]Kuhn, D. (1986). Education for thinking. Teachers College Record, 87, 495–512, p. 499.

[84]McPeck, J. E. (1992). Thoughts on subject specificity. In S. P. Norris (Ed.), The generalizability of critical thinking: Multiple perspectives on an educational ideal (pp. 198–205). New York: Columbia University, p. 200.

[85]Frederiksen, N. (1984). Implications of cognitive theory for instruction in problem solving. Review of Educational Research, 54, 363–407, p. 391.

[86]Voss, J., Blais, J., Means, M., Greene, T., & Ahwesh, E. (1989). informal reasoning and subject matter knowledge in the solving of economics problems by naïve and novice individuals. In L. Resnick (Ed.), Knowing, learning, and instruction: Essays in honor of Robert Glaser (pp. 251–282). Hillsdale, NJ: Lawrence Erlbaum, p. 233.

[87]Chi, M. T. H. (1989). Learning from examples via self-explanations. In L. Resnick (Ed.), Knowing, learning, and instruction: Essays in honor of Robert Glaser (pp. 251–282). Hillsdale, NJ: Lawrence Erlbaum, p. 260.

[88]Ibid, p. 260.

[89]Gardner, H. (1991). *The unschooled mind: How children think and how schools should teach.* New York: Basic Books, p. 3.

[90]Zenger, J. H. (1996). Then: the painful turnabout in training; Now: A retrospective. *Training and Development,* 50, (1) January, p. 48.

[91]Ibid, pp. 48–49.

[92]Ibid, p. 49.

[93]Ibid, p. 49.

[94]Ibid, p. 50.

[95]Ibid, p. 48.

[96]Phye, G. (1997). Inductive reasoning and problem solving: The early grades. In *Handbook of academic learning* (pp. 451–471). San Diego: Academic Press, p. 453.

# 2

# Transfer of Learning: What It Is and Why It's Important

*We talk about "transfer of learning" when . . . learning is displayed in a situation some-*
*what different from that in which the original learning occurred. If the transfer situa-*
*tion is so different that the use of learning encounters some barrier or difficulty, we speak*
*of "problem solving." When the situation is greatly different and the distance of trans-*
*fer needed is greater still, we speak of creativity.*

—Wilbert McKeachie, *Teaching and Learning*
*in the College Classroom*[1]

What kind of learning made it possible for someone to see that lightning is in fact a "big spark," or that the process of metal rusting is in fact "slow combustion," or to see that the development of the reciprocating gasoline engine required that it be seen as a series of "controlled explosions"? The answer is transfer of learning. These apparently simple examples of transfer, however, are not as simple as they appear to be. Despite years of research in psychology, education, and other fields, transfer remains a mysterious process. In explaining transfer, I will be presenting a framework largely missing from standard accounts. But it's a crucial framework, for our very future depends on our ability to transfer our learning.

Transfer refers to how previous learning influences current and future learning, and how past or current learning is applied or adapted to similar or novel situations. Transfer, then, isn't so much an instructional and learning technique as a way of thinking, perceiving, and processing information. Therefore it's fundamental to *all* learning. Without it we couldn't engage in our everyday thinking and reasoning nor even acquire the most basic of motor skills; transfer is responsible for the simplest of ideas and for the highest achievements of humankind.

## THE BASICS OF WHAT TRANSFER OF LEARNING IS

In one sense, we are all experts in transfer, yet in another and more important sense, we are all lacking in higher order transfer skills. The more skilled we are in transfer, the more creative and efficient is our thinking and performance. Transfer is a deceptively simple concept. The simple aspect of transfer of learning is exemplified whenever we say, for example, *it's like . . . it's equivalent to . . . for example . . . it's akin to . . . for instance . . . it's the same as . . . by the same token . . . similarly . . . in the same way . . . it reminds me of . . . it resembles . . . it's comparable to . . . or, it's analogous to . . . .* Transfer involves the use of figurative language with analogies and metaphors; the deceptive aspect of transfer is that when we simply say "it's like," it's the *same* transfer of learning that Albert Einstein used in creating his theory of relativity.

The word *transfer* is derived from *trans*, meaning *across* or *over*, and *ferre*, meaning to *bear*, thus, *to carry over*. In both a trivial and a profound sense—as no situation is ever exactly the same—all learning is transfer of learning. In short, virtually all learning involves *carrying over* previous learning to new situations. Failure to carry over previous learning all too frequently leads to rigid patterns of behavior and thinking. In psychology we use the term *functional fixedness* to describe such rigid patterns. For example, when you're in a hotel room and you need to tighten a screw on your computer case but you don't have a screwdriver, many of us wouldn't think of using (or 'seeing') a dime, or a fingernail file or a credit card as a screwdriver.

We constantly transfer our previous learning and experience in order to more quickly and efficiently learn a new skill. A person who plays the piano, for example, will learn to play an accordion more quickly and efficiently than a person who has no experience with the piano. Similarly, experience with ice skating can decrease the learning time of a person learning roller skating. There's a game called Short Tennis for children. It's a mini version of regular tennis and is constructed to retain most of the movement elements of regular tennis. It has a smaller court, smaller rackets, and lower net height, and a foam rubber ball. Recent research demonstrates that skills and movements learned by children in Short Tennis later transfer to Lawn Tennis.[2]

A fundamental transfer-of-learning task confronting education today is the need to improve computer competency. Thus the challenge facing all computer instruction is to teach not merely the keystrokes (training) necessary to perform program tasks but to develop mental models of the underlying structure (learning) of the different user interfaces. Complicating this issue is the problem of having to deal with multiple hardware architectures, operating systems, and user interfaces. But with the trend of moving toward common user interfaces based on graphics such as Microsoft *Windows*, transfer of learning is accelerated. Just as many countries have been changing language-based road signs to include icons (i.e., signs with the word *Food* are paired with a picture of a dinner plate, connoting a restaurant), to make the information understood by a wider audience, computer software designers have likewise found that pictures or icons can do the same for learning programs. As experience increases, users realize that the underlying structure among apparently different applications are similar. The primary differences reside in terminology (semantics) and keystrokes, while the end result is identical.

One application included with the basic Windows program is Notepad, a small miniprogram designed to function like the hard copy paper note pad. The menu structure in Notepad is simple, with headings for File, Edit, Search, and Help. Once familiar with Notepad, a user can begin using a more complex word-processing program, such as WordPerfect for Windows, and be capable of at least transferring the fundamental tasks of typing and editing text, opening and saving files, printing, cutting, and pasting text from one section to another because WordPerfect also contains File, Edit, and Help menus, virtually identical to those in Notepad. Properly instructed, a user should be capable of transferring to an entirely new word processor, spreadsheet, or database program with relative ease. A final example of transfer is the ability to expand the skill of searching a simple index on a computer to that of scanning and exploring worldwide indexes on the Internet. This example of transfer can be traced back to one's previous ability to use the index in a book. Negative transfer may also occur, however, in the transition from one operating system or program to another, particularly when different terminology and procedures are emphasized.[3]

If everything were different from everything else—which in fact it is to one degree or another—we would be unable to function; we would experience what psychologist and philosopher William James in another context called a "blooming, buzzing, confusion." Transfer thus reduces our world to manageable proportions; it makes the world familiar. Transfer, the seeing of similarities, creates categories and concepts for us, and it is responsible for our creating *generic* or general structures of thinking.[4] Thus the concept of transfer of learning, although simple, is crucial to all learning from the lowest level of skill to the highest reaches of theoretical thinking.

The traditional view of transfer is that it's a special case of learning. There are many researchers, including myself, however, who for some time now have seen learning as a special case of transfer. One early researcher, George Ferguson, noted that, "It has long been apparent to . . . myself and to others that transfer is the more general phenomenon and learning a particular case."[5] This is important because it means that any discussion of learning assumes transfer.

It is a truism in the psychology of perception to say that our directly perceived world is in flux, and our brains render our world constant or *invariant* by seeing regularity within this flux. In the perceptual realm, recurrent regularities are transfer-generated cognitive stabilizations of our constantly changing environment. Because nothing ever repeats itself exactly the same way or in exactly the same context, the essential problem in transfer is when and how something is perceived as being the *same as* or *equivalent to* something else. To say that X is like Y isn't the simple problem that it appears to be.

Because on a basic level transfer appears so simple and commonsensical, we may all too often do the opposite of what appears to be obvious. Negative transfer from our past experience frequently occurs. What appears to be logical, or reasonable, or just plain commonsense, however, is all too often counterintuitive; or in the absence of adequate knowledge, predictions of when transfer will occur may be counterintuitive or incorrect, leading to negative transfer. Novices and children—lacking sufficient knowledge—often transfer inappropriately, as when a penguin *is not* seen as a bird, or a whale *is* called a fish, or when a bat *is* seen as a bird. On perceptual grounds only, who would think a deer and a whale would be the *same*? These inappropriate transfers are the consequence of not possessing sufficient knowledge and theory of the phenomena we are attempting to transfer (see chapters 6 and 9). Though not complex, transfer isn't a simple matter.

Transfer is the neurocognitive mechanism underlying many phenomena (see chapter 11). Because of its fundamental nature, transfer is known by many names. Transfer is the basis of mental abstraction, analogical relations, classification, generalization, generic thinking, induction, invariance, isomorphic relations, logical inference, metaphor, and constructing mental models. The very concept of *inference* is a metaphor. Etymologically, it's a reference to the "transfer" or "carrying over" meaning from one situation to another. Indeed, transfer is so fundamental that to explain it is to repeat the *same* thing over and over, using different terms from different fields, in different contexts, on different levels of abstraction, and in different orders of magnitude.

Think of the basic structure of transfer being characterized by the arithmetical form of $2 + 2 = 4$, and just as we can plug apples, peaches, pears, plums, and Buicks into this abstract structure, so, too, we plug into the general transfer form: abstraction, analogical relations, archetypal thinking, classification, generalization, generic thinking, induction, invariance, isomorphic relations, logical inference, metaphor, and mental models. The $2 + 2 = 4$ is an example of generic thinking. By such transfer thinking, if you understand one of these concepts, you can generally understand the other. It's a kind of repetition. To say that I am repeating the *same* thing, however, is not to say that I am *simply* repeating the *exact* same thing. In mathematics such repetition is called the *differentiation of an invariant* through its various mathematical forms; it's like counting from 10 to 100, then counting from 100 to 1000; that is, 10 *is to* 100 *as* 100 *is to* 1000. In other areas transfer may be known as variation on a theme. Or it can be seen as different archetypes or proverbs all expressing the same meaning.

The research on teaching for transfer clearly shows that for transfer to occur, the original learning must be repeatedly reinforced with multiple examples or similar concepts in multiple contexts, and I would add, on different levels and orders of magnitude. Teaching that promotes transfer, then, involves returning again and again to an idea or procedure but on different levels and in different contexts, with apparently "different" examples. The great psychologist Jean Piaget referred to this method as epigenetic, as a kind of spiral where each new turn is a higher order manifestation of the order below it, just as 2 *is to* 4 and 4 *is to* 8 (see chapter 12). The bare-bones essence of transfer, then, is simple: it's *equivalence* and it can be summarized by the "=" sign. In order to further understand transfer of learning, it's useful to briefly look a little more technically at the levels and kinds of transfer of learning.

## EVOLUTION OF TRANSFER FROM RATS
## TO CHIMPS TO HUMANS

From the most primitive of life-forms to the best and the brightest of humankind, transfer ability varies. This variation in ability at transfer is, in part, founded on biological evolutionary advances that are hard-wired into our brain. For example, if a rat is taught to respond to the image of a triangle drawn with solid line $T_1$, when shown a "different" triangle drawn with lines made up of a series of dots $T_2$, it is unable to recognize $T_1$ as the *same* object as $T_2$. Similarly, a rat trained to respond to a white triangle with black background will not respond to a black triangle with white background.

A chimpanzee and a small child, however, will respond to both triangles as the *same* object; they will transfer their experience. On a more abstract level, when we recognize a familiar melody played in a new key, or in a different octave, we are engaging in transfer because the new melody is in fact not the *exact same* set of notes that we are familiar with. Transfer can also be seen in the ability of some people to "see sounds" or to "hear colors." This is known as cross-modal synesthesia. Such people literally have their neurological "wires crossed." A variant of synesthesia in us "normal" people results in experiencing the sound of the word "we" as being "brighter" and "higher" than the word "do."

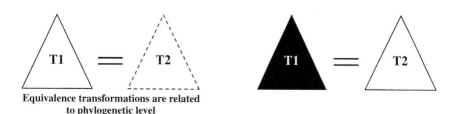

Equivalence transformations are related
to phylogenetic level

**FIGURE 1**
The evolution of sameness: sameness.

**FIGURE 2**
The evolution of sameness: abstract transposition.


The capability to transfer sounds into colors, to perceive "different" melodies, or the transposition of different octaves into the *same* musical experience, appears to be built into both single brain cells and hardwired into our neurological pathways. Once again the capacity for transposition is related to one's place on the evolutionary scale. If a rat is trained to go toward a light of intensity $L_1$ and to avoid intensity $L_2$, which is twice the intensity of $L_1$, and is then presented with intensity $L_3$ and $L_4$, where $L_4$ is twice the intensity of $L_3$, the rat will not respond.

Chimpanzees and young children will make the transposition. They will consider intensity $L_1$ in the first situation the *same* as intensity $L_3$ in the second situation. Put in analogical terms, $L_1:L_2$ as $L_3:L_4$. This is the same process as hearing a melody played in one key as being the *same* melody played in a different key, even though not a single note in the new octave is the same as the notes in the old octave.

Transfer is integrally responsible for classifying things. We generally place something into a category by its similarity to things in that category. The Nobel Laureate in economics, Frederick von Hayek, in his little known book, *The Sensory Order: An Inquiry into the Foundations of Theoretical Psychology*, sees transfer as being hardwired into our neurological system. Under the heading, "The Nervous System as an Instrument of Classification," Hayek says, "A wide range of mental phenomena, such as discrimination, equivalence of stimuli, generalization, transfer, abstraction and conceptual thought may all be interpreted as different forms of the same process of classification which is operative in creating the sensory order."[6] Certainly von Hayek himself, writing in both economics and psychology, possessed a high level of transfer expertise.

In a very early article, I also considered transfer to be a general phenomenon, seeing it as a form of analogical reasoning.[7] I suggested that transfer "may be equated with the well known constructs of stimulus generalization, constancy, transposition phenomena, isomorphic relations, metaphor, abstraction, transfer, and the more recent signature of science, model," and I have since continued to do research on transfer in both a theoretical and applied manner. I also believe that there is sufficient evidence showing that the basic structure of transfer is hardwired into our brains (see chapter 11).

# A GENERAL SCHEME FOR UNDERSTANDING THE LEVELS AND KINDS OF TRANSFER

An important ingredient in understanding something is to know where it belongs in a larger scheme and to become familiar with its parts. Knowing what kinds of tools are available for a particular kind of job, for example, not only allows us to select the tool that will do the best job, but it provides us with a framework and a plan for how to do the job. It follows that tools create (and limit) the possibilities for what and how a job can be done. The same is true for the concepts and words that we describe tools with. The more extensive vocabulary we have, the more ways we have for seeing, describing, and doing something.

It is now time to spell out what I see as the six levels of transfer. They comprise a kind of simple taxonomy (a taxonomy is a system of classification): Level 1, nonspecific transfer; Level 2, application transfer; Level 3, context transfer; Level 4, near transfer; Level 5, far transfer; and, Level 6, displacement or creative transfer. Such a "system" has generally been missing in the transfer literature. Although there are labels for different kinds of transfer, such as lateral transfer and vertical transfer, there is no system of classification directly based on a precise degree of similarity.

*Level 1: Nonspecific transfer.* Because all learning depends on some connection to past learning, all learning in this sense is transfer of learning. Although this is true and profoundly necessary, it's also somewhat trivial in terms of our everyday experience of transfer.

*Level 2: Application transfer.* This refers to applying what one has learned to a specific situation. For example, after having learned about a word-processing system, one is then able to apply the learning to actually operating a word processor. This may seem to be an outrageously condescending example, but I assure you that this level of transfer is a problem in the learning of many tasks.

*Level 3: Context transfer.* This level refers to applying what one has learned in a slightly different situation. Often a change in context, though the learned task is exactly the same, may result in lack of transfer. An analogy to a change in context interfering with transfer is "place learning" in psychology. Sometimes what is learned is welded to the place where it is learned, because the physical place provides the cues necessary for retrieving the learning. Most people have had the experience of not recognizing someone even though they are looking right at them. This often happens when we have no experience of or expectation for the person being in a particular place.

*Level 4: Near transfer.* This refers to when previous knowledge is transferred to new situations that are closely similar but not identical to previous situations. A person's experience in roller skating when transferred to ice skating is an example of near procedural transfer. Learning to calculate the amount of floor tile needed for a living room using your prior classroom experience in figuring the area of rectangles is another example. As obvious as this may seem, many of us don't even make this simple kind of transfer either.

*Level 5: Far transfer.* This refers to applying learning to situations that are quite dissimilar to the original learning. Examples like seeing lightning as a big spark and other similar transfers often involved in invention and product development.[8] What we ordinarily call analogical reasoning is clearly evident in this level of transfer thinking.

*Level 6: Displacement or creative transfer.* This refers to transferring learning in a way that leads to more than the insight of "that is like this." In the interaction of the newly discovered similarity between the old and the new, a new concept is created.

Each level of transfer just described is based on judgments of similarity. But just how similar something is to another thing is largely a subjective matter, and there is no simple way to determine how quantitatively similar something X is to another something Y. This is, after all, the very problem of transfer: what do we mean when we say something is *similar* to something, or is *like* something else? There is no simple way to say if something is a case of *near* transfer or *far* transfer. The essential problem of similarity or equivalency has yet to be solved. Until some genius solves this problem, the psychologist Walter Weimer's succinct conclusion will have to suffice: "Stimuli are equivalent, in the final analysis, only because they mean the same thing."[9] I will address the relationship of meaning to transfer in chapter 7.

Knowledge base greatly influences whether something is considered near or far transfer. What is near transfer to an expert may be far transfer to a novice. This is why the identical elements theory of transfer is not as simple as it first appears to be (see chapter 5). Since nothing—by definition—is identical to anything else, identical elements are in fact only similar elements. This fact is often overlooked, especially when designing instructional programs. Thus, much of the perception of similarity, like beauty, is in the mind of the perceiver, not in the concrete features of an object or event.

I consider levels 1 and 2 as essentially simple learning, not transfer proper at all; level 3 is simply the application of learning, reserving level 4 as near transfer, and levels 5 and 6 as far transfer. Finally, I would like to note that what I consider to be significant transfer is transfer that requires the learning of something new in order to make the transfer. Levels 4, 5, and 6 typically require such new learning. Without the requirement of new learning, the transfer in my view is not transfer but simply applying the *same* learning.

In the same way that understanding the levels of transfer of learning allows us to recognize how, when, and where transfer occurs, so does understanding the kinds of transfer of learning. Transfer can be classified into two basic categories: (a) the type of knowledge that the transfer is based on and (b) the specific kinds of transfer. The first category corresponds to the five types of knowledge that I describe in chapter 6 (declarative, procedural, strategic, conditional, and theoretical knowledge); the second category is based on transfer itself. I should point out that none of the kinds of transfer are necessarily mutually exclusive.

1. *Content-to-content transfer* is making use of what we know in one subject area to the learning of another area. Content knowledge is what I describe in chapter 6 as declarative knowledge. Declarative-to-declarative transfer occurs whenever existing knowledge of some content area facilitates or interferes with simple learning. It also refers to learning new knowledge that may be somewhat different from the original learning. Knowledge about proteins, fats, and carbohydrates from chemistry, for example, will be useful in health education. Knowing how small groups work will help in understanding business meetings. Content or declarative knowledge may provide us with a general framework, it may help us to elaborate, or it may provide an analog for a second content area.

2. *Procedural-to-procedural transfer*, also known as *skill-to-skill transfer*, refers to using the procedures learned in one skill area in another skill area. For example, skills used in riding a bicycle typically transfer to driving a motorcycle or driving a car. Procedures are sequences of actions. Sequences learned on one computer program may transfer to operating another similar program.

3. *Declarative-to-procedural transfer* occurs when learning *about* something helps in actually doing something. For example, knowledge about computers enables us to learn programming procedures; knowledge about corporate stocks enables us to more proficiently play the stock market.

4. *Procedural-to-declarative transfer* is when practical experience in an area helps us to learn more abstract knowledge of the area. Practical experience in constructing electronic circuits, for example, will help in learning theoretical knowledge of electronics; knowledge of programming may help in learning computer theory.

5. *Strategic transfer* is when knowledge about our mental processes, such as how we learn or remember, is gained through monitoring our mental activities during learning. Knowledge of how we solved one problem may transfer to the solving of another problem.

6. *Conditional transfer* is when knowledge concerning when to apply the knowledge learned in one context may be appropriate for transferring it to another context.

7. *Theoretical transfer* is understanding deep level relationships of cause and effect in one area that can be transferred to another. Recognizing that a spark and lightning are the same, that combustion and rusting are the same, and that the inverse square law applies to planets and the tides, are all examples of theoretical transfer.

8. *General or nonspecific transfer* is when previous knowledge that is not specific to the training situation transfers to other situations even though no ap-

parent similarities exist between the old and the new situations. The first kind of content-to-content knowledge described above is such an example of non-specific transfer. General transfer is often described under the concepts of "learning to learn" and "warm-up effects."

9. *Literal transfer* is using knowledge or a procedure directly in a new learning situation. In studying about the American Revolution you might learn that wars are caused by competition to control natural resources. Then in studying World War I, you might look for competition to control natural resources as an explanation of the cause. Literal transfer can be seen as a form of near transfer.

10. *Vertical transfer* refers to prior learning transferred to new learning that is higher in a knowledge hierarchy, or learning that presupposes the prior learning. Learning in which prerequisite skills are necessary requires vertical transfer. For example, to calculate percentages, you must already know how to divide and multiply.

11. *Lateral transfer* is when previous learning is transferred to the same level in a hierarchy. The above example of transferring roller skating skills to ice skating is an example of lateral transfer, as is transferring the known laws of the flow of liquid to a theory of heat conduction.

12. *Reverse transfer*, sometimes called *backward transfer*, occurs when existing (prior) knowledge is modified and re-viewed in terms of its similarities to the new information. Backward transfer reverses the direction of the typical view of process transfer.

13. *Proportional transfer* is a more abstract transfer. Recognizing a melody played in a different octave or key is an example.

14. *Relational transfer* can be illustrated by mathematical analogies. In biology, this kind of structure is called a homology, a correspondence in form of external appearance between two species as with the wing of a bird and the fin of a fish, even though the underlying causal mechanisms are different. Both share a similar structure, but there's no underlying causal relationship. Relational transfer is seeing the same structure between two things.

Now that the basics for understanding what transfer is have been outlined, we can proceed to initially understand the importance of transfer.

## IMPORTANCE OF TRANSFER OF LEARNING

As I have shown in the opening of this chapter, so pervasive is the transfer function, that it shouldn't come as a surprise that its effects are equally pervasive. We constantly reason in everyday life using transfer (see chapter 4). The history of science, invention, technology transfer, and everyday life is replete with people who are good at transfer. We often develop and see new things in terms of past experience, as being *like* something we are already familiar with. When cars were first invented, they were seen as "horseless carriages." With the advent of the computer age, we now have electronic "mail" sent via our computer terminals. Small laptop computers are called electronic "notepads" in analogy with paper note pads. The development of a technology capable of analyzing the complex structure of our DNA has found its way into the court room. Each person's DNA code is unique to them *like* fingerprints: thus we call it DNA "fingerprinting."

In addition, when we learn from history (if, indeed, we do), it involves transfer. In fact, the only way we can learn from history *is* by transfer. There's no other way. We do it by seeing the past as relevant to or as being *like* the present, that is, by transferring past events to present situations. This is the very definition of transfer of learning (see chapter 5). As obvious as it may now appear, history isn't typically thought of as transfer of learning. Learning from history, however, *is* transfer of learning; it's the very paradigm of transfer: past knowledge influencing present learning.

Many advances in science are made on the basis of a simple *it's like* type of transfer. The invention of a new representation (e.g., Einstein's theory of relativity, Darwin's theory of evolution) seems to involve a basic insight into the nature of the problem to be solved. Einstein is famous for his use of everyday mental images of concrete situations and analogies for thinking about abstract problems. Charles Darwin transferred the idea of the selective (i.e., artificial) breeding of animals to his development of the principle of natural selection to his theory of evolution. In place of a farmer selectively picking what genetic traits of an animal are to be reproduced or enhanced, Darwin saw that nature or natural selection was at work in the place of the farmer. It seems simple now, but it wasn't then.

The great physicist Louis De Broglie noticed that the mathematical equations of another well-known physicist, Neils Bohr, who described the orbits of an electron, were the *same* equations used to describe the vibrating waves of a violin string. With this transfer of his learning, De Broglie revolutionized atomic physics and laid the foundations of quantum mechanics. It may well be that the inventing of such representations by transfer of learning is the highest intellectual achievement.

In school, students often learn essentially the same concept in different courses, but these concepts are given different labels by different disciplines, so children are not aware they are learning the same concept. Teachers, too, seldom recognize the similarities that exist across disciplines. It is never pointed out, for example, that the concept of *learning* in psychology, *socialization* in sociology, *adaptation* in biology, and *acculturation* in anthropology are very *similar* concepts. *Learning* is the process of acquiring knowledge or skill through practice, training, or experience; *socialization* is the process whereby individuals assimilate the values and behavior patterns of their culture and social position; *adaptation* is the alteration in an organism that results from natural selection enabling the organism to survive; *acculturation* is the process of adopting cultural traits or social patterns of another culture. Such a systems approach to learning is cognitively and instructionally beneficial in a number of ways.

First, learning the above four individual concepts requires a certain amount of memory space. If, however, students can see how the four concepts of learning, socialization, adaptation, and acculturation are essentially the *same*, they can "chunk" them into one concept and thus ease the load on memory. Second, once the four concepts are seen as being *alike*, they become associated with each other and other material associated with them facilitates memory retrieval. Third, the four concepts are now cognitively integrated for a deeper understanding, with each individual concept reinforcing the other. Fourth, because the four concepts aren't identical, certain aspects from one of the concepts may reveal something new about the other that was not known prior to the transfer. Transfer of learning is thus not only extremely economical in terms of an individual's learning resources, it creates creativity and learning itself; it helps us to efficiently store, remember, integrate, process, and retrieve information.

Finally, one form of transfer is the use of analogies and metaphors. Reasoning on the basis of analogy is called analogical reasoning, a kind of reasoning in which one thing is inferred to be similar to another thing on the basis of a shared, common, or similar structure. A well-known analogy is the use of knowledge about the human eye that was transferred to the development of the camera:

| *Human eye* | → | *Camera* |
|---|---|---|
| *lens* | → | *lens* |
| *retina* | → | *film* |
| *inverted image* | → | *inverted image* |
| *eyelid* | → | *lens cap* |
| *lens accommodation* | → | *focus* |
| *pupil dilation* | → | *aperture* |

Without going into the fine distinctions traditionally made by linguists, grammarians, and philosophers on the differences between analogies, metaphors, and similes, it's sufficient for our purposes here to understand that the transfer function undergirds analogical and metaphorical reasoning and many other similar processes that are called by different names when they are used in different ways. Some years ago, I suggested that analogical reasoning was not just a kind of literary style of reasoning but was fundamental to all learning.[10] Since that time, many researchers have concluded that analogical reasoning is a central mechanism—if not the primary mechanism—in learning, thinking, and reasoning.[11] Finally, the use of analogies and analogical transfer is increasingly being used in the classroom for teaching science, and is often viewed as one of the primary means of drawing on students' existing knowledge.[12]

## TRICKS OF THE TRADE: NOW YOU SEE IT, NOW YOU DON'T

Not only does most research show that both the failures and successes in achieving transfer overwhelmingly come from learning situations involving the most basic levels of learning, but as some researchers clearly suggest, even most of the transfer studies that do manage to demonstrate some low level of transfer don't deserve to be called transfer of learning. With some reservations, I tend to concur. This is what the issue is all about.

Douglas Detterman is one exponent of the view that most of the transfer studies that do manage to demonstrate some low level of transfer don't deserve to be called transfer of learning.[13] I say he is one proponent of this view because there aren't many. Considered the Holy grail of education, the transfer catechism doesn't have many critics.

Not only is it important to include critics of a particular point of view, it's unforgivable not to. Anything else is propaganda, not science or scholarship. More pragmatically, we learn as much from critics—perhaps more—than we do from advocates. Before continuing with Detterman's criticisms, however, it's useful to briefly look at one early critic whose view is virtually never cited in the literature, and whose view makes Detterman's criticism pale by comparison. Whereas Detterman's criticisms center on the instructional methods used in transfer research, Edward Kelly's[14] claim is much more radical. He rejects the very idea of transfer, claiming that "the concept of transfer does not serve any educationally useful purpose." He maintains that transfer is "an empirically meaningless or a worthless notion."[15] This is not just rhetoric. Kelly has his logical and philosophical reasons. First he says that the term *transfer* is simply a metaphor; that nothing actually gets transferred or "moved" from one domain or thought to another. His position is that all prior learning either simply enhances or, conversely, inhibits learning; he finds it impossible to learn anything without past learning's influence. Therefore the concept of transfer of learning has no special merit or claim. For Kelly, all is learning—clear and simple. Kelly further objects to the term *use*, as in using past knowledge, and to the term *apply* as in applying past knowledge. He says that these terms and the very concept of transfer are vague, ambiguous, and trite.

Although logically there is some truth to Kelly's criticisms, at the risk of dismissing him too quickly, to explore them here in more depth would take me too far afield. Suffice it to say, that in a round-about way he would agree with the view of this book and a few other researchers like Gick and Holyoak "that no empirical or theoretical chasm separates transfer from the general topic of learning,"[16] and that "A theory of Transfer is of necessity a theory of learning and inference."[17] In my view, Detterman's criticisms are more to the immediate point.

Detterman's view is based on his review of many typical studies of transfer. In one representative study, children were taught to transfer general principles from one situation to a different one. A child would learn to stack tires on top of each other, which would then let a doll reach a shelf where other tires were to be stacked. A similar problem involved requiring the child to stack bales of hay on top of each other so that a farmer doll could then reach a tractor. Three sets of such problems were used where the general principles of stacking, pulling, or swinging were the same. It can be seen that the surface structure for each story in the set was different, but the structure was the same. If a child was not able to solve a problem, the experimenter demonstrated the solution to them. Children were always asked to repeat the solution to the problem, at which time the next structurally identical problem was presented. Given this methodology, it's not surprising, says Detterman, that these children learned the "rules of the game" over the three problem sets. Learning the rules of the game, however, is not what most would consider transfer of learning. Such experiments, says Detterman, are more a demonstration of rule induction than transfer.

In another representative study of college students, subjects saw solutions to different kinds of algebra word problems to which they solved either equivalent or very similar problems. The equivalent problems were identical except for using different numbers. Nothing else was different. Four such experiments showed that students could solve equivalent problems only when they had the sample problems available to them while solving the similar problem. Subjects infrequently solved the similar problems, even under the best of conditions. As Detterman points out, the result of these kinds of studies is not likely to surprise algebra teachers, but it surprised him.

A close look at the famous 1908 experiment of Charles Judd, who first challenged Thorndike's identical elements model, suggests that transfer not only occurs on the basis of identical elements between two problems, but also can occur via the abstract general principle underlying a phenomena (see chapter 5).[18] In Judd's experiment two groups of boys threw darts at an underwater target. In the experimental group, the boys were told about how water reflected light and that the principle of refraction would be useful for hitting the target. The control group of boys practiced but received no instruction. The transfer test was simply hitting the targets at different depths. The experimental group outperformed the control group on the so-called transfer tests.

Detterman says that the result is not surprising, because the experimental manipulation was essentially to teach the experimental group a strategy and to *tell them to use it*. But this hardly constitutes transfer, he says. Although it shows that the strategy taught was successful at producing improved performance and that subjects followed directions when told to use the strategy, he notes that, like the representative studies above, Judd's experiment in fact doesn't show anything approaching spontaneous or significant transfer. This is why transfer experiments, more frequently than not, don't in fact show transfer.

Instruction on refraction of light by water should have been given in a situation where it wasn't possible for subjects to directly make the connection between the experiment and the instruction. The idea of general transfer is for subjects to use a previously learned principle in a new situation. Teaching the principle in such close association with testing for transfer is not much different from actually telling subjects that they should use the principle just taught them. And telling a subject to use a principle is not transfer. It's simply following instructions.[19]

Detterman's criticism may be summarized as follows: When subjects (a) *are told* that previous material may be useful in the solution of a new problem, (b) are *informed* about strategies and methods known to improve learning on specific kinds of material, (c) are *instructed* to use those strategies on that material, (d) have the similarity *pointed out to them* "in some not-so-subtle way," (e) *or given other hints* about the similarity between the problems to be solved, Detterman says it "hardly seems reasonable to refer to the solution of the new problem as the result of transfer."[20] He goes on to suggest that studies claiming transfer can be said to have achieved transfer only by using "the most generous of criteria and would not meet the classical definition of transfer." He concludes by saying that in all the studies he is familiar with, transfer is achieved only by using the above kinds of "tricks," as he calls them. In keeping with the title of the heading for this section, what Detterman is saying in so many words is that what most call *teaching for transfer,* is in fact *teaching the actual transfer itself.* He also concludes his review of the research by saying that when transfer does occur, "it requires heroic efforts to produce and even with [such] draconian measures, the amount of transfer is small."[21] What more is there to say?

## CONCLUSION

Let me close by noting that in slow-changing traditional societies, there's much less need for transfer of learning. The demands of our modern civilization, however, make transfer increasingly important. In our highly complex, rapidly changing, Information Age, the ability to transfer or generalize from the familiar to the less familiar, from the old to the new, not only renders our world predictable and understandable, but is a necessity for our adaptation to the technological and global demands of the 21st century.

### Notes

[1]McKeachie, W. J., Pintrich, P. R., Lin, Y. G., & Smith, D. A. F. (1986). *Teaching and learning in the college classroom: A review of the research literature.* National Center for Research to Improve Postsecondary Teaching and Learning, p. 33.

[2]See Coldwells, A., & Hare, M. E. (1994). The transfer of skill from short tennis to lawn tennis. *Ergonomics, 37,* 17–21.

[3]I would like to thank Mr. David Allie of Phoenix Systems for these examples from his introductory material on transfer of learning in teaching computer competencies.

[4]See, for example, Haskell, R. E. (1989). Analogical transforms: A cognitive theory of the origin and development of transformation of invariance, Part I, II, *Metaphor and symbolic activity*, 4, 247–277; See also Hayek, F. A. (1952). *The sensory order: An inquiry into the foundations of theoretical psychology.* Chicago: University of Chicago Press; Marks, L. E., & Bornstein, M. H. (1987). Sensory similarities: Classes characteristics and cognitive consequences. In R. E. Haskell (Ed.), *Cognitive and symbolic structures: The psychology of metaphoric transformation* (pp. 49–65). Norwood, NJ: Ablex.

[5]Ferguson, G. A. (1963). On transfer and the abilities of man. In R. G. Grose & R. C. Birney (Eds.), Transfer of learning: An enduring problem in psychology (pp. 181–194). New York: D. Van Nostrand, p. 185.

[6]Hayek, F. A. (1952). *The sensory order: An inquiry into the foundations of theoretical psychology.* Chicago: University of Chicago Press, p. 55.

[7]Haskell, R. E. (1968). Anatomy of analogy: A new look. *Journal of* Humanistic *Psychology*, 8, 161–169.

[8]See Chapter 6 in Haskell, R. E. (1998). *Reengineering corporate training: Intellectual capital and transfer of learning.* New York: Quorum Books.

[9]Weimer, W., & Palermo, D. S. (Eds.). (1974). *Cognition and the symbolic processes.* Hillsdale, NJ: Erlbaum, p. 429.

[10]Haskell, R. E. (1968). Anatomy of analogy: A new look. *Journal of* Humanistic *Psychology*, 8, 161–169; Haskell, R. E. (1989). Analogical transforms: A cognitive theory of the origin and development of transformation of invariance, Part I, II, *Metaphor and symbolic activity*, 4, 247–277; Haskell, R. E. (Ed.). (1987). *Cognition and symbolic structures: The psychology of metaphoric transformations* (pp. 257–292). Norwood, NJ: Ablex Pub.

[11]*See, for example, Brown, D. E., & Clement, J. (1989). Overcoming misconceptions via analogical reasoning: Abstract transfer versus explanatory model construction. Instructional Science, 18, 237–261; Halford, G. S. (1992). Analogical reasoning and conceptual complexity in cognitive development. Human Development, 35, 193–217.*

[12]The literature on using analogical transfer in the classroom is quite large. But, see for example, Gilbert, S. W. (1989). An evaluation of the use of analogy, simile, and metaphor in science texts. *Journal of Research in Science Teaching*, 26, 315–327; Iding, M. K. (1993). Instructional analogies and elaborations in science text: Effects on recall and transfer performance. *Reading Psychology*, 14(1), 33–55; Klauer, K. J. (1989). Teaching for analogical transfer as a means of improving problem-solving, thinking and learning. *Instructional Science*, 18, 179–192; Mason, L. (1994). Analogy, metaconceptual awareness and conceptual change: A classroom study. *Educational Studies*, 20(2), 267–291; Mason, L., & Sorzio, P. (1996). Analogical reasoning in restructuring scientific knowledge. *European Journal of Psychology of Education*, 11(1), 3–23; Suber, P. (1988). Analogy exercises for teaching legal reasoning. *Journal of Law and Education*, 17, 91–98; Suzuki, H. (1994). The centrality of analogy in knowledge acquisition in instructional contexts. *Human Development*, 37(4), 207–219; Thagard, P. (1992). Analogy, explanation, and education. *Journal of Research in Science Teaching*, 29, 537–544.

[13]Detterman, D. K. (1993). The case for the prosecution: Transfer as an epiphenomenon. In D. K. Detterman & R. J. Sternberg (Eds.), *Transfer on trial: Intelligence, cognition, and instruction* (pp. 1–24). Norwood, NJ: Ablex.

[14]Kelly, E. L. (1967). Transfer of training: An analytic study. In B. P. Kosimar & C. J. B. MacMillan (Eds.), *Psychological concepts in education.* Chicago: Rand McNally, p. 50.

[15]Ibid, p. 50.

[16]Gick, M. L., & Holyoak, K. J. (1987). The cognitive basis of knowledge transfer. In S. M. Cormier & J. D. Hagman (Eds.), *Transfer of learning contemporary research and application* (pp. 9–45). New York: Academic Press, p. 10.

[17]Ibid, p. 13.

[18]Judd, C. H. (1908). The relation of special training and general intelligence. *Educational Review*, 36, 42–48.

[19]Another, but nontransfer-related, problem with Judd's experiment—and according to Detterman, with many other transfer experiments—is that the experimenters were not blind to the subjects' conditions. That is, apparently the same experimenter that gave instructions on re-

fraction were the same who tested the subjects for transfer. Not being blind to the conditions, the data may be entered with systematic bias. Moreover, experimenters may subtly influence their subjects performance. As Detterman correctly concludes, transfer experiment shouldn't be conducted without using a double-blind procedure, especially when assessing for general transfer.

[20]Detterman, D. K. (1993). The case for the prosecution: Transfer as an epiphenomenon. In D. K. Detterman & R. J. Sternberg (Eds.), *Transfer on trial: Intelligence, cognition, and instruction* (pp. 1–24). Norwood, NJ: Ablex, p. 11.

[21]Ibid, p. 14.

# To Teach or Not to Teach for Transfer: That Is the Question

*Individual differences in transfer will not be explained until there is a more complete explanation of the fundamental operations that compose it.*

—Douglas Detterman, *Transfer on Trial*[1]

So what lessons are we to learn from the long history of research on the failure to achieve transfer outlined in chapter 1? Edward Thorndike, the eminent experimental psychologist who initiated the experimental research on transfer of learning, concluded as early as 1901 that transfer from instructional settings does not occur. His findings were so discouraging that—even then—he counseled his graduate students at Columbia University's Teachers College to teach specifically for each specific situation and not to depend on transfer. More recently, after reviewing the decades of research since Thorndike on transfer and having taught for years, Douglas Detterman (discussed in chapter 2) concludes similarly.

Detterman concludes so pessimistically and straightforwardly that I will quote him at length. His conclusions are so personally revealing and potentially damaging that out of professional concern, I contacted him to see if he minded my using the following quote in a book that would be read, not just by fellow researchers and colleagues, but by a public audience.[2] Bravely, he didn't mind my quoting him. This is what he concludes. He says that when he began teaching,

> I thought it was important to make things as hard as possible for students so they would discover the principles for themselves. I thought the discovery of principles was a fundamental skill that students needed to learn and transfer to new situations. Now I view education, even graduate education, as the learning of information. I try to make it as easy for students as possible. Where before I was ambiguous about what a good

paper was, I now provide examples of the best papers from past classes. Before, I expected students to infer the general conclusion from specific exaamples. Now, I provide the general conclusion and support it with specific examples. In general, I sub-
scribe to the principle that you should teach people exactly what you want them to
learn in a situation as close as possible to the one in which the learning will be applied. I don't count on transfer and I don't try to promote it except by explicitly pointing out where taught skills may be applied.[3]

This is discouraging to hear. Like Detterman, however, it's clear that many
other instructors, though more privately, have likewise changed their teaching style. On many college and university campuses, faculty (including myself) are being pressured to lower the level of their courses, while at the same
time grade inflation is a national issue.[4]

Further, says Detterman, the failure of transfer isn't confined to students.
"To my knowledge," he says, "there is no convincing body of evidence showing college professors, to say nothing of college graduates, regularly applying old learning to new, novel situations." In short, says Detterman, "We replay
most of our behaviour exactly as we learn it [italics added]."[5] Unfortunately, from my
review of the research, from my years of teaching, and given the current educational Zeitgeist, I generally agree with his observations and conclusions.
Depending on how transfer is defined, I would disagree with him on one
point. Most college professors are in fact somewhat proficient at transfer or
they would not have achieved becoming a professor. Most are proficient, however, only within their specialized areas of expertise (see chapter 6), otherwise, Detterman's conclusion is perhaps correct for most professionals.

A clear implication of Detterman's observation of a lack of transfer even
among teachers is that before students can be expected or taught to transfer
their learning, teachers also need to become proficient at transfer thinking.
Although not encouraging to contemplate, for years it has been known that
the general academic quality of those enrolling in teacher education programs in the U.S. "is lower than that of students enrolled in other university
programs."[6] More recently, reviewing the research on teacher education candidates, Lasley and Williams, as well as others note the consistent findings
that "Many, if not most, teacher education students still function at a cognitive level approximating the concrete operations stage"[7] of mental functioning as measured by Piagetian cognitive tests. Cognitive functioning at a concrete level is not conducive to general transfer. I would like to make it clear,
however, that this isn't to say that there aren't extremely bright and competent individual teachers. There are. And many of them.

Piaget's cognitive stages of development are well known and cited in every
introductory psychology text on the market. According to Piagetian tests, mature reasoning is indicated by functioning on the "formal operational stage"
of development. These stages are widely thought to be "naturally" occurring.
As I will point out in later chapters, however, Piaget's cognitive stages of de-

velopment as naturally occurring stages have been seriously questioned by rigorous recent research. Current thinking is that the differences between stages may be due to the quality of the knowledge base and/or memory capacity, not to naturally occurring maturational changes. Whatever the causes of the stages, the Piagetian tests do reflect relative levels of mental functioning in culturally significant realms. And reaching a formal operational stage of development is generally implicated in success at transfer.

In an attempt to achieve transfer, numerous educational fads and miracle methods are claimed to work. At the opposite extreme of computational methods is the fanfare surrounding what is variously termed "accelerated," "integrative," or "superlearning" programs. Such programs are actually a mix of a number of traditional and nontraditional components, including playing baroque music, reciting poetry, the use of meditation and mental imaging techniques, as well as other "feel good" methods like eating pastries while learning. Though accelerated learning programs have been in use for over 10 years now, they appear to be the current fad—in a long history—of trendy methods purporting to achieve superior learning and transfer. Accelerated learning programs have been used in Fortune 500 companies, government agencies, and in public school systems on a large scale.

Most of the evaluation research conducted on such superlearning programs has been fraught with numerous and serious methodological problems. Aside from the traditional subjective evaluations by participants in these courses, there are hardly any rigorous studies on such programs. As with many miracle methods and programs, participants and their supervisors in an Eastman Kodak program reported enjoying the training and believed they had learned more than from traditional training methods. But an excellent study on accelerated learning, conducted at the Eastman Kodak Corporation by Robert Bretz and Richard Thompsett,[8] published in the *Journal of Applied Psychology*, and using experimental and control group design, found no evidence for the superior learning or transfer attributable to the accelerated learning methods.

Now it might be asked, if participants enjoy such miracle programs, and perhaps learn as much from them as more traditional methods, why not use them? The answer is simple: the cost is much higher than typical training programs. For example, in the Kodak study the teacher–participant ratio for the accelerated learning approach was approximately 1/10, as compared to a 1/44 ratio for the traditional approach, plus other equipment costs. Much of the information about miracle educational methods belongs more to the category of rumor than of valid evaluation of their effectiveness. The only thing that's accelerating and super about most of these programs are their cost.

So where do we go from here, educationally speaking? The long answer to this question is what this book is all about; the short answer is as follows.

## INSTRUCTIONAL PROSPECTUS
## FOR THE 21ST CENTURY

Given our individual and cultural set of values, expectations, and social conditions, the conclusion reached by Detterman, myself, and others is perhaps
the most objective and honest evaluation of *current* educational outcomes.
The reasons for this current state of affairs are many. In general, U.S. culture
is pragmatic, expects instant success, is generally anti-intellectual, having little tolerance for anything that isn't "concrete," that isn't immediately "useful,"
and for anything that's called "theoretical" and "abstract." As Howard Gardner and others have historically observed, we consider street smarts more important than book learning, which won't get you anywhere, and that college
professors are absentminded and live in an Ivory Tower. In addressing these
stereotypes, Robyn Dawes aptly relates a story that "in the 1940s and early
1950s, the owners of some small farms in New Hampshire whom I knew were
fond of misquoting |Benjamin| Franklin and contemptuous of 'book learning':
their land is now owned by a neighbor's son who went to college instead of
acquiring 'experience' " (see chapters 9 and 10).[9] Those growing up in our society receive very mixed messages about education.

In addition our educational institutions are increasingly required to take
on responsibilities that used to be the province of the family and even religion; our schools are now not only required to be therapeutic communities
but much of their "instructional" time—the shortest of any industrialized nation—is increasingly used as therapeutic time. Compounding these demands upon our educational institutions, our society transmits an ambivalence about the role of schools and the value of education. As Gardner points
out, on a rhetorical level there's little disagreement about the importance of
education. Yet the extent to which education is in fact valued in our society
has been called into question for many decades. Given this historical view of
knowing and knowledge, it's no wonder that we engage in little transfer. Until we come to terms with these issues, Detterman's prescription for teaching
is sad—but sage—advice for most current instructional situations.[10]

In an information age, our ambivalence about learning has become dan-
gerously counterproductive. In an age where we must be increasingly able to
analyze and think about information, transfer ability becomes increasingly
important. As a society we are going through profound changes. This is no
less true of the business world where most of our students will work. The business workforce is increasingly made up of *knowledge workers*, people who have
and are able to analyze information. As a society, our anti-intellectual orientation is counterproductive. I find it somewhat more than a little ironic that
those on the vanguard of business are now implementing what are called
learning organizations, and with knowledge considered the engine of such organizations, enabling them to compete in a global marketplace. This knowledge is being termed *intellectual capital*. At first glance, the phrase *intellectual cap-*

*ital* perhaps sounds like an oxymoron, or worse yet, a phrase conjured up by some esoteric postmodern Marxist humanities professor. But it isn't: Intellectual capital is increasingly used by hard-headed, bottom-line business executives. In fact, in 1989 the phrase intellectual capital was boldly spread across the cover of *Fortune* magazine.[11]

Despite the widespread—but quite understandable—conclusion by many researchers that "a long line of research (starting with the work of Thorndike and James) casts a gloomy pall on the prospect of general transfer,"[12] what I will be outlining in the remaining chapters of this book is a framework for achieving general transfer. I will suggest that to achieve general transfer requires the following learning and instructional principles, principles that other philosophies of education, in various ways and forms, have previously suggested. The difference is that this time around the principles are specifically connected to transfer and to the latest research supporting the eleven principles that I outline, not just to educational "philosophies." The principles I'm about to suggest could be considered both "old time schooling" principles and as what in the past was called progressive education. It was advocated by the philosopher and educator John Dewey (1859–1952), and as Gardner has correctly lamented, the progressive approach to education ultimately defeated Dewey and many of his followers.

Dewey's approach was defeated because a progressive education "requires teachers who are well trained . . . a community beyond the walls of the school . . . And . . . a student body sufficiently motivated and responsible so that it can make the most of the opportunities offered and accept the responsibilities it entails"[13] (see chapters 7 and 8). Although my approach to transfer does not directly evolve from this progressive educational philosophy, many of its requirements and principles are similar. I should clarify, however, that I am not referring to what has often been called "progressive education," which included instructional methods like "open classrooms" and unstructured "discovery" learning. As I noted in the Introduction, this theory of transfer does not necessarily imply the use or nonuse of any particular method of teaching.

As I indicated in the Introduction, many of the principles that I've derived from the research may not be popular with the current educational and social Zeitgeists, and some may appear obvious. Be that as it may, the fact is they are not practiced in most educational settings. In broad outline, here is a preview of what's required.

1. *Learners need to acquire a large primary knowledge base or high level of expertise in the area that transfer is required* (see chapter 6). To some, this requirement may not seem to be any great news. But to those engaged in higher education or those who read the *Chronicle of Higher education* and keep abreast of educational issues, it's clear that either by design or by default or both, that learning strategies have been *in* and that requiring learners to master a large knowl-

edge base has been *out* for quiet some time. Education has tended to reflect our technological society. Somehow, learning a number of skills and simple facts is supposed to add up to significant knowledge and transfer. It doesn't.

2. *Some level of knowledge base in subjects outside the primary area is necessary for significant transfer* (see chapter 6). Peripheral or oblique knowledge often provides important links to a primary area of knowledge that makes it possible to engage in transfer; if we're to be serious regarding the much written-about interdisciplinary curricular and integrative learning where we make transfer discoveries and educate generalists, then a knowledge base outside one primary area becomes a necessity.

3. *An understanding of the history of the transfer area(s) is vital.* Without at least a general grasp of the history of an area, transfer may be incorrect or inadequate (see chapter 5).

4. *Motivation, or more specifically, a "spirit of transfer," is a primary prerequisite for transfer to occur* (see chapter 7). Without this affective or emotion/feeling-based foundation, the impetus to transfer is unlikely to occur (see chapter 7).

5. *Learners need to understand what transfer of learning is and how it works.*

6. *An orientation to think and encode our learning in transfer terms is necessary, for significant transfer doesn't happen automatically* (see chapters 7 and 8). How we encode new information determines how we retrieve and apply it.

7. *Cultures of transfer need to be created* (see chapter 8). To one degree or another, transfer is supported or inhibited by the group or culture in which learning takes place. Accordingly, we need to develop cultures of transfer.

8. *An understanding of the theory underlying the transfer area is crucial* (see chapter 9). By grasping the theory of an area, one can see and make the appropriate transfer.

9. *Hours of practice and drill are requisite* (see chapter 10). This in turn requires hours of self-conscious learning and discipline. Fundamental have to be learned thoroughly before significant and creative transfer can occur (see chapter 10).

10. *Significant transfer requires time to incubate; it tends not to occur instantaneously.* In our society we typically transmit to students expectations of instant knowledge and success. Expecting such instant results and gratification, learners often quit trying to transfer. Research shows that expertise requires incubation time.

11. *Finally, and most importantly, learners must observe and read the works of people who are exemplars of transfer thinking.* This means reading systems thinkers, accounts of scientific discoveries, of invention and innovation; it means reading the great poets. Poets are masters of transfer.

If all of this seems similar to an "old time" schooling philosophy, so be it. It's what's required if we want to achieve transfer. If we look at those who do transfer well, they have not done so simply with learning strategies or by observing what they are doing as a set of metacognitive skills.

I might also note at this point that I am not naive enough to believe that the principles I advocate will be adopted in any large-scale fashion, at least not any time soon. Nevertheless, the extent to which a learner, a teacher, or a school adopts these principles is the extent to which transfer will occur—and only to that extent. Nothing else will work. Nothing else has ever worked.

Although none of these principles are novel and may seem overly simple, in the succeeding chapters I will show why and how each is specifically related to and is important for transfer. Indeed, the very idea of transfer implies that every new idea is based on or has continuity to past ideas. What would an entirely new idea look like, and how would we recognize it? From time to time—and in bits and pieces—others have advocated most of what I have outlined as prerequisites for learning and transfer.

These requirements constitute what I consider to be a general theory of transfer. Learning strategies alone will not suffice to insure transfer. They are important, however, in augmenting transfer once the general theory of transfer outlined in this book has been adopted. Accordingly, strategies and heuristics constitute a special theory of transfer that I will outline in a future volume. Based on the research, I don't think I am overstating the case to say that unless we adopt in some manner the eleven principles of transfer outlined above, we will at best continue to be limited to the lowest levels of simple transfer. And we'll only achieve those levels at great human and financial cost. The chapters to follow will further explore, delineate, and reinforce these eleven principles of transfer on which effective education and our future as a species is dependent.

## IMPLICATIONS FOR INSTRUCTION
## AND A PRESCRIPTIVE REMEDY

That transfer seldom occurs in any significant way is repeatedly shown in both laboratory research and in the classroom. What's learned in the classroom may not transfer outside the classroom, and what's learned outside the classroom may not transfer to inside the classroom. Many students in grade school who learn how to multiply, add, and subtract numbers are unable to multiply, add, and subtract real items in their everyday life. The converse is also true. Studies show that street children who do complex mathematical calculations in their street business are unable to do the same math problems when presented with them formally in a classroom situation.[14] This concreteness of reasoning embodies the very essence of the transfer problem: that learning isn't only welded to subject matter, but is often welded to the physical place where the learning occurred, and how it's encoded during the learning process. This is a serious finding because a failure to transfer means a failure to think.

During the early years of life, children learn and transfer at an incredibly rapid rate in their natural, everyday setting. In fact children are often too good at transfer. In terms of language usage, children's transfer may often be logically correct but conventionally wrong. For example, from the point of view of the conjugation of *big, bigger, biggest*, children logically transfer this learning and say *good, gooder, goodest*, which, of course, in terms of conventional grammar is inappropriate transfer. Yet it's a logically correct conjugation. When formal schooling begins, however, little significant transfer occurs from instruction. The question is, What's going on here—or, rather, what's not going on? First, learning in natural, everyday situations seems to be a kind of learning that's almost qualitatively different from formal learning (I will address this issue in chapter 8). But even in a natural environment, learning often doesn't transfer very far—either conceptually or in terms of physical place.

Also implied in my general approach to transfer is that transfer isn't based on the learning of skills and strategies. If it's not already obvious, strictly speaking, the term *skills* belongs more to a *vocational training* approach to instruction than to a *learning* or education approach, a distinction I will make central to this book. Both in the United States and in England, government-supported youth training and employment training skills programs are increasing. These programs are based on the belief that if the "same skill" occurs in several contexts, then there can be general skills taught for transfer across the different situations. Mixing concrete and mixing ingredients for a cake, for example, can both be described in terms of their similar mixing and measuring skills. Accordingly, the assumed outcome is that a person trained in the mixing of concrete can be expected to be more successful in his or her initial attempts at mixing a cake than would be a person without the skills of mixing or measuring.

Intuitively, such a skills approach seems obviously correct. Empirically, however, they lack theoretical support. As Carole Myers notes, "The difficulty is, that while many activities may be described in the *same* (italics added) way, they need not involve the same psychological process".[15] Mixing cakes and concrete make different demands on the individuals in terms of (a) the scale of the operation, (b) judgments to be made, (c) motor skills used, (d) operation of equipment, and (e) use of tools. Though such skills can be described in *similar* terms, the similarity often occurs at such a high level of abstraction that the expected transfer doesn't take place.

An interesting article in the *Oxford Review of Education* summarizes my approach to transfer. The author says of the instructional process that "whatever else is involved in it, it is about the individual person and his development; and . . . only that which is more than simply a skill can contribute to that development, the continual forming and reforming of the person" (see chapters 7 and 8).[16] The term *skill* is used these days in a myriad of contexts. We talk of writing skills, reading skills, thinking skills, and interpersonal skills. There is hardly an activity not described as a skill. The indiscriminate use of the term skill confuses and blurs the distinction between things which really are skills with things which are not. Although it is true that in order to read well one has to bring something other than skills to the reading, this "something other" is the individual reader as a human being with values, beliefs, and knowledge. Being able to apply all the technical skills of word, sentence, and paragraph construction, etc., will not make you a good reader, any more than knowing all the so-called interpersonal relations skills will make you good at interacting with others. As a technological society, we tend to believe that step-by-step techniques will conquer all. It's as if painting by numbers will create a great artist, or that accumulating a bunch of skills will lead to insight and significant transfer. It hasn't. And it won't.

As I noted in the introduction, the theory goes against not only many of our historical and contemporary values, but against what most of the historical and contemporary artificial intelligence research seems to indicate. If we base our view of education and transfer on what the preponderance of rigorous research appears to show, then we are left with Detterman's apparently justifiable conclusions (cited in chapter 2): teach a subject matter step-by-incremental-step, sticking as closely to the concrete facts as possible and be content that transfer of the learning is unlikely to occur. The problem is, what are the consequences of accepting such an approach to education?

Despite the preponderance of negative findings on transfer and similar teaching experiences, I'm not as pessimistic as Detterman about the *possibility* of achieving transfer. My optimism is conditional, however, upon the eleven principles that I've derived from the research and outlined above and that I'm convinced are the conditions required to achieve transfer. Let me briefly reiterate them: (a) acquire a large primary knowledge base or high level of expertise in the area that transfer is; (b) acquire some level of knowledge base in subjects outside the primary area; (c) acquire an understanding of the history of the transfer area(s); (d) acquire a "spirit of transfer"; (e) understand what transfer of learning is and how it works; (f) develop an orientation to think and encode learning in transfer terms; (g) create cultures of transfer; (h) understand the theory underlying the transfer area(s); (i) engage in hours of practice and drill; (j) take time for the learning to incubate; (k) observe and read the works of people who are exemplars of transfer thinking. Superficial, short-run, isolated learning strategies will not suffice as the history of transfer research and teaching experience tellingly reveals. In the following chapters I will present what I consider to be a prescriptive, concrete, and useful theory of transfer.

## FROM RESEARCH TO USEFUL THEORY

It is important to explain why I am convinced that my approach to transfer is the only course of action that ensures transfer. First, the so-called facts of the transfer findings don't speak for themselves. We interpret them. Second, in between the cracks of the preponderance of findings demonstrating that transfer seldom occurs, there is other evidence that I have gathered and co-alesced into a counter interpretation which says that the ability to transfer can be taught and learned. But only with the principles that I have enumerated.

Third, and perhaps most importantly, it has been assumed by most researchers—including myself—and educational experts, but probably by a lesser number of classroom teachers (but often for the wrong reasons), that instructional methods should be directly designed on detailed research findings; that the form of instruction should follow what we have discovered about the structure of how information flows in our brains. As Douglas Medin and Anthony Ortony have noted,

> Logical and psychological accounts of certain phenomena need not necessarily be compatible. It is now generally accepted that psychologically plausible accounts of certain phenomena are at odds with purely logical analyses. People are not wetware instantiations of formal systems, be they logical or statistical, as a wealth of research on judgment under uncertainty has shown.[17]

In other words, if we find that the structure of information flow in the brain or mind is of the form $f>p>q>z$, then instructional methods should be designed in the same $f>p>q>z$ sequence. I now have grave reservations about this assumption, at least for most instructional purposes, and especially for general transfer. To be informed by cognitive and brain research findings is one thing, to construct a detailed instructional model based on them, is quite another thing. The implications of not directly basing a theory of instruction on the details of research findings are profound—and perhaps more importantly, dangerous.

The implications of such an approach are dangerous because an approach not directly based on research findings can all too easily lead to an "anything goes" philosophy of education. But nothing could be farther from my intent. Scattered throughout the educational literature, I was gratified to find precedents for my view of designing instructional theory. In 1963, the well-known educational psychologist, Lee Cronbach, maintained that, "Formal psychological theory is not, and may never be, able to calculate a prescription for teaching; its service is to point out factors requiring adjustment and to suggest provisional tries."[18] In 1964, another educational researcher noted that, "it is not to be assumed that the architectonics of knowledge is necessarily the same as the architectonics of instruction,"[19] which is to say that the structure of our cognitive processes are not necessarily the appropriate structures on which to base a theory of instruction.

Another well-known educational researcher and practitioner, David Ausubel, maintained a similar stance. Engaging in transfer thinking himself, Ausubel says,

> Educational psychology is unequivocally an applied discipline, but . . . it is not general psychology applied to educational problems—no more so than mechanical en-

gineering is general physics applied to problems of designing machinery or medicine is general biology applied to problems of diagnosing, treating, and preventing human diseases.[20]

In other words, instructional theory building and methodology is itself a separate and valid level of investigation. The apparent simplicity of these statements masks their profound importance. Their simplicity, however, does perhaps in part explain why they have not been widely acknowledged. It's thus important to reiterate: What these researchers are saying is that using the detailed computational research findings on how the mind works may not be the best data for designing effective instructional methods; what we know about how the mind is structured isn't necessarily the model on which to base the structure of teaching. Unfortunately, these insights have generally been ignored by psychological and education specialists and theorists. I intend to take these insights seriously.

From a slightly different but corroborating perspective, recent research on reasoning provides additional support for my approach to an instructional theory of transfer. Medin and Ortony suggest that we need

> to acknowledge, as has been acknowledged in other areas of psychology, that *logical* and *psycho*logical [italics added] accounts of certain phenomena need not necessarily be compatible. It's now generally accepted that psychologically plausible accounts of how we reason are at odds with purely logical analyses.[21]

As I will outline in more detail in chapter 6, many of us don't reason with rules of logic but with mental models. We are not simply wetware instantiations (i.e., organic examples) of formal computational systems, be they logical or statistical, as a wealth of research on judgment under uncertainty has shown.

In other words, our model of the mind as functioning like a computer (that is, a "wetware" instance of a computer) operating in a minute, sequential, logical, step-by-logical-step fashion, guided by sets of formal rules, doesn't appear to conform to how we reason in everyday life. In short, what's formally logical may not be *psycho*-logical. Still more recently, Graeme Halford argued "that much of human reasoning, including what's often called logical inference, is essentially analogical. It is performed by using schemas from everyday life as analogs,"[22] not formal or abstract rules of reasoning. In other words, our reasoning in everyday life—more often than not—doesn't follow the rules that constitute formal or computational logic (see chapter 6). In large measure, this is why courses in formal logic do not seem to transfer to everyday reasoning.

Thus designing instructional material in minute, sequential steps directly based on research of how our cognitive processes may appear to work—and I stress "may appear to work" as there is beginning to be serious dissent that the computational view of mind—may not always be the most efficient model for learning or for instruction. What I suggest is that basing our models of learning and instruction on cognitive findings isn't the appropriate approach if we want to achieve significant transfer. Moreover, the step-by-step approach to learning and current cognitive theories are biased toward a conscious level of mental processing, despite the fact that it's well accepted in cognitive psychology that our conscious "channel" is a limited one compared to our nonconscious processing of information. I suggest that a conscious step-by-step approach to learning tends only to result in near transfer. Far transfer depends much more on a nonconscious processing of information than does near transfer. A more naturally holistic, nonprogrammed, approach to transfer is the way we "naturally" learn as we go about our everyday business; it's the way children master, order, and transfer the complex and huge amount of information they structure into something called language. What's needed, then, is an instructional framework that's soundly informed by cognitive research findings, but which isn't mired in, and modeled on, the details of that research.

Current standard instructional approaches that involve a very concrete, sequential, step-by-step type of instruction are similar to the programmed text approach to learning during the behaviorist-dominated 1960s and early 1970s, leaving little or nothing to be inferred by the learner. Lohman notes that the line between instructional and general experimental psychology is often difficult to detect. He observes,

> Topics such as mathematical problem solving and reading comprehension that were once the provincial concern of educators now occupy center stage in the new psychology of thinking and problem solving. The gap between psychological theory and educational practice has not been this narrow since the turn of the century.[23]

A detailed programming approach is more of a *training* than a *learning* approach. As such, like most training approaches, the emphasis—though not exclusively—is on instructional method and design, rather than on the learner as the central cause of learning. I should note at this point that a general theory of transfer doesn't preclude the more traditional detailed and programmed-instruction approach to learning in some situations and subject matters. A programming type of approach is basically relevant to lower level, more concrete, and detailed tasks. Jobs, or knowledge bases, that involve detail and that are technical are often best taught with this approach, at least initially.

Recent evidence indicates a conscious, sequential, and goal-oriented approach during problem solving can decrease the acquisition of mental schemas, and that this significantly reduces the quality of transfer. This is because learners tend to work backward from their goal, which is very demanding on mental resources and tends to inhibit the acquisition of mental schemas.[24] To break everything down into discrete tasks and procedures results in never-ending lists, as the programmed learning texts movement of a few years ago demonstrated. Moreover, even when programmed texts are successful, it's difficult to move beyond them. And when we do move beyond them, we don't move very far. Moreover, although teaching specific strategies is a viable approach for some situations, there are just too many of them, and we don't know when or to what extent or under what conditions they work.

The findings from cognitive science and artificial intelligence have been applied successfully to programming computers, and this model is being applied to learning and instruction. The formal discipline theory of transfer (see chapter 5), which held that we automatically learn and transfer based on the inherent properties of certain disciplines like Latin and math, is alive and well in the guise of computer programming models. As Ann Brown and Joseph Campione observed, "If the Greeks thought that instruction in mathematics teaches one to think, and the 19-century classicists set great store by learning Latin, 20th-century psychologists place their faith in computer programming."[25] A further down-side of adopting an artificial intelligence model of learning is that if curricular were designed on the basis of these otherwise useful and excellent programming methods, it would increase the time required to learn any given subject at least 10-fold, because unlike computers, we are not rapid calculators that can consciously recall long strings of rules and integrate them.

Chair of Psychological and Quantitative Foundations department in the College of Education of the University of Iowa, Lohman similarly recognizes in his insightful article, "Encouraging the development of Fluid Abilities in Gifted Students," that applying computational findings to educational practice is often problematic. He says, "Although this work is theoretically encouraging, it's unlikely that it will have a significant impact on practical efforts to assess transfer. Why? First, a detailed task analysis requires an incredible amount of work."[26] Thus such an approach would not generally be educationally feasible. Breaking learning down into minute components very quickly reaches a point of diminishing returns. Something has to be left to the inference process of the human mind. Because something is found to be valid or true, it doesn't necessarily follow that it's useful. A further problem is that learners conceptualize *similarity* differently. There's no guarantee that learners represent tasks in the same way as the theorists or educators who construct them. Research demonstrates that learners of diverse abilities recognize similarity and solve transfer problems in many different ways. All computational theories of transfer suffer from these limitations. This is why it's important to have a general theory of transfer.

Again, with the exception of inherently technical material, such as learning mathematics, accounting, and other similar material, a more holistic, nonconscious approach is often more effective. Even in these fields, however, on a higher level—after the basics have been repetitively practiced—many innovators function holistically. It's clear from reading the accounts of great innovators that they didn't come up with their discoveries by sequential processing; however, they may then need to be back-translated into more manageable sequential, analytical, and technical terms. From a transfer perspective, adding up little bits of information will not lead to a big piece of knowledge, just as adding up little bits of knowledge will not lead to innovation and discovery.

## CONCLUSION

From the time of Socrates to the present, the basic transfer question has been, What is it that enables a person with specific knowledge, learning, understanding, or skills learned in one area and/or social context to adapt, modify, or extend it in such a way as to be able to apply it to other areas? This is of course the central and long-standing issue that this book addresses. Transfer of learning must be raised to a principle, and change what it means to learn, to be educated, and to think. There really is no other viable choice for us as individuals, as a nation, or as a global society.

## Notes

[1]Detterman, D. K. (1993). The case for the prosecution: Transfer as an epiphenomenon. In D. K. Detterman & R. J. Sternberg (Eds.), *Transfer on trial: Intelligence, cognition, and instruction* (pp. 1–24). Norwood, NJ: Ablex, p. 21.
[2]Personal communication, March 1999.
[3]Detterman, D. K. (1993). The case for the prosecution: Transfer as an epiphenomenon. In D. K. Detterman & R. J. Sternberg (Eds.), *Transfer on trial: Intelligence, cognition, and instruction* (pp. 1–24). Norwood, NJ: Ablex, p. 16.
[4]See Haskell, R. E. (1997). Academic freedom, tenure, and student evaluations of faculty: Galloping polls in the 21st century. *Educational Policy Analysis Archives*, 5(6). [Peer-reviewed journal]. Available: *http://olam.ed.asu.edu/epaa/v5n6.html*
[5]Detterman, D. K. (1993). The case for the prosecution: Transfer as an epiphenomenon. In D. K. Detterman & R. J. Sternberg (Eds.), *Transfer on trial: Intelligence, cognition, and instruction* (pp. 1–24). Norwood, NJ: Ablex, p. 16.
[6]Reyes, D. J. (1987). Cognitive development of teacher candidates: An analysis. *Journal of Teacher Education*, Mar/April, 18–21, p. 18.
[7]Lasley, T. J., Williams, S. J., & Hart, P. M. (1991). Nonexamples: Why teachers don't use them and why teacher educators should. *Mid-Western Educational Researcher*, 4, 2–6, p. 4; see also Wyatt, M. L. (1982). *Formal-operational thinking and the role of training*. Doctoral Dissertation, Mississippi State University.
[8]Bretz, R. D., & Thomsett, R. E. (1992). Comparing traditional and integrative learning methods in organizational training programs. *Journal of Applied Psychology*, 77(6), 941–951.
[9]Dawes, R. M. (1994). *House of cards: Psychology and psychotherapy built on myth*. New York: Free Press, p. 109.
[10]When I say *most* instructional situations I refer mainly to educational administration and organizational system pressures that preclude an instructor from requiring of students what is needed to achieve transfer.
[11]*Fortune* (1989). October 23rd.
[12]Singley, M. K., & Anderson, J. R. (1989). *The transfer of cognitive skill*. Cambridge, MA: Harvard University Press, p. 230.
[13]Gardner, H. (1991). *The unschooled mind: How children think and how schools should teach*. New York: Basic Books, p. 195.

[14]Scribner, S., & Cole, M. (1973). Cognitive consequences of formal and informal education. *Science*, 182, 553–559; Scribner, S., & Cole, M. (1981). *The psychology of literacy*. Cambridge, MA: Harvard University Press.

[15]Myers, C. (1992). Research Core skills and transfer in the youth training schemes: A field study of trainee motor mechanics. *Journal of Organizational Behavior*, 13, 625–632.

[16]Hart, W. A. (1978). Against skills. *Oxford Review of Education*, 4, 205–216, p. 213.

[17]Medin, D., & Ortony, A. (1989). Psychological essentialism. In S. Vosniadou & A. Anthony (Eds.), *Similarity and analogical reasoning*. New York: Cambridge University Press, p. 182.

[18]Cronbach, L. J., Hilgard, E. R., & Spalding, W. B. (1963). Intellectual development as transfer of learning. In L. J. Cronbach, E. R. Hilgard, & W. B. Spalding (Eds.), *Educational psychology* (314–348). New York: Harcourt, Brace, & World, p. 13.

[19]Phenix, P. H. (1964). The architectonics of knowledge. In *Education and the structure of knowledge* (45–74). Phi Delta Kappa Symposium on Educational Research, University of Illinois. Chicago: Rand McNally, pp. 45–74.

[20]Ausubel, D. P. (1977). The facilitation of meaningful verbal learning in the classroom. *Educational Psychologist*, 12, 162–178, pp. 174–5.

[21]Medin, D., & Ortony, A. (1989). Psychological essentialism. In S. Vosniadou & A. Anthony (Eds.), *Similarity and analogical reasoning* (pp. 179–195). New York: Cambridge University Press, pp. 182–183.

[22]Halford, G. S. (1992). Analogical reasoning and conceptual complexity in cognitive development. *Human Development*, 35, 193–217, p. 193.

[23]Lohman, D. (1993). Learning and the nature of educational measurement. *National Association of Secondary School Principles*, 77, 41–53, p. 42.

[24]Pierce, K. A., Duncan, M. K., Gholson, B., Ray, G. E., & Kamhi, A. G. (1993). Cognitive load, schema acquisition, and procedural adaptation in nonisomorphic analogical transfer. *Journal of Educational Psychology*, 85, no. 1.

[25]Brown, A. L., & Campione, J. C. (1984). Three faces of transfer: Implications to early competence, individual differences, and instruction. *Advances in Developmental Psychology*, 3, 143–192, p. 144.

[26]Lohman, D. F. (1992). Encouraging the development of fluid abilities in gifted students. In N. Colangelo, S. G. Assouline, & D. L. Ambroson (Eds.), *Talent development: Proceedings from the 1991 Henry B. and Jocelyn Wallace national research symposium on talent development* (pp. 143–162). New York: Trillium Press, p. 151–152.

# Transfer and Everyday Reasoning: Personal Development, Cultural Diversity, and Decision Making

*Although it might seem that the use of individual instances would be restricted to novel situations, there is evidence that particular events may be tremendously important in people's lives and may condition their responses to a number of different situations.*

—STEPHEN READ, *Once Is Enough: Causal Reasoning from a Single Instance*[1]

Recall that the initial paradox of transfer is that although transfer has been clearly demonstrated throughout the history of transfer research, it seldom occurs as the result of formal instruction; nevertheless, it occurs widely in everyday life. In fact, it occurs pervasively in everyday reasoning about events and people. Without exaggeration, transfer in everyday reasoning is so pervasive that this chapter could all too easily become a book in itself. In fact, this book can be seen as a development of this chapter. When transfer occurs in everyday reasoning, however, we often fail to recognize it as transfer. This is partly because of how we understand the concept of transfer. As I pointed out in chapter 2, when we cite an "example" or an "instance" of phenomena we typically don't consider it to be transfer, but a metaphor or an analogy. Furthermore, an *example* or an *instance* of something is simply considered a member of the *same* category and therefore—by definition— is not transfer. However, because nothing is ever absolutely the same as anything else, when we create an example or see something as an instance of something else, we are generalizing by focusing on the similarities between the example or the instance and the general category we consider them to be instantiations of. It follows then that when we use examples and instances of an event, we have already engaged in transfer thinking. Consequently, our everyday reasoning is replete with transfer. Of necessity, it can be no other way.

## REASONING ABOUT EVERYDAY EVENTS

Transfer is no more evident than in our everyday use of language. Our language is a veritable quarry of transfer. We say, do you *feel warm, cold, bitter, tender, hard, irritated, wounded, refreshed*, or *excited*? Are you going *up* in the world or *down*? Are you an *upright, downcast, stable, grasping, tight, dull, sharp* person? Are you a *cog* in the *wheel*? Do you *fit* in? During the last year, did you make a *hit, play* on the team, play to *win, slug it out, strike out*, or reach a *stalemate*? Are you *on the ball, selling* yourself, and being *sold* on an idea? We talk about *social scales, ladders of success, hierarchies, climbers, rising* and *falling stars*, and about *pitfalls*. The list is endless. It is generally accepted that language grows on the basis of transfer. These linguistic transfers, however, are more than simple "figures of speech"; they are powerfully influential in learning, thinking, and reasoning.[2] And they point to a more fundamental cognitive process by which we reason in everyday life: reasoning by similarity. In short, transfer.

David Rumelhart, well known in the field of cognitive psychology of reasoning, suggests that much of our everyday thinking is based on simple similarity relations:

> Most everyday reasoning probably does not involve much in the way of manipulating mental models. It probably involves even less in the way of formal reasoning. Rather, it probably involves assimilating the novel situation to other situations that are in some way similar—that is, reasoning by similarity. Now, it is possible to see a continuum of possible situations for reasoning by similarity involving at one pole what might be called remembering and at the other what might be called analogical reasoning. In between, we have such processes as generalizing, being reminded, and reasoning by example.[3]

Our use of similarity, it seems, is systemic in our everyday reasoning. We could say that our mental manipulation of similarity is the foundation of reasoning itself.

That reminds me: How often do we say, "Oh, that reminds me of the time when. . . ." or "Here we go again. He's acting just like he did when. . . ." or "She's acting just like Mary"? Most of us have also had the experience of responding to a friend or colleague in the same way that we responded in the past to our brother or sister or to our parents. And how often have we had the experience of instantly liking or disliking someone we just met. We don't have to be Sigmund Freud to realize that when such situations happen they are typically because we are reminded in some way—either in appearance, mannerism, or emotional style—of a sibling, parent, or person in our past that we either liked or disliked. We then often base our responses to others on these ostensibly *similar* situations from our past experience. These *re-mindings* function as examples and instances and mental models for us to reason and make decisions about people and situations. I will illustrate later in this chapter that many governmental and social policy decisions are based on transfer from single instances in a decision makers' experience or knowledge base.

In the context of therapy, Freud called these reminders, "transference phenomena." Transference is when a patient transfers, projects, or attributes the characteristics of a significant other, say a parent, onto the therapist, and as a consequence reacts to the therapist as he or she would to the significant other person. Continuing a long line of clinical research, there has recently been considerable experimental data on this kind of transfer thinking in everyday interaction with others. Reporting in the *Journal of Personality and Social Psychology*, Susan Andersen and her colleagues wrote, "Mental representations of significant others serve as storehouses of information about important individuals from one's life. Interestingly, these representations can also be triggered by a new person and applied to this person in the context of everyday interpersonal relations."[4] She found that this tends to occur when there are similarities between the present and past experiences of the person doing the transferring. Past experiences that are transferred onto our everyday social judgments have implications not only for our present social perceptions but for our memory of past events.

## REASONING WITH SINGLE INSTANCES

We often place as much if not more credence on a single instance than we do on theory or logic. We use these single instances as metaphors or analogies. In terms of reasoning from base rates (i.e., on the probability of an event being true based on its actual frequency of occurrence), instead we often reason with a single instance. For example, from a base rate perspective, if I say there's a person standing on the other side of a door, and all I say is that the person is 85 years old, and I then ask someone to describe that person, not knowing anything else, in terms of probabilities, the person should describe "a female," since females tend to live longer than males. Most people make wild guesses, or say they can't possibly make an intelligent guess as they don't have sufficient information. Similarly, people will often not buy automobile X because of a single negative instance in their experience—perhaps a neighbor who had an X and it was a lemon—despite research in *Consumer Reports* indicating that in terms of the probabilities (or base rate) X is a very reliable car.

Stephen Read, a psychologist at the University of California, Los Angeles (UCLA),[5] and others[6] have been conducting research on our use of single instances in reasoning and decision making. This single-stance research has several implications. Somewhat counterintuitively, it's often the simple observations in life that carry profound consequences. One implication is that it provides insight into the bases on which we respond to others in social situations. Another implication is that reasoning on the basis of a single instance is applicable to the logical problem of induction and inference. It has long been known that our penchant to generalize from a few instances to a new instance is highly variable—and problematic. At times, we are quite willing to generalize from one or two cases, whereas other times we will not generalize even from a large number of cases. Perhaps the most important implication, as Read points out, is that

> In the past, researchers and theorists have tended to focus on people's use of abstract rules and strategies in causal reasoning. Such a focus is far too narrow. There are good reasons to think that a great deal of people's everyday causal reasoning is firmly grounded in their concrete knowledge of the world. If one truly wishes to understand how people explain and predict the behavior of others, one must devote far more effort to studying the ways in which people actually use their knowledge of the world.[7]

Although reasoning on the basis of a single instance may sound like it's "reasoning for dummies," it isn't. As Socrates said over two thousand years ago, "I am myself a great lover of these processes of division and generalizations; they help me to speak and to think. And if I find any man who is able to see 'a One in Many' in nature, him I follow, and walk in his footsteps as if he were a god."[8] As it turns out, we do use our particular knowledge of the world by transferring it to many different situations.

In an early study entitled, "Seeing the Past in the Present: The Effect of Association to Familiar Events on Judgments and Decisions,"[9] Thomas Gilovich asked twenty male sportswriters to rate descriptions of hypothetical football players. They were asked to rate them as being more or less likely to be excellent players. The raters were more apt to rate the hypothetical players as more likely to be excellent players when the description of the hypothetical player contained superficial associations (similarities) to highly successful professional players that the raters were familiar with. For example, when a hypothetical player was described as attending the same school as a real successful professional player, the subject was more likely to predict that the player would be successful. The raters used such phrases as "he's like . . .," "he reminds me of . . .," or "he's in the mold of . . . ." Unlike many psychological experiments, these raters were not first-year college students but professional sportswriters and football coaches. In a second experiment by Gilovich, political science students' predictions for a hypothetical foreign policy crisis was shown to be dependent on whether the superficial features of the crisis called to mind World War II or Vietnam.

Unfortunately, because of the design of Gilovich's studies, it's possible that his subjects were relying on some kind of abstract, schematic knowledge (based upon a number of past instances) rather than on a single concrete instance. Read rectified this problem and basically found the same results. In one study he asked subjects to learn about some strange behavior in a novel situation by six members of a preliterate tribe. Some of the tribe members had performed a bizarre ritual and some had not. The subjects were then asked to predict if other members of the tribe would perform the ritual. They were then presented with descriptions of several other tribes of people and asked to predict whether these latter tribe members would engage in the same behaviors as the previous tribe members.[10] The use of strange and novel behavior was to reduce the subject's use of familiar knowledge so that their prediction would be the consequence of single-instance reasoning and not on the basis of past schematic knowledge. The subjects were more likely to predict that another tribe member would perform the ritual if the tribe member was similar to the other members who had performed the ritual. Thus the subjects based their prediction on the single instance that they were aware of.

While the findings are consistently clear, reasoning on the basis of a single instance is, like most human behavior, dependent on a number of factors or variables. Saying that single-instance reasoning is dependent on a number of factors is another way of saying that the answer to any question always "depends" on the situation. For example, we are more likely to base our prediction that someone will behave like someone in our past experience on the basis of a single instance if the similarity between the two situations are thought to be causally related. That is, if a hypothetical football player is described as having the same reflexes, body build, past performance record, and was trained by the same coach, we are more likely to use this single instance than if we simply are told that the hypothetical player comes from the same town (though, unfortunately, this isn't always true). Read notes a second "it depends." It seems that we are increasingly likely to use a single, similar instance to base our reasoning on as the situation becomes more complex. We tend to dislike complexity and need to reduce it to manageable proportions. Transfer reduces this complexity. Sometimes it does well; at other times it doesn't.

A final implication that I briefly noted above is that cognitive and artificial intelligence researchers have tended to focus on our use of abstract rules and strategies in our reasoning. It has always been assumed, for example, that courses in logic teach us how to think and reason more validly in everyday life. But what we learn in logic courses doesn't seem to transfer very well. To assume that the study of logic transfers is equivalent to the old formal discipline theory of transfer (see chapter 5), where transfer is considered to be inherent in the subject matter. Recent research suggests that what most of us use when reasoning—including many scientists—are what have been termed pragmatic reasoning schemas,[11] and mental models.[12] Pragmatic reasoning schemas include what are called permission schemas and causation schemas.

A permission schema takes this form: if a given action is taken, then some precondition must be met. For example, if a person is in a bar drinking beer, then the person must be at least 21 years old. A causation schema takes this form: if a given event occurs, then some particular outcome will follow. For example, if a person exercises daily, then the person will tend to be in good physical shape. We can see that reasoning with pragmatic schemas are in fact mental models based on our past experience and our accumulated knowledge base (see chapter 6). We are coming to realize that "much of human reasoning, including what is often called logical inference. . . . is performed by using schemas from everyday life as analogs."[13] Similarly, the cognitive psychologist David Rumelhart notes that "most of the reasoning we do apparently does not involve the application of general-purpose reasoning skills. Rather, it seems that most of our reasoning ability is tied to particular bodies of knowledge."[14]

## LEGAL REASONING AND TRANSFER

The finding of similarity or difference is the key ingredient in legal reasoning. Thus much of legal reasoning is based on transfer. Legal reasoning is also largely based on reasoning from a single or a few instances, as Edward Levi[15] observed years ago and others have more recently noted.[16] Levi observes that "the basic pattern of legal reasoning is reasoning by *example* [italics added]. . . . The finding of *similarity* or *difference* [italics added] is the key step in the legal process".[17] Attorneys and judges are always arguing whether some previous case is applicable to a current case. In short, what they are doing is arguing whether the previous case is *similar* or *is like* a current case in order to render a decision on the particular case or to judge whether it is congruent with a certain legal principle or rule. Judges often check their reasoning about a particular case by looking at their reasoning on similar cases. Even reasoning on the basis of legal principle is in fact transfer reasoning. As one legal scholar notes, "The requirement that judges should decide cases 'on principle' is related to the idea of fairness, which demands that the *like* [italics added] cases should be treated *alike* [italics added]."[18] He goes on to recognize that the basis on which similarity is recognized and judged relevant remains a mystery. He says it is not "possible to formulate any rule for determining the relevant similarities among cases."[19]

Just as language develops by way of similarity transfer, so too does law frequently develop by similarity transfer from particular cases. In 1869, a case known as *Adams v. New Jersey Steamboat Co.*[20] extended the reach of liability law by seeing a new claim as being similar to a previous one. A passenger sued a steamboat company because he had money stolen from his berth (room). There was no precedent for the liability of steamboat owners. There was law on innkeeper liability. After a careful comparison and mapping of the different aspects of the new case with an already accepted case, a judge reasoned the steamboat company was liable. It was, after all, nothing but a "floating inn." This may seem obvious now, but it wasn't obvious then. Neither was it always accepted that a corporation is considered by the law as a "person, as it often is now."

In another example, a medical patient sued his doctor and the hospital for theft.[21] What did they steal from him? They stole some of his body tissue. His tissue was developed into a therapeutic cell line and patented without his knowledge. The legal question is, was it in fact a theft? It seems it may at least have been "like" a theft. The patient went in for a fairly routine operation and typically any tissue a surgeon removes during an operation is thrown out. In this case, however, the physicians discovered a unique biochemical substance in the patient's tissue. So they didn't throw it away. Unbeknownst to the patient, the hospital kept the tissue, duplicated it and used it, making financial gain from it. The hospital claimed it was not "theft" but "garbage" since the patient did not ask for it to be saved. I would argue that the best lawyers are those who are good at transfer thinking.

I am not advocating that we should reason on the basis of only a single or a few instances from our past experience, only that this is in fact the way most of us do reason in most situations, and therefore we should understand this kind of transfer reasoning. If most of us reason using single instances as mental models and pragmatic reasoning schemas—and there's considerable evidence that we do—then as Howard Gardner notes, "the kinds of principles devised by logicians—and invoked by researchers like Piaget—will turn out to have only limited applicability to how we reason in the real world."[22] The implications seem clear at least for the initial stages of instruction.

If we think about it for a moment, our not reasoning from abstract principles and formal logic but instead from concrete situations makes sense from an evolutionary perspective. After all, our systems of formal logic and abstract reasoning developed long after our more primitive and concrete mode of reasoning was well established. The downside of this is that such transfer thinking doesn't always serve us very well. In general, however, transfer reasoning on the basis of a few instances has proven itself throughout evolution to be quite vital to everyday reasoning and thus for the development of the species. As Read and many others have pointed out, however, individuals using transfer reasoning "may respond to irrelevant aspects of a situation and behave inappropriately."[23] This is called negative transfer, and it has profound implications for our own personal development and for living and working with others.

## PERSONAL DEVELOPMENT, HUMAN DIVERSITY, AND THE PROBLEM OF OTHER PEOPLE'S MINDS

Although it may not be completely apparent at this point, transfer is integral to our personal development (see chapter 7). The general approach I advocate implies that acquiring significant ability at transfer is the function of the whole person, not a modular add-on part of the personality. To say that transfer is a function of the whole person, however, isn't just a nice humanistic philosophy of transfer, it's a statement as close to empirical fact as we'll ever come. In one way or another, personal development is the consequence of knowledge (call it information, if you like)—knowledge of things, knowledge of knowledge, sometimes called meta-knowledge (see chapter 6), knowledge of self, and knowledge of others (see chapters 7 and 8). Thus there are two basic paths to personal development. The first concerns developing our individual selves through general knowledge; the second path is development through interaction based on knowledge of others. For some reason, general knowledge as a path to personality development is widely recognized. These two paths, general knowledge and knowledge of others, are not, of course, mutually exclusive.

The second path, involving our social knowledge of others presents us with the problem of how it's possible to know and understand them. In essence, the problem is because I can't get inside your mind or your feelings, I can't know exactly the pain, oppression, or pleasures you are feeling or have felt, and you can't know exactly what I'm experiencing. This is no small matter for either everyday communication, and child development,[24] not to mention romance relationships, friendships, and profound philosophical systems of thought.[25] For centuries, in one way or another, thinkers have pondered the problem of how we understand others. One of these major thinkers was Gottfried Wilhelm Leibniz (1646–1716), a German philosopher and mathematician. His philosophy of monadology (a monad is a hypothetical indivisible, impenetrable unit that floats around the universe that's somehow coordinated with other monads) suggests that we are all *like* isolated monads floating in the universe, ultimately unconnected to each other. The fact is, we are all monads unable to know what's in another person's mind or what they are feeling. So how is it that we can know, understand, and empathize with others?

One of the solutions to this problem is what the German philosopher Immanuel Kant (1724–1804) called *analogies of experience*. Analogies of experience refers to the fact that I have certain experiences that I *infer* are *similar* to yours. I can, therefore, understand you by analogy, by transferring or mapping my experiences onto yours. Analogies of experience are perhaps our first transfers. Not the most reliable of methods, but what else do we have? Even in science and logic, the use of inference is the basic problem of knowing; how we know what we think we know. The transferring of experience is the basis of our human sense of caring, empathy, and compassion for others. It is interesting to note that a child's sense of other minds doesn't develop until about age four. More importantly, sociopathic personalities don't have this capacity. This is why they have no conscience. Sociopaths can inflict pain on another and not be bothered by it; they experience no moral conflict. Sociopaths thus lack the ability to *generalize* themselves, to *transfer* or generate *analogies of experience*, and thus to psychologically and emotionally connect to others. This is the profound personal importance of transfer.

Through our transfer ability, we sharpen our sense of relation to others. Likewise with the transfer approach that I outline in chapter 8 on cultures of transfer, transfer often occurs only in connection with others. In large measure, the social context we are in defines and reinforces who we are, what we are, and what we do; we are moved to do nothing, or we are moved to develop our potential, to develop a spirit of transfer. We need to facilitate this transfer in such a way that it becomes self-sustaining and self-generating. In this 21st century, the problem of understanding each other is an increasingly important one, with the significant demographic changes that are already occurring, and that will continue to occur in our society along with an increasing globalization of our individual, social, economic, and political experience. We need to develop ways to understand transfer in relation to this diversity and difference. If we don't develop ways to cope with these "21st-century problems" then misunderstanding and conflict will continue to consume us as it has throughout the history of our species, when either nature or culture creates difference.

We have different cultural "minds" and experiences that we must learn to understand. Many ethnic minorities have maintained that white people can never know what it's like, for example, to be a black person. The assertion implies that whites have nothing in their experience that enables them to understand what it means to be black. Certainly this is true on a level. But not on an absolute level. If we are to survive we must understand the others' experience. But how do we do this? A couple of white people have dyed their skin in order to have the experience of being black.[26] Their experience was instructive. Given that it isn't practical for each of us to dye our skins, or surgically change the shape of our eyes, there's a "master" (read: generic) blueprint of understanding others that can be found in philosophy. I have always believed that within philosophy are found the "master blueprints" of most human issues. Philosophy is a kind of master language, as it were, that can be transferred to many areas. After all, it's from philosophy that all the modern sciences are derived. As the original science, philosophy has worked out the problem of inferring other people's feelings and thoughts more extensively and systematically than have other disciplines, such as psychology. This blueprint is known as the problem of other minds.[27]

The essential solution to the problem of other minds are our *analogies of experience*: that I have certain *similar* experiences to yours. When you prick your finger with a pin or experience some other kind of pain, because I'm not you, how do I know what you are experiencing? Simple. I've pricked my finger at some time in my life and have experienced pain. I can thus know what you are experiencing—or at least this is the closest I will get to understanding your experience. Similarly, although I am a white person and have not experienced the exact oppression that a minority has, I've nevertheless experienced oppression in my life. At least to the degree of my experience, to the degree of my sensitivity, to the degree that I can use my imagination to trans-

fer my experience of oppression, I can understand what it means to be an ethnic minority. What else do we have but analogies of experience to understand
others?

It should be clear that the process I'm describing here is transfer. To the
extent that we have in common certain *similar* cultural, social, group, family,
or individual experiences, and can recognize them, is the extent to which we
can understand each other; to the extent that we are sensitive and have the
capacity to transfer, is the extent to which we can understand each other.
There is, however, a dangerous downside to analogies of experience. It's
called negative transfer. Negative transfer is inappropriately transferring *like-
nesses* that should not be transferred because they are not in fact the *same*. It's
the flip side of positive transfer. Such transfer is the result of overgeneralization. Negative transfer is probably at least as prevalent as positive transfer.

A serious and negative implication of transfer for an increasingly global,
diverse, and multicultural society is ethnic prejudice. When we meet a few
members of a minority group who act in a certain way, there's often the tendency to generalize or transfer this experience to other members of the group
whom we have not met. This is what prejudice is, a prejudgment. As some instructional practitioners have recognized, "A very subtle carry-over from one
situation to another is seen in the transfer of attitudes. Prejudices and biases about one ethnic group are likely to transfer (or generalize) to other groups
with like characteristics, and other groups that are perceived to have similar
characteristics."[28] The negative transfer of our analogies of experience can
lead to serious misunderstandings. Counterintuitively, we can also engage in
negative transfer, even when making what we intend to be positive transfer.

My closest, and most enduring friend, for example, is a black man. We have
been friends for over 20 years. Although his early childhood experience was
that of growing up in a black ghetto, he now holds two doctoral degrees—
one in education and one in psychology—and has published a considerable
amount on race relations.[29] In our early professional lives, he and I taught at
the same college together. We immediately liked each other. We both were
interested in psychology, sociology, and philosophy. Since I grew up in a lower socioeconomic class—a white "ghetto"—many of our early experiences
were also similar. Having never considered myself prejudiced, and in my in-
experience as being the good "liberal," I saw him just as a "human being," not
a black man. Indeed, I saw no "Jews," "Hispanics," or "Asians"—only human
beings. Like a good liberal, I believed in a universal humanity—which meant
that we are all *the same*. Of course, on one level this is true: we are all human
beings. In point of fact, I saw him as-a-human-being *just like* me. The only *difference* being that, by random evolutionary circumstance, he "just happened"
to have dark skin. In overtransferring this universal analogy of experience, I
was denying his *differences*. The fact is, he isn't simply a human being (i.e., a
"white" human being with dark skin); he's a human being with a "different"
cultural heritage and experience based on the color of his skin. Until I un-

derstood this difference, I was not only doing him an injustice, I really didn't understand him. Though I must admit, he understood me very well. Minorities seem to understand the majority more than the majority understands minorities. After all, minorities experience both worlds.

We can use (transfer) my relationship with my black friend as a prototype or model of the essential everyday problem in transfer thinking: the problem of perceiving and assessing similarity and difference. On the one hand everything is the *same*, yet on the other hand, everything is *different*. There's no scientific "metric of similarity," no quantitative method for concluding whether something is more similar than different or more different than similar. Further, diversity isn't just something we visually see; it's something that makes us—uniquely—who we are. In all that we do and think, we need to be acutely aware of negative transfer—even negative transfer that can result from "good" motives, like my seeing my friend as just another human being.

In today's world, it's difficult to imagine anyone unfamiliar with traditional attitudes and behaviors underlying prejudice and discrimination. Because the stereotypes are so well known, I will not explain them all in detail. Instead, in Figure 3 I summarize many of the significant beliefs and stereotypes of prejudice. I do this for a reason that will become clear in a moment.

Substitute the Figure 3 legend to read: *Sexual stereotypes and dynamics of discrimination* instead of Racial. Each stereotype and dynamic can be transferred to attitudes on sexism. In mapping these two worlds upon each other, we can learn a great deal either about sexism that we knew only to be true about racism (or vice versa) or by juxtaposing the two areas we can learn something about both areas that we may not have known before.

The racism and sexism stereotype connection isn't a novel example, of course. At least since 1944, in a piece by the Swedish sociologist Karl Gunner Myrdal entitled, "A Parallel to the Negro Problem," the transfer of the dynamics of racism to sexism had been recognized. Myrdal not only drew the racial parallel to women but to the treatment of children as well.[30] The anthropologist Ashley Montague in his book on race entitled, *Man's Most Dangerous Myth*, wrote a chapter titled, "Antifeminism and Race Prejudice: A parallel."[31] At the close of the 1960s, Jerry Farber published a book with the provocative title, *The Student as Nigger*,[32] which demonstrated parallels between the treatment of blacks and the treatment of students. The transfer of knowledge about racism to sexism has not been overlooked by contemporary feminist thinking. Farber's book later inspired a similar piece by the feminist, Naomi Weisstein, with the equally provocative title, "Woman as Nigger."[33] Neither was it overlooked by the early suffragette movement where the parallels were often pointed out. Reading these pieces can be quite instructive in terms of transfer thinking.

Juxtaposing racism and sexism and comparing them allows us to inductively recognize a general scheme, a general systems dynamic recognizing equivalent power relations in two "different" systems. Working deductively

1. Biological
   a.   innately inferior
   b.   behavior largely genetic
   c.   innately week "willed"
   d.   biologically "unclean"

2. Psychological
   a.   inferior mental capacity
   b.   childlike ideas and behaviors
   c.   not control strong emotions
   d.   religiosity/superstitious

3. Psychiatric
   a.   prone to psychiatric disorder
   b.   keep they busy so will not deteriorate
   c.   disobeying as mental disease

4. Education
   a.   denied access
   b.   separate but equal
   c.   largely only trainable

5. Economic
   a.   considered property
   b.   menial jobs
   c.   cheap labor

6. Relations to Dominant Race
   a.   not trusted
   b.   mutually uncomfortable
   c.   to serve the master
   d.   must obey

7. Socialization Process
   a.   must know their "place"
   b.   treated as child
   a)   socialized into the dominant reality
   d.   lack of positive role models

8. Civil Rights of Discrimination
   a.   separate facilities, etc.
   b.   denied right to vote
   c.   laws made by dominant group

9. *Reasons for Emancipation*
   a.   technology made slavery obsolete

10. Proof of Inferiority
    a.   deny equal opporunity...
    b.   ...socialize as inferior...
    c.   ...then use as proof of inferiority

11. Reasons for Prejudice and Discrimination
    a.   need a status inferior
    b.   competition for economics
    c.   social isolation leads to stereotypes

12. Conditional Non-prejudice
    a.   tokenism
    b.   as mascots

13. Psychodynamic Effects of Oppression
    a.   anger-out/anger-in
    b.   identification with dominant values
    c.   sabotage: passive resistance

**FIGURE 3**
Racial stereotypes and dynamics of discrimination.

from a general systems perspective we may deduce that because the two phenomena are about power relations, we are immediately *cued* to assume that racism and sexism are essentially the same. The above example is a method to begin to think in transfer terms. In any passage or description about a given topic, it is often useful to substitute the main subject or noun for another noun, or subject.

Furthermore, has the lack of understanding one another, the problem of other minds, not been responsible for many of the eternal issues between females and males? In modern times, beginning with the suffragette movement of the early 1900s, through the 1960s women's liberation movement to the current feminist movement, women have made it clear that males tend not to understand the female experience. Likewise, women tend not to understand the male experience. In a very real sense we are Liebnitz's monads, isolated from each other's experience. Focusing on "difference" for a moment, a male can never know what it's like to be female, and a female can never know what it's like to be male. Hence the eternal conflict between man and woman—and most of it due to lack of transferability; in this case the trans-fer of analogies of experience. If we are to survive, however, we must under-stand the others' experience. The existential fact is, each of us is a subculture of one.

Whether we like it or not, diversity is not only here to stay, it has always existed. Despite the fact that gender, social, and cultural diversity often cre-ates conditions of extreme conflict, over the long haul diversity has a posi-tive function. Perhaps this is why evolution selected for diversity. Genetical-ly, we know that a gene pool without diversity or variability tends to be unstable and more likely to undergo extinction under conditions of a chang-ing environment. A diverse or variable gene pool is one of the primary sources of biological creativity. The same is true of our cultural "gene pool."

## SOCIAL POLICY DECISION MAKING
## AND TRANSFER THINKING

The use of single-instance reasoning has implications well beyond its use by the person in the street. A number of studies on analogical transfer have noted that governmental policymakers often make use of single instances in their experience as analogs on which to base their decisions and policies of current crises. For some years, Donald Schon has observed,

> When we examine the problem-setting stories told by the analysts and practitioners of social policy, it becomes apparent that the framing of problems often depends on metaphors underlying the stories which generate problem setting and set the direction of problem solving.[34]

It's well known that military leaders often make strategy decisions on the ba-sis of a single instance in military history. Heads of governments, too, use this type of transfer thinking. Read notes that as a result of the perceived simi-larity between Woodrow Wilson's (1856–1924, 28th U.S. president) situation and James Madison's, Wilson became quite concerned about the possibility of war with Great Britain. As a consequence, he went to great lengths to avoid it. Wilson held a Ph.D. and was a noted scholar. Still he reasoned on the ba-sis of a single instance, an instance that occurred some 100 years earlier in quite different historical circumstances. Wilson's reasoning is not an isolat-ed instance among policy and governmental decision makers.

Keith Holyoak, a leading cognitive psychologist at UCLA, and Paul Tha-gard, a philosopher at the University of Waterloo, in their book *Mental Leaps: Analogy in Creative Thought*, note a number of instances of high-level policy be-ing made on the basis of one or two similar historical instances.[35] In 1950, North Korea invaded South Korea, and President Harry Truman had to decide how to respond to this invasion. Although South Korea was thought to be of no significant strategic value, Truman was psychologically captured by certain historical incidents that had preceded World War II which he saw as analogous to the North Korean invasion. In particular, there had been the Japanese invasion of Manchuria, the Italian attack on Ethiopia, and the annexation of Austria by Germany. Truman saw the invasion of South Korea as just the beginning of a series of hostile acts like those that led to World War II, just as more recently, George Bush saw Saddam Hussein's invasion of Kuwait as reminiscent of Hitler.

The importance of transfer of learning in thinking about everyday, social, and political life on the basis of history is exemplified by discussions surrounding the build-up and entrance into the 1991 Persian Gulf war. In a fascinating experiment on analogical transfer entitled, "If Saddam Is Hitler Then Who is George Bush?"[36] Barbara Spellman and Keith Holyoak of UCLA systematically examined the prelude to the Gulf War, which engendered a widespread use of analogy in argument and persuasion by governmental leaders and the press. The authors point out that "Hawks" transferred their knowledge of World War II to the situation, seeing Saddam Hussein as an emerging Hitler about to swallow up neighboring countries. The "Doves" transferred their knowledge of Vietnam, seeing the situation as an unpopular and drawn-out war in which the United States had no business being involved. People's understanding of the analogies of the situation depended on their assessment of the similarities and differences between World War II and the situation in the Persian Gulf. President Bush was ultimately successful in convincing members of Congress and most of the American public, as well as the leaders of other Western nations that the World War II analogy was sound. The pragmatic impact of this analogical transfer was the initiation of war. The authors note that "it would not be an exaggeration to say that the U.S. went to war on the basis of an analogy."[37] The same kind of transfer reasoning was used by decision makers in decisions regarding U.S. involvement in El Salvador.[38]

That politicians make policy decisions on the basis of past historical and political events isn't surprising. It seems that the academic background of many officials in the U.S. State Department and other government positions is history and political science. This is the knowledge base from which they construct their transfer thinking. In addition to explicit sociohistorical instances, policy making also involves implicit transfers. One widespread implicit transfer is seeing a nation or an organization as a rational individual, a questionable model at best, especially given what we know about how many individuals make decisions. In any event, we can gain insights into organizational behavior by transferring some of what we know about the behavior of nation states, social movements, or biological populations to our understanding of organizations. Understanding control in government has been modeled by transferring what we know about the human nervous system. An excellent and lucid example of transferring knowledge about the human nervous system to governmental structures was detailed some years ago by the general systems theorist Karl Deutsch in his classic book, *The Nerves of Gov-*

*ernment: Models of Political Communication and Control*, where he mapped how bureaucracy is structured and functions on a model of the human nervous system.[39] More recently, other systems theorists who study organizational behavior have transferred knowledge from other specific for understanding organizations.[40]

Given the pervasiveness of transfer thinking in policy and decision making, it is imperative to understand how transfer thinking—both positive and negative—works. More often than not, such transfer thinking is badly done in the area of social policy and decision making. Occasionally, it's apparently done well. In their excellent analysis of policy makers' use of analogical reasoning using historical data, Keith Holyoak and Paul Thagard describe the interesting case of George W. Ball, who served as Under Secretary of State in the Johnson administration, and who was a master of analogical reasoning with historical and political data. The authors go on to say that George Ball was one "who history must now credit as the greatest American political analogist of his time."[41] They conclude this on the basis of Ball's past "correct" (as it historically just happened to turn out) analogical analyses of political events that he arrived at his correct predictions by following what the authors recommend as the most effective method of analogical reasoning. The flaw is that while history has shown the correctness of Ball's past predictions, it cannot be concluded that the analogical reasoning he used was in fact the correct causal reasoning. The sample is obviously too small and the analysis was after the fact.[42]

Typically, however, transferring historical knowledge is so badly done that the historian, James Banner, in a recent article published in *The Public Historian*, has proposed a "history watch." Banner says, "Experience has decisively shown that the current use of historical knowledge within and outside government is appallingly bad."[43] He goes on to recommend

> a kind of History Watch, Shadow Council of History Advisors, or Historical Analogy Police—a voluntary, self-supporting, unaffiliated committee of historians prepared to assess the use of history by senior national policymakers. Its members would function something like those of the Shadow Open Market Committee, a group of roughly eight monetarists from universities, banks, and economic organizations who since 1973 have regularly evaluated the decisions of the Open Market Committee of the Federal Reserve Board.[44]

The Shadow Committee meets and issues public reports on federal monetary policy. Though their reports are rarely heeded by the Federal Reserve Board, the Shadow Committee is known as a serious, responsible bird-dog of the Federal Bank and is frequently cited by the press.

Those more knowledgeable in political history than I could undoubtedly document a vast array of specific examples of transfer reasoning by policy makers. At this point I will leave it to these individuals to further document such examples. To document a wide array of such cases would be instructive. We could learn a great deal about transfer reasoning and how historical conditions are validly and invalidly applied to contemporary situations, which in turn could alter future decisions and policies in a useful way.

Like these policy makers, humans as social beings, professionals, and as teachers are constantly using past experience to make a point in personal conversations and in the classroom when providing examples to our students. And like these policy makers we are using the same mental transfer processes. We need to know on what basis we select the examples we use and how valid they are (see chapters 9 and 10).

So the question remains, On what bases do we make these transfers from history and everyday life? The following chapters will answer this question. In the meantime, we can now begin to appreciate the momentous import of transfer thinking in everyday life.

# Notes

[1]Read, S. J. (1983). Once is enough: Causal reasoning from a single instance. *Journal of Personality and Social Psychology*, 45, 323–334.

[2]SeeLakoff, G., & Johnson, M. (1980). *Metaphors we live by*. Chicago: University of Chicago Press.

[3]Rumelhart, D. E. (1989). Toward a microstructural account of human reasoning. In S. Vosniadou & A. Anthony (Eds.), *Similarity and analogical reasoning* (pp. 298–312). New York: Cambridge University Press, p. 301.

[4]Andersen, S., Noah, M., Glassman, S., Chen,S., & Cole, S. W. (1995). Transference in social perception: The role of chronic accessibility in significant-other representations. *Journal of Personality and Social Psychology*, 69, 41–57, p. 41.

[5]Read, S. J., & Cesa, I. L. (1991). This reminds me of the time when . . .: Expectations and failures in reminding and explanation. *Journal of Experimental Social Psychology*, 27, 1–25; Read, S. J. (1984). Analogical reasoning in social judgment: The importance of causal theories. *Journal of Personality and Social Psychology*, 46, 14–25.

[6]Gilovich, T. (1981). Seeing the past in the present: The effect of association to familiar events on judgments and decisions. *Journal of Personality and Social Psychology*, 40, 797–808.

[7]Read, S. J. (1983). Once is enough: Causal reasoning from a single instance. *Journal of Personality and Social Psychology*, 45, 323–334, p. 334.

[8]Plato in Gilovich, T. (1981). Seeing the past in the present: The effect of association to familiar events on judgments and decisions. *Journal of Personality and Social Psychology*, 40, 797–808.

[9]Gilovich, T. (1981). Seeing the past in the present: The effect of association to familiar events on judgments and decisions. *Journal of Personality and Social Psychology*, 40, 797–808.

[10]Read, S. J. (1984). Analogical reasoning in social judgment: The importance of causal theories. *Journal of Personality and Social Psychology*, 46, 14–25.

[11]Cheng, P. W., Holyoak, K., Nisbett, R. E., & Oliver, L. M. (1986). Pragmatic versus syntactic approaches to training deductive reasoning. *Cognitive Psychology*, 18, 293–328.

[12]Johnson-Laird, P. N. (1983). *Mental models*. Cambridge, MA: Harvard University Press.

[13]Halford, G. S. (1992). Analogical reasoning and conceptual complexity in cognitive development. *Human Development*, 35, 193–217, p. 193.

[14]Rumelhart, D. E., & Norman, D. A. (1981). Analogical processes in learning. In J. Anderson (Ed.), *Cognitive skills and their acquisition* (pp. 335–359). Hillsdale, NJ: Lawrence Erlbaum, p. 338.

[15]Levi, E. H. (1949). *An introduction to legal reasoning*. Chicago: University of Chicago Press.

[16]Sunstein, C. R. (1993). On analogical reasoning. *Harvard Law Review*, 106, 741–791; Marchant, G., Robinson, J., Anderson, U., & Schadewald, M. (1991). Analogical transfer and expertise in legal reasoning. *Organizational Behavior and Human Decision Processes*, 48, 272–290.

[17]Levi, E. H. (1949). *An introduction to legal reasoning*. Chicago: University of Chicago Press, p. 1–2.

[18]Golding, M. P. (1984). *Legal reasoning*. New York: Alfred A. Knopf, p. 64.

[19]Golding, M. P. (1984). *Legal reasoning*. New York: Alfred A. Knopf, p. 64.

[20]Golding, M. P. (1984). *Legal reasoning*. New York: Alfred A. Knopf, pp. 46–47.

[21]*Moore v. Regents of the University of California*, 793, p. 2479 (California 1990).

[22]Gardner, H. (1985). *The mind's new science: A history of the cognitive revolution*. New York: Basic Books, p. 370.

[23]Read, S. J. (1983). Once is enough: Causal reasoning from a single instance. *Journal of Personality and Social Psychology*, 45, 323–334, p. 334.

[24]Dunn, J. (1995). Children as psychologists: The later correlates of individual differences in understanding of emotions and other minds. *Cognition & Emotion*, 9(2–3), 187–201.

[25]Morick, H. (1967). *Wittgenstein and the problem of other minds*. New York: McGraw-Hill.

[26]See Griffin, J. H. (1961). *Black like me*. Boston, MA; Houghton Mifflin; and Halsell, G. (1969). *Soul sister*. New York: World Pub.

[27]See, for example, Morick, H. (1967). *Wittgenstein and the problem of other minds*. New York: McGraw-Hill.

[28]Di Vesta, F. J., & Thompson, G. G. (1970). *Educational psychology: Instruction and behavioral change*. New York: Appleton-Century-Crofts, p. 257.

[29]Gresson, A. D. (1995). *The recovery of race in America*. Minneapolis, MN: University of Minnesota Press; Gresson, A. D. (1987). Transitional metaphors and the political psychology of identity maintenance. In R. E. Haskell (Ed.), *Cognition and symbolic structures: The psychology of metaphoric transformation* (pp. 163–186). Norwood, NJ: Ablex.

[30]Myrdal, G. (1944). A parallel to the Negro problem. In G. Myrdal (Ed.), *An American dilemma*. New York: Harper Row.

[31]Montague, A. (1964). *Man's most dangerous myth: The fallacy of race* (4th ed.). Cleveland: World.

[32]Farber, J. (1969). *Student as nigger*. North Hollywood, CA: Contact Books.

[33]Weisstein, N. (1969). Woman as nigger. *Psychology Today*, 3, 20–22, 58.

[34]Schon, D. (1979). Generative metaphor: A perspective on problem-setting in social policy. In A. Ortrony (Ed.), *Metaphor and thought* (pp. 254–283). New York: Cambridge University Press, p. 255; See also Schon, D. (1963). *Displacement of concepts*. London: Tavistock Publications.

[35]Holyoak, K., & Thagard, P. (1995). *Mental leaps: Analogy in creative thought*. Cambridge, MA: MIT Press.

[36]Spellman, B. A., & Holyoak, K. J. (1992). If Saddam is Hitler then who is George Bush? Analogical mapping between systems of social roles. *Journal of Personality and Social Psychology*, 62(6), 913–933, p. 913.

[37]Ibid, p. 913.

[38]See Gilovich, T. (1981). Seeing the past in the present: The effect of association to familiar events on judgments and decisions. *Journal of Personality and Social Psychology*, 40, 797–808.

[39]Deutsch, Karl (1966). *The nerves of government: Models of political communication and control*. New York: Free Press.

[40]See examples in Tsoukas, H. (1993). Analogical reasoning and knowledge generation in organization theory. *Organization Studies*, 14, 323–346.

[41]Holyoak, K., & Thagard, P. (1995). *Mental leaps: Analogy in creative thought*. Cambridge, MA: MIT Press, p. 163.

[42]See my review of Holyoak & Thagard's book: Haskell, R. E. (1996). Review of *Mental leaps: Analogy in creative thought* by Holyoak, K. J. & Thagard, P. (1995). *Journal of Metaphor and symbolic activity*, 12, 89–94.

[43]Banner, J. Jr. (1993). The history watch: A proposal. *The Public Historian*, pp. 15, 48, 54.

[44]Ibid, pp. 48, 49.

# CHAPTER 5

# A Brief History of Transfer and Transfer as History

*When I reason in terms of genetic psychology, I always keep in the back of my mind something based on the history of science or the history of mathematics, because it is the same process.*

—Jean Piaget[1]

In this chapter, I will outline a brief history of transfer research and coalesce the central issues and problems in the literature. This is both appropriate and necessary, for it is, after all, in the very nature of the theory of transfer presented in this book that to understand transfer it's necessary to understand its history. The very definition of transfer—applying what we have learned in the past to understanding and grasping the present—is learning from history, both individually and culturally. Learning from history, then, is the very exemplar of transfer.

In studying the history of Greece in the fifth century B.C. through Thucydides, we can transfer this historical analyses to today's world. In studying Thucydides, says Anthony Flew, we find it "much easier to grasp general and perhaps universal principles in detachment from the particular cases in which at the time the passions are most strongly engaged.[2] Flew illustrates this by observing,

> What, for one, could be more relevant to any consideration of the pre-invasion confrontation of Soviet with Czechoslovak representatives at Cierna and Tisouin 1968 than the Melian Dialogue of Thucydides, referring to events of 416 B.C.? Both the Melians and the Czechoslovaks tried to appeal to moral ideals–justice and "socialism with a human face," respectively. But both the Athenians and the Soviets, disclaiming any reference to their services in their respective Great Patriotic Wars, instead insisted on talking of the interests of a great power within its own sphere of domination.[3]

Unfortunately, we do not generally learn from history. To cite the well-worn words of the philosopher George Santayana (1863–1952): "Those who cannot remember the past are condemned to repeat it."[4]

From a transfer perspective, it's an ironic twist that those who cannot remember the past are condemned not to transfer their learning. In terms of transfer, the only thing we learn from history is that we don't often learn from it. No wonder we fail to find so little transfer on either the social or personal level. We in the United States tend to dislike history; we are an ahistorical people. We tend to live in a constricted present, future, and pragmatic tense: for us, history, is the day before yesterday.

But learning from history—whether it be in scholarship, understanding cultural events, running a business, or in one's personal life—is the very basis of transfer. Thomas Peters and Robert Waterman in their book, *In Search of Excellence: Lessons from America's Best-Run Companies*, cite Michael Thomas, a former successful investment banker and author, lamenting the educational background that many business majors receive. Thomas says they "lack liberal arts literacy . . . [and] . . . need a broader vision, *a sense of history*, perspectives from literature and art."[5] Again, success at achieving transfer requires of us a sense of history, a sense of history on the social, personal, and subject matter levels because this is what makes transfer possible.

I've included this chapter on the history of transfer not only for the general reasons just stated, but for the same reasons that scholarly journal articles in the social and behavioral sciences typically begin with a brief section on the history of the problem: The history section serves a number of purposes. First, it delineates the problem and its themes, letting the reader know where the author is going; second, sound scholarship is based on knowing what the origins of a problem are; third, it puts the current approach to a problem in perspective; fourth, it in turn prevents our reinventing the wheel; and fifth, knowing the history of an area tends to prevent faddish approaches to a problem. Certainly, both education and psychology have had no shortage of fads that reinvent a wheel—albeit usually an inferior one. Finally, knowing the history of an area or of one's profession is often necessary for correctly reading the classic material in one's area or profession.

For example, in reading Gordon Allport's classic work, *Personality: A Psychological Interpretation*, and using examples from it in my classes, I cite a line from his book which says "one of the outstanding problems in the psychology of learning is transfer of training."[6] Note here his use of the term *training* and not *learning* when referring to transfer. When I used this quote in my classes, just after I had lectured on what I consider to be an important distinction between *training* on the one hand, and *education* and *learning* on the other (see chapters 1 and 2), I had to clarify Allport's use of the term *training*. If I had not been familiar with the history of the transfer of learning literature when reading Allport, as well as being familiar with his theoretical orientation, I may have misinterpreted or misunderstood his meaning (see chapter 9). First, I knew that Allport did not mean "training" in the narrow sense, he really meant "learning." Second, I knew this because I was aware not only of his theoretical orientation but of the fact that at the time he was using the term in 1937, the phrases *transfer of training* and *transfer of learning* were often used interchangeably. Using the term training in the context of my lectures without explaining the history would have confused my students. History is always present in the current moment. Ironically, in order to completely understand a present moment in time requires that we bring history along with us.

## TEXTS ON TRANSFER OF LEARNING

Given the widespread recognition of the importance of transfer of learning, we might think that educational books would be filled with the subject. Until very recently, however, the last comprehensive nonedited research-based volume on transfer was published in 1965.[7] Since then, two major edited research-based volumes on analogical transfer in cognitive psychology and two general books in the business training literature have appeared, indicating renewed interest in transfer.[8] None have appeared in the educational literature.

As Richard Clark and Alexander Voogle noted in their review of the educational literature, in textbooks transfer is only given cursory mention.[9] Seventy-one years after Edward Thorndike's research, George Haslerud in his 1972 book on creativity and transfer noted in the introduction that, "Chapters on transfer in most texts for the psychology of learning or educational psychology must be described as perfunctory. . . . They usually fail to emphasize the importance of the topic, to integrate transfer into the rest of psychology, and especially to indicate how it can aid application of knowledge."[10] In a 1976 text on educational psychology, the subject index had no heading for transfer of learning.[11] In 1983, Nathaniel Gage and David Berliner, authors of perhaps the leading educational psychology textbook, state in their chapter on transfer, "This chapter may be the most important in this section on learning. It is also one of our shortest chapters. This unhappy state of affairs occurs because we do not know what to tell teachers other than to think long and hard about this topic."[12] Finally, Stephen Cormier and Joseph Hagman noted that for many years, "it was difficult to locate references to transfer in the indexes of books on cognitive psychology."[13] Clearly this lack is significant. Even now, no major nonedited volume on transfer in the instructional field has been published.

## GENERAL HISTORY

In reviewing the vast literature on transfer over the past nine decades since the classic statements of Edward Thorndike and Robert Woodworth, and of Charles Judd, eight outstanding observations stand out.[14] The first observation is the widespread recognition of the profound importance attributed to transfer; the second is that until about the last 10 years or so, transfer had not been included in cognitive psychology research. Only recently has cognitive psychology begun to recognize transfer, largely under the rubrics of analogical transfer and analogical reasoning; the third is that the term transfer appears nearly omnimeaningful, with no systemic taxonomical framework to guide its multiple definitions and uses; the fourth is inconsistent with the first observation, namely, an almost complete absence of conceptual and theoretical development of transfer as an *educational principle* in the 90 plus years since its empirical and experimental inception; fifth is the observation that until recent years, the educational field has ceased to generate useful transfer findings or applications; sixth is the many names under which the transfer of learning has paraded; seventh is that transfer has been largely missing in the pages of educational textbooks; and finally, the eighth observation is that there has been no comprehensive educational text on transfer.

Beginning in the 1960s, up through about the mid-1980s, research into transfer of learning steadily declined. According to Richard Clark and Alexander Voogel's 1985 review of the educational literature, in the years from 1971–1974, 31 documents were published on transfer; in the years from 1975–1978, the number dropped to 24; and from 1979–1982, there were only 13 published articles.[15] Why this occurred has partly to do with the identical elements model it was based on (see below) and partly due to a change in instructional focus, a focus on skills and competencies. As Brown and Campione note: "In the rush to demonstrate hitherto unsuspected early competencies, somehow the concept of transfer lost out."[16] The figures in Clark and Voogel's review, however, are somewhat misleading, because the apparent decline in transfer research was the consequence of a semantic problem: different fields have labeled transfer differently. Since Clark and Voogel's review, there has been, by comparison, a near explosion of articles relating to transfer.

As early as 1963, Cronbach recognized this problem, observing that "reasoning ability, intellectual power, mastery of the great disciplines, functional skills in problem solving—whatever the name, the aim is transfer."[17] Transfer research was being conducted under such headings as stimulus generalization, constancy, transposition phenomena, isomorphic relations, metaphor, analogical reasoning, assimilation, and a host of others. As Wilbert McKeachie has pointed out, "Frequently we fail to recognize it because we hide it under other names."[18] From very early on, the term transfer of learning has been primarily concerned with teaching and learning in the classroom, not with studying the cognitive mechanism underlying it. But this soon changed. As Cormier and Hagman noted, "A new upsurge in interest in transfer of learning has occurred among researchers with a cognitive or information-processing approach to human learning."[19] These studies have certainly been helpful in understanding transfer, but they have proved difficult to translate into instructional terms.

More recently, because of a general recognition of the cognitive operations involved in transfer, it has been extended to include the research literature on metaphorical, analogical reasoning, and the study of figurative language, though these areas still primarily focus on the structures and cognitive processes involved in encoding and retrieval of information that operate during learning, not on the implications for instruction.[20] Historically, there have been a number of models of transfer that have influenced instruction for transfer.

## SEVEN MODELS OF TRANSFER

I'll now briefly outline what I consider to be the seven major models of transfer. Historically, however, only the first four have been recognized as primary models.

### Formal Discipline Model of Transfer

The formal discipline approach to transfer grew out of ancient and classical educational theory, where it was believed that training in certain formal disciplines such as geometry or mathematics, or learning Latin—by their very nature—enabled the mind to transfer what was learned. It was thought by some that the internal logic or structure of the discipline or material being studied by the learner would automatically transfer to everyday reasoning and performance. The internal structure of certain formal disciplines were thought to be similar to our inherent cognitive structures (or faculties, as they were then called) and to inherent structures in our environment. Learning Latin, for example, was thought to be sufficiently similar to all language learning so that learning Latin would transfer to the learning of language in general. It doesn't. Similarly, it was thought that courses in logic taught people how to think. They don't.

From the beginning, very little rigorous research supported the formal-discipline approach to transfer in most instructional situations. Today, the formal discipline approach is considered antiquated, if not a "dead horse,"—though there remain what are called critical thinking programs that often assume that transfer will occur by teaching general thinking skills. Again, it doesn't. The research findings show that the current cottage industry of teaching general thinking, critical thinking, and general writing skills don't easily lead to transfer; as we have seen, learning typically remains welded to the specific context in which the subject matter was learned. There are exceptions to these findings, but they are not directly applicable to most learning environments.

It is clear that the formal discipline model of transfer does not address the issue of similarity; rather it simply assumes that transfer is somehow present in the structure of the discipline itself. The instructional implications of the apparent failure of the formal discipline model is that we can't assume transfer will automatically occur as the consequence of teaching any subject, or that learning a particular subject itself will train the mind. Despite these negative findings, I will revisit in a moment the question of whether this model may still be a valid and useful one.

## Identical Elements Model

The identical elements model was launched by the laboratory research of the psychologist Edward Thorndike in 1901.[21] Interpreting Thorndike's research (perhaps incorrectly), his findings ostensibly demonstrated that for transfer to occur there must be a common set of very concrete identical elements between two experiences or learning events; hence, it has become known as the identical elements model of transfer. The classical formal discipline model was diametrically opposed to Thorndike's identical elements model. An educational battle ensued. Lacking research support for the formal discipline model, Thorndike's identical elements model won, hands down, spelling the demise of the formal discipline approach to transfer.

Strictly speaking, the identical elements model does not constitute a theory of transfer, but simply posits the necessity of identical elements within a learning theory framework. The identical elements model was, however, supported by a wealth of research and was theoretically extended and integrated by the classic work on a matrix of similarity by the renowned psychologist, Charles Osgood.[22] Essentially, there has since been no theoretical development of Osgood's quantitative work, though a great deal of work is currently being done on the concept of similarity.[23] Despite its apparent simplicity, the concept of similarity continues to be a very problematic concept with a long history in philosophy.[24] Thorndike's findings led to a pessimistic view of the possibility of teaching for general transfer (see chapter 1). Despite this, the identical elements model has exerted near total hegemony over curriculum design and textbook chapters on transfer, continuing until present day. In fact, the identical elements model of transfer, remark researchers Anita Woolfolk and Lorraine Nicolich, has "probably had more impact on education than any other research conducted by psychologists"[25] in the twentieth century. As I'll point out below, though this model remains forceful, there are signs of its being seriously downgraded.

In the classic identical elements model of transfer, similarity is usually defined by the measurement of the response strength to a given stimulus. But as it has been pointed out, this approach to a definition of transfer tends to be circular, because transfer itself is defined by response strength.[26] This model also assumes that the perception of similarity exists objectively in the external world, an assumption that's highly questionable. Moreover, the Identical Elements Model leads only to simple and "near transfer" at best and does not lead to synthesizing and integrating information across domains.

## General Principle Model

Since the beginning, the identical elements model was seriously challenged by Charles Judd's classic research in 1908, which suggests that transfer not only occurs on the basis of identical elements, but also by way of understanding the abstract general principle underlying a phenomenon which can then be applied to situations that do not possess obvious identical elements, or at least no obvious concrete ones. In other words, a general (abstract) principle can be transferred to different particular (concrete) events. In this model, transfer was considered to be more abstract, rather than a concrete set of elements.[27]

In Judd's early experiments, groups of young children aimed and threw darts at an underwater target. The experimenter instructed some of the subjects on how water refracted light. Understanding the principle of refraction was found to promote transfer in hitting their underwater target. The control group practiced but received no instruction.[28] The test for transfer was to successfully hit targets at varying depths. The experimental group outperformed the control group on the transfer tests. Like the formal discipline model, but unlike the identical elements model, Judd's model held that attitudinal or dispositional characteristics of the learner (e.g., motivation) are important factors in transfer (see chapter 7). Judd's model replaced the old battle between the formal discipline and the identical elements model. The identical elements versus general principle battle still rages today.

The general principal model of transfer posits the use of abstract and general principles that underlie a given transfer, but not via the mechanisms by which the similarity is apprehended. Nevertheless, Judd's model should be considered a precursor of the current cognitive approach to transfer because, first, unlike the identical elements approach, it is concerned with what is in the learner's head, not just the featural similarity of the instructional material. Second, it can be considered a precursor to the metacognition approach (see below) because it recognizes that transfer can be promoted by indirect processes, namely, the use of strategies such as directing the subjects "attention" to a task and thereby facilitating what are now called metacognitive strategies. In theory at least, this approach can lead to "far transfer."

## Stimulus Generalization Model

Almost from its inception, transfer research has been related to the concept of stimulus generalization and continues to be so today, though mostly by experimental learning theorists. The concept of stimulus generalization comes out of behaviorist laboratory research on Pavlov's classical conditioning paradigm. Stimulus generalization is the evocation of a nonreinforced response to a stimulus that is very *similar* to an original conditioned stimulus.[29] It is typically measured with a few test trials, whereas transfer is typically mea-

sured by the acquisition of new responses or the attachment of older responses to *new* stimuli. In brief, stimulus generalization can be viewed as
the basic physiological "learning theory," underpinnings, or microtheory
explaining how transfer, based on identical elements, occurs. As Richard
Thompson observed in 1965, "An adequate neurophysiological theory of
stimulus generalization might well facilitate analyses of the more complex
processes of learning."[30] Stimulus generalization occurs automatically in response to a similar stimulus without the "new" stimulus being previously reinforced (i.e., without specifically learning the "new" item). Stimulus generalization is the exception to the rule that no learning occurs unless it is
specifically reinforced.

The stimulus generalization model presupposes concrete identical elements that enable generalization to occur. Despite the fact that the identical
elements model provided the primary model for instructional transfer for
years, its theoretical basis—stimulus generalization—did not help a great
deal as a tool for instruction. As Ellis noted, the researcher involved in basic
research is more likely than the applied researcher to investigate the processes underlying transfer and to attempt a formalization of those processes
separate from the "more inclusive concept of the transfer of learning,"[31] as an
instructional concept.

## The Cognitive Information-Processing Model

As transfer historically evolved, its origins lay squarely within the applied instructional arena of education; only secondarily did its origins lie within behaviorist laboratory research and later in cognitive psychology. As I have
noted, cognitive psychology has not historically considered transfer within its
purview. For many years it was difficult to find references in the indexes
of books on cognitive psychology. Currently, however, transfer figures prominently in many areas of cognitive research, but with few exceptions
researchers have not primarily been concerned with transfer as an instructional process but rather with laying the foundation for an information-processing framework that explains the acquisition, processing, and retention
of information. Until recently, cognitive psychology had no theory of transfer
per se.[32]

Since about 1985, renewed interest in the mechanisms underlying transfer is to be found in the cognitive psychology arena and other areas concerned
with the processing and transfer of information. As I already briefly noted, the
problem of transfer is found under different research labels. One central area
in contemporary cognitive psychology is schema research.[33] Basically, a
schema is a hypothetical cognitive structure by which information and knowledge is thought to be organized and processed; new information is assimi-
lated, learned, and interpreted in terms of relevant pre-existing schemata. In
transfer of learning terminology, previous learning is transferred onto new sit-

uations. As such, much of the early research on schemata is in fact transfer research, but without articulating the precise structures responsible for the transfer.[34] More recently, however, the theoretical base of schema transfer has included what are termed *isomorphic relations* (where stories of identical structure but different content are used to test for transfer), artificial intelligence computations,[35] metaphorical reasoning, analogical reasoning[36] and exemplification (i.e., the cognitive function of examples),[37] and others.[38]

The cognitive model essentially deals with the issue of similarity in two ways. First, through an *implied* and indirect similarity contained in the theoretical construct of schemata and in strategy-transfer, (i.e., pre-existing schemata or previous learning) are brought to bear on the acquisition and comprehension of new information by assimilating learning into previous learning structures, and by applying previous strategies to new situations using rules. The schema approach does not account for the underlying processes by which subjects discover or cognitively recognize similarity or when to apply a rule.

## The Metacognition Model

A further area that uses a cognitive approach to facilitate transfer is called metacognition. The metacognition model is composed of self-monitoring strategies, leading to learners transferring these strategies within and across tasks or learning domains. Metacognitive research is viewed by many as the "new approach to" transfer.[39] Strategies include learners asking questions of themselves that are self-reflective on their learning process (i.e., self-monitoring to observe what they are doing while learning). Strictly speaking, the metacognitive approach is not a part of cognitive psychology research but is more aligned with education strategies. The metacognition and strategy approach to transfer deals with general strategies that seem to *promote* transfer but, again, leave the theoretical cognitive development and understanding of the processes underlying transfer unexplained. Discovering strategies of how transfer can be promoted is nevertheless important instructionally.

## The Instructional Model

The educational concept of transfer of learning has been undergoing a relatively unnoticed paradigm shift. With few exceptions, most of the research into discovering the underlying mechanisms of how to achieve transfer has been in cognitive psychology, not in educational research. Thus the term transfer of learning, the original superordinate and applied educational construct, has been in danger of becoming a fragmented and a subordinate process subsumed under the cognitive research labels outlined above. With few exceptions, it is by far the case that historically the educational field has not made use of cognitive research findings. Beginning about 1979, however, educational researchers began to become aware of these data and to think about building upon them.

This shift from transfer as an *applied* instructional concept to a cognitive and metacognitive mechanism has constituted a paradigm shift. This shift is double edged, however. On the positive side, it shifted emphasis from a cognitively uninformed instructional view of transfer to a more research-based view of the cognitive processes underlying transfer. For years, it was repeatedly pointed out that to simply exhort educators to "teach for transfer" was neither sufficient nor effective.[40] On the negative side, pure research into the cognitive mechanisms underlying transfer has inappropriately subsumed the applied instructional approach to transfer.[41] As I argued in chapter 3, if instructional methods were designed—as some are already—on the basis of the otherwise useful and excellent cognitive research and artificial intelligence findings, the time to learn any given subject would increase by at least tenfold because, unlike computers, we are not rapid calculators that can recall long strings of rules and integrate them. With the exception of material that is inherently technical, like learning mathematics, a more general approach will be more effective, given that we do not have an infinite amount of time to teach each course or concept.

Findings from the now competing paradigms of transfer need to be incorporated in some manner as explanatory lower-order mechanisms into a new theoretical base for an instructional model or theory of transfer. These research findings need to be incorporated in order to maintain the cognitive validity of an *instructional* model of transfer. Applied research needs to be conducted on the instructional model of transfer as well. To transfer David Ausabel's argument that educational psychology is not simply general psychology applied to educational problems any more than mechanical engineering is simply general physics applied to problems of designing machinery, an instructional theory of transfer is not simply applied learning theory or applied cognitive psychology.[42] This is why it's important to have a general instructional theory or model of transfer.

## GENERAL MODELS OF MIND

To further understand the history of transfer, it will be useful to review four basic "philosophical" views or models of mind. It will be useful as these four models have influenced not only how we understand transfer but where we look for it and, consequently, how we teach for it. In explaining these views, I'll be radically distilling them. These four models can be categorized into two basic camps: Those who believe that the processes responsible for transfer reside largely (though not exclusively) inside the mind and those who believe they reside largely outside the mind.

In the first model, the rationalist view, cognitive processes are limited by general properties of the mind itself that impose constraints on what we can experience. For example, rationalists assume that the learning of language depends on innate abilities and mental structures that organize linguistic information. Because these mental structures are innate they don't have to be learned. A rationalist model requires that we look for shared mental structures that a learner can carry over from their initial learning to the transfer situation. The transfer process largely depends on inherent structures inside the mind.

In the second model, the empiricist view, cognitive processes are seen as created by external stimuli. This model would include the classic empiricist analysis of transfer by Edward Thorndike in 1901, as well as his "identical elements" view that was a response to the formal discipline view that transfer automatically occurs by studying certain disciplines. An empiricist model requires that we look for external elements or components between two situations or objects that overlap in similarity. The transfer process largely depends on structures inherent in the external object or situation that then create internal mental structures, in this case, transfer. From the perspective of the theory of transfer I have presented in this book, the empiricist view is a limited one, applying largely to training and other more concrete learning situations. (See chapters 11 and 12.)

The third model is a social and historical view of the mind. It assumes that transfer processes largely reside in the social and interpersonal world of human interaction. This model focuses attention on structures constructed in social activities. In this model, transfer depends primarily on our having participated in a social (or work) activity that includes the very structures that form, facilitate, and cue transfer. Thus transfer depends on structures *in the situation* that are primarily socially defined. (I will address this model in chapter 8).

The fourth model is an ecological view of the mind. It assumes that "transfer" is inherent in the external physical world, but not only in the social world. Here, transfer does not have to be constructed by mental processes. An ecological model focuses on structures in the physical world itself. Equivalencies and invariants result from direct perception rather than being mediated by mental representations. Invariance is not constructed or deduced, it is "out there" to be "picked-up" by the brain. In this model, "picking-up" invariants that exist in the world *is* transfer. Strictly speaking, "transfer" does not exist because there is nothing to transfer.

Historically, a common mistake has been taking only a single view of mind and applying it to transfer. But transfer is complex and multifaceted. It is more useful to see each model of transfer as addressing one of the many facets of transfer.

## NEO-IDENTICAL ELEMENTS MODEL REVISITED

The identical elements model of transfer remains forceful in modern cognitive psychology research, though not exclusively in its original form. In Mark

Singley and John Anderson's complex computational system of what they call "production rules," they clearly state that

> what we have presented is a modern version of Thorndike's theory of identical elements. We have identified the elements of cognitive skill to be production rules, (essentially "if . . . then" statements) which, as noted elsewhere are simply computationally enhanced versions of the stimulus–response bonds proposed by Thorndike.[43]

Gray and Orasanu also recognize that the cognitive approach to transferring "goals," "selection rules," and other cognitive "operators" is a common elements approach, which "puts the cognitive science approach squarely in the tradition of Thorndike's identical elements model of transfer, the difference being that the cognitive identical elements are much more abstract."[44]

Similarly, the body of research into analogical reasoning and isomorphic transfer does not focus on general strategies to promote transfer, but on the apparent cognitive basis of transfer; namely, the perception of identical elements underlying the transfer function. Both are squarely based on perceiving similarity that's apparently "out there" to be picked up. These studies tend to construct story plots and descriptions of scientific processes, which run parallel to each other (i.e., they have structurally identical narrative structure). Thus the story plot and descriptions of scientific processes are structurally isomorphic. Experimentally presented to subjects in differing forms and under varying transfer conditions, responses to the various levels of similarity are measured and analyzed. By presenting multiple sets of analogical or isomorphic parallels between descriptions of situations or events, researchers measure and study how subjects map and transfer the common elements among the sets. Findings from these analogical reasoning and isomorphic relations studies have been incorporated into the development of a theory of analogical transfer.

Thus, most of the analogical reasoning and isomorphic relations approaches, based on concrete features of similarity, are in effect a neo-identical elements approach to transfer, with many of the same limitations of Thorndike's original identical elements model. It can nevertheless be a productive approach; first, because it deals with a more complex set of elements than did Thorndike, and, second, because the complexity is coupled with more sophisticated and insightful experimental designs. These designs lead to increased understanding of the cognitive processes underlying some transfer; for example, findings of the relative cognitive function of surface as opposed to deeper structural similarity relations involved in transfer.

Nevertheless, on a more macro- or broader cognitive level, the common elements approach to transfer is proving limited in some of the physical concrete domains to which it is presumably suited. From research on industrial flight simulators, where it has historically been assumed that the physical simulator should be as "identical" to the real flight situation as possible (called full fidelity), findings suggest that "the issue of common elements or full fidelity has not been supported by much of the transfer of learning research."[45] This is not to imply, however, that the common elements theory has no utility. A common elements approach can be useful in many learning contexts. In any event, it is clear that nearly all cognitive research into analogical reasoning is in fact a neo-identical elements approach to transfer.

Recently Ann Brown suggested that analogical transfer must be based within a framework of theories of learning. More importantly, she demonstrates from her research, which goes beyond common elements and metacognition approaches, that young children can engage in transfer generated from a "deep structure" level of conceptual understanding *even when unsimilar surface elements between tasks would contraindicate transfer.*[46] (See chapter 6.) Brown's work is fundamental for an instructional theory of transfer and is the intellectual progeny of Judd's challenge to the identical elements model.

## THE FORMAL DISCIPLINE MODEL REVISITED

I conclude this chapter by revisiting the old formal discipline model of transfer. To read the educational and cognitive literatures today, it's clear that just about everyone considers the formal discipline model a dead issue, as little research has confirmed this approach to transfer. Scattered throughout the literature, however, have been murmurings of its continued validity.[47] Nevertheless, as Nathaniel Gage and David Berliner noted, despite the fact that the formal discipline model virtually disappeared after Thorndike's identical elements studies,

> It still keeps popping up . . . usually in different forms in different decades. To hear the advocates of computer programming talk, learning to program can improve students' performance in other areas of thinking. This expectation is based on the old formal discipline doctrine, where the learning of Greek and Latin was thought to transfer to learning other languages. Thorndike would have taken a dim view of these claims.[48]

Indeed, Thorndike would have taken a dim view of the neo-formal discipline model claim that computer programming inherently contains transfer structures that transfer to reasoning in general.

At least as early as 1937, Gordon Allport suggested that the formal discipline model should not be entirely dismissed.[49] As Henry Ellis noted in 1965, the formal discipline model may not yet be a dead issue but simply needs to be reformulated, along with the identical elements model, to determine the conditions under which each might be useful.[50] Typically, the classic formal discipline model of transfer has been misunderstood. In a 1974 article in the *Journal of Educational Psychology*, Joseph Rychlak, Nguyen Duc Tuan, and William Schneider revived the formal discipline model with new evidence. As the authors point out, it has generally been thought that the formal discipline model held that transfer would occur by a kind of cognitive osmosis; that simply by learning Latin, the very structure of the discipline would be somehow automatically absorbed and transferred.[51] The formal discipline model has also maintained that simple long, hard, and repetitive practice in a discipline would result in transfer, somewhat like developing a muscle.

In actuality, many theorists and educators within the formal discipline model camp held that a teacher could do nothing but show a student the way; students had to bring about their own learning and development. In point of fact, the formal discipline model assumed a meaningful, motivated learning on the part of the student, not a passive learning, where information is poured into the student. Rychlak, Duc Tuan, and Schneider define meaningfulness of learning in terms of intrinsic reinforcement value, or "likability" of the material to be learned. In a series of experiments, they found evidence for the formal discipline model of transfer. They suggested that a strong affective or "feeling" component is prerequisite to transfer, raising the question of whether such an affective component could be the historical source and underpinning of the formal discipline model. Rychlak, Duc Tuan, and Schneider also found that with an affective base, transfer did not depend on any apparent similarity relations. Gordon Allport found the same thing. It is also in keeping with what I refer to as the spirit of transfer (see chapter 7). More recently, there are additional indications that the formal structures of certain other disciplines may in fact transfer to everyday reasoning.

In this regard, it is interesting to note that although the structure of mathematics does not seem to generally train the mind for transfer to everyday reasoning, Geoffrey Fong, David Krantz, and Richard Nisbett, in an article entitled, "The Effects of Statistical Training on Thinking about Everyday Problems," suggest that learning probability statistics may generally transfer to everyday reasoning.[52] They found that students were able to benefit from abstract training in statistical principles. They trained students on the law of large numbers (i.e., that larger sample sizes result in more reliable predictions than small sample sizes), together with several training examples from a given domain (e.g., sports). Considerable subsequent transfer of these principles occurred. It was theorized that subjects learned the law of large numbers in abstract form. In other words, knowledge was learned and stored in abstract, content-free form; it wasn't welded to the learning context.

Darrin Lehman, Richard Lempert, and Richard Nisbett suggested that the structures contained in certain other formal disciplines can in fact transfer to everyday reasoning. In their article on the effects of graduate training on reasoning, the authors maintain that their experiments support the doctrine of formal discipline.[53] They suggest that having learned the rules of one field, students were able to solve problems outside that field using what they had learned in the first field. They conclude that this supports the doctrine of formal discipline. Others are also just beginning to rethink the formal discipline model of transfer. This is especially the case in the more formal approach to reasoning held by computational oriented researchers.

On the basis of his research, Paul Klaczynski suggests that domain-independent (formal) rules may be acquired not only in domains that are themselves relatively content free (like math) but that, under certain conditions, formal rules also may be acquired from training in content-specific areas.[54] More surprisingly, in discussing their work on what they call production rules (i.e., mentalistic abstractions containing variables, goal structures, and "if . . . then" rules), Singley and Anderson suggest

> Given that productions have these features, it might in principle be possible to revive the doctrine of formal discipline in our framework by finding a production system cast at a high enough level of abstraction so that it applies profitably to a wide range of problems. In fact, such production sets have already been identified.[55]

Computational models, then, can be seen not only as limited reformulations of the identical elements model but also of the classic formal discipline model. The primary difference is that in computational models of mind, neither affect nor motivation is included. The classic formal discipline model involves learner characteristics, whereas the computational model is simply an information-processing model. Thus, the computational approach is not so much a reformulation of the classic formal discipline model as it is a possible computational explanation of the cognitive mechanisms underlying the formal discipline model of transfer.

## CONCLUSION

At this point it should be noted that the transfer models suggest that transfer has been approached in seven basic ways: (a) that transfer exists as an *inherent formal property* of certain disciplines; (b) that transfer occurs by the recognition of *concrete identical elements* between two stimuli existing in concrete reality; (c) that transfer results from the application of *general principles* from particular events; (d) that transfer occurs by *stimulus generalization* (e) and the induction of *cognitive schemas*; (f) that transfer is promoted by the delineation and use of *metacognitive strategies*; and (g) that transfer is a property of individual learner characteristics.

It will become clear in the following pages that each model has a role to play in transfer. Each model may be more appropriate for certain kinds of transfer material (e.g., technical vs. theory based), for near and far transfer, or for different learning situations. Some models, however, are more significant for general transfer. In the following chapters, I advocate the latter.

## Notes

[1] Piaget, J. (1980). The psychogenesis of knowledge and its epistemological significance. In M. Piattelli-Palmarini (Ed.), *Language and learning: The debate between Jean Piaget and Noam Chomsky* (pp. 23–52). Cambridge, MA: Harvard University Press, p. 151.

[2] Flew, A. (1995). Higher education, the individual, and the humane sciences. In J. W. Sommer

(Ed.), *The academy in crisis: The political economy of higher education* (pp. 95–126). London: Transactions Publishers.

[3]Flew, A. (1995). Higher education, the individual, and the humane sciences. In J. W. Sommer (Ed.), *The academy in crisis: The political economy of higher education* (pp. 95–126). London: Transactions Publishers, p. 112–113.

[4]Santayana, G. (1905). *The life of reason*. London: Constable, p. 284.

[5]Peters, T. J., & Waterman, R. H. (1982). *In search of excellence: Lessons from America's best-run companies*. New York: Harper & Row, p. 35.

[6]Allport, G. W. (1960). *Personality: A psychological interpretation*. New York: Henry Holt. [Original work published 1937]

[7]Ellis, H. C. (1965). *The transfer of learning*. New York: MacMillan Company.

[8]Cormier, S. M., & Hagman, J. D. (Eds.). (1987). *Transfer of learning contemporary research and application*. New York: Academic Press; Singley, M. K., & Anderson, J. R. (1989). *The transfer of cognitive skill*. Cambridge, MA: Harvard University Press; Analoui, F. (1993). *Training and transfer of learning*. Brookfield, MA: Avebury; Broad, M. L., & Newstrom, J. (1992). *Transfer of training: Action-packed strategies to ensure high payoff from training investments*. New York: Addison-Wesley. See also, Grose, R. G., & Birney, R. C. (Eds.). (1963). *Transfer of learning: An enduring problem in psychology*. New York: D. Van Nostrand.

[9]Clark, R. E., & Voogel, A. (1985). Transfer of training principles for instructional design. *Education Communication and Technology*, 33, 2, 113–123.

[10]Haslerud, G. M. (1972). *Transfer, memory and creativity*. Minneapolis: University of Minnesota Press, p. vii.

[11]Lindgren, H.C. (1976). *Educational psychology in the classroom*. New York: John Wiley.

[12]Gage, N. L., & Berliner, D. C. (1983). *Educational psychology*. London: Houghton-Mifflin, p. 351.

[13]Cormier, S. M., & Hagman, J. D. (Ed.). (1987). *Transfer of learning contemporary research and application*. New York: Academic Press, p. 1.

[14]Thorndike, E. L., & Woodworth, R. S. (1901). The influence of improvement in one mental function upon the efficiency of other functions. *Psychological Review*, 8, 247–261; Judd, C. H. (1908). The relation of special training and general intelligence. *Educational Review*, 36, 42–48.

[15]Clark, R. E., & Voogel, A. (1985). Transfer of training principles for instructional design. *Education Communication and Technology*, 33, 2, 113–123, p. 122.

[16]Brown, A. L., & Campione, J. C. (1984). Three faces of transfer: Implications to early competence, individual differences, and instruction. *Advances in Developmental Psychology*, 3, 143–148, p. 148.

[17]Cronbach, L. J. (1963). *Educational psychology*. New York: Harcourt, Brace & World, p. 314.

[18]McKeachie, W. J. (1987). Cognitive skills and their transfer: discussion. *International Journal of Educational Research*, 11, 707–712, p. 707.

[19]Cormier, S. M., & Hagman, J. D. (Ed.). (1987). *Transfer of learning contemporary research and application*. New York: Academic Press, p. xi.

[20]See Haskell, R. E. (Ed.). (1987). *Cognition and symbolic structures: The psychology of metaphoric transformation*. Norwood, NJ: Ablex; Honeck, R. P., & Hoffman, R. R. (1980). (Eds.). *Cognitive psychology and figurative language*. Hillsdale, NJ: Lawrence Erlbaum; Ortony, A. (Ed.). (1979). *Metaphor and thought*. Cambridge, UK: Cambridge University Press; Vogniadou, S., & Ortony, A. (1989). (Eds.). *Similarity and analogical reasoning*. Hillsdale, NJ: Lawrence Erlbaum; Pollio, H. R., Barlow, J. M., Fine, H. J., & Pollio, M. R. (1977). *Psychology and the poetics of growth: Figurative language in psychology, psychotherapy and education*. Hillsdale, NJ: Lawrence Erlbaum.

[21]For further brief historical views of the transfer literature relating to laboratory research approaches (e.g., gestalt school) see Cormier, S. M., & Hagman, J. D. (Eds.). (1987). *Transfer of learning contemporary research and application*. New York: Academic Press; Ellis, H. C. (1965). *The Transfer of Learning*. New York: MacMillan Company.

[22]Osgood, C. (1949).The similarity paradox in human learning. *The Psychological Review*, 56, 132–143.

[23]See Tversky, A. (1977). Features of similarity. *Psychological Review*, 84, 327–351; also, Vosniadou,

S., & Anthony, A. (Eds.). (1989). *Similarity and analogical reasoning.* New York: Cambridge University Press. Because of the central importance of *similarity* in the understanding of transfer, I will further elaborate on it in a future volume.

[24]See for example, Goodman, N. (1952). On likeness of meaning. In L. Linsky (Ed.). *Semantics and the philosophy of language.* Urbana: University of Illinois Press; Quine, W. (1953). *From a logical point of view.* New York: Harper Torchbooks.

[25]Woolfolk, A., & Nicolich, L. M. (1980). *Educational psychology for teachers.* Englewood Cliffs, NJ: Prentice-Hall, p. 267.

[26]Ellis, H. C. (1965). *The transfer of learning.* New York: MacMillan Company.

[27]Judd, C. H. (1908). The relation of special training and general intelligence. *Educational Review,* 36, 42–48.

[28]Detterman severely, and correctly, critiques Judd's experiment as not in fact being a test of transfer. I nevertheless use it here as it is part of the standard currency in the literature and is virtually always cited as an example of transfer by abstract principle.

[29]Mostofsky, D. (Ed.). (1965). *Stimulus generalization.* Palo Alto, CA: Stanford University Press; Kalish, H. (1969). Generalization as a fundamental phenomenon. In M. H. Marx (Ed.), *Learning processes* (pp. 259–275). New York: Macmillian.

[30]Thompson, R. F. (1965). The neural basis of stimulus generalization. In D. I. Mostofsky (Ed.), *Stimulus generalization* (pp. 178–155). Stanford, CA: Stanford University Press, p. 154.

[31]Ellis, H. C. (1965). *The transfer of learning.* New York: MacMillan Company, p. 84.

[32]Brown, A. L., & Campione, J. C. (1984). Three faces of transfer: Implications to early competence, individual differences, and instruction. *Advances in Developmental Psychology,* 3, 143–148; Crisafi, M. A., & Brown, A. L. (1986). Analogical transfer in very young children: Combining two separately learned solutions to reach a goal. *Child development,* 57, 953–968.

[33]See, for example, Thorndyke, P. W., & Hayes-Roth, B. (1979). The use of schemata in the acquisition and transfer of knowledge. *Cognitive Psychology,* 11, 82–106; Elio, R., & Anderson, J. R. (1981). The effects of category generalizations and instance similarity on schema abstraction. *Journal of Experimental Psychology: Human Learning and Memory,* 7, 397.

[34]See, for example, Hayes, J. R., & Simon, H. A. (1977). Psychological differences among problem isomorphs in N. J. Castellan, D. B. Pison, & G. R. Potts (Eds.), *Cognitive theory* (Vol. 2, pp. 21–41). Hillsdale, NJ: Lawrence Erlbaum Associates; Simon, H. A., & Hayes, J. R. (1976). The understanding process: Problem isomorphs. *Cognitive Psychology,* 8, 165–190.

[35]See, for example, Winston, P. H. (1980). Learning and reasoning by analogy. *Artificial intelligence and language processing,* 23, 689–703.

[36]Gamlin, P. J. (1989). Promoting the generalization of knowledge: A developmental approach to teaching metaphorical thinking. *Canadian Journal of Special Education,* 5, 101–113.

[37]See, for example, Catrambone, R. (1994). Improving examples to improve transfer to novel problems. *Memory and Cognition,* 22(5), 606–615.

[38]See, for example, Gentner, D. (1983). Structure-mapping: A theoretical framework for analogy. *Cognitive Science,* 7, 155–170; Gick, M. L., & Holyoak, K. J. (1987). The cognitive basis of knowledge transfer. In S. M. Cormier & J. D. Hagman (Eds.), *Transfer of learning contemporary research and application.* New York: Academic Press; Holyoak, K. J. (1985). The pragmatics of analogical transfer. In G. H. Bower (Ed.), *The psychology of learning and motivation* (59–87). New York: Academic Press; Holyoak, K. J., Junn, E. N., & Billman, D. O. (1984). Development of analogical problem-solving skills. *Child Development,* 55, 2042–2055; Haskell, R. E. (1989). Analogical transforms: A cognitive theory of the origin and development of transformation of invariance. Part I, II. *Metaphor and Symbolic Activity,* 4, 247–277; Holyoak, K. J., & Koh, K. (1987). Surface and structural similarity in analogical transfer. *Memory and cognition,* 15(4), 332–340; Reed, S. K., Ernst, G. W., & Banerji, R. (1974). The role of analogy in transfer between similar problem states. *Cognitive Psychology,* 6, 436–450; Rumelhart, D. E., & Norman, D. A. (1981). Analogical processes in learning. In J. R. Anderson (Ed.), *Cognitive skills and their acquisition* (pp. 335–359). Hillsdale, NJ: Lawrence Erlbaum Associates; Rumelhart, D. E., & Abrahamson, A. D. (1973). A model for analogical reasoning. *Cognitive Psychology,* 5, 1–2; Spencer, R. M., & Weisberg,

R. W. (1986). Context-dependent effects on analogical transfer. *Memory and Cognition*, 14(5), 442–449; Sternberg, R. J., & Rifkin, B. (1979). The development of analogical reasoning processes. *Journal of Experimental Child Psychology*, 27, 195–232; Vosniadou, S., & Ortony, A. (Ed.). (1989). *Similarity and analogical reasoning*. New York: Cambridge University Press.

[39]See, for example, Borkowski, J. G. (1985). Signs of intelligence: Strategy generalization and metacognition. In S. R. Yussen (Ed.), *The growth of reflection in children* (pp. 105–144). New York: Academic Press; Belmont, J. M., Butterfield, E. C., & Ferretti, R. P. (1982). To secure transfer of training instruct self-management skills. In D. K. Detterman & R. J. Sternberg (Eds.), *How and how much can intelligence be increased?* (pp. 147–153). Norwood, NJ: Ablex; Flavell, J. H., & Wellman, H. M. (1977). Metamemory. In R. V. Kail & J. W. Hagen (Eds.), *Perspectives on the development of memory and cognition* (3–33). Hillsdale, NJ: Lawrence Erlbaum; Nickerson, R. S., Perkins, D. N., & Smith, E. E. (1985). Problem solving, creativity, and metacognition. In R. S. Nickerson, D. N. Perkins, & E. E. Smith (Eds.), *The teaching of thinking* (pp. 64–110). Hillsdale, NJ: Lawrence Erlbaum Associates.

[40]See, for example, Perkins, D. N., & Salomon, G. (1987). Transfer and teaching thinking. In D. N. Perkins, J. Lochhead, & Bishop, J. (Eds.), *Thinking: The second international conference* pp. 285–303). Hillsdale, NJ: Erlbaum.

[41]See, Royer, J. M. (1979). Theories of the transfer of learning. *Educational Psychologist*, 14, 53–69.

[42]Ausubel, D. P. (1968). Cognitive structure and transfer. *Educational psychology: A cognitive view*. New York: Holt, Rinehart & Winston.

[43]Singley, M. K., & Anderson, J. R. (1989). *The transfer of cognitive skill*. Cambridge, MA: Harvard University Press, p. 222.

[44]Gray, W. D., & Orasanu, J. M. (1987). Transfer of cognitive skills. In S. M. Cormier & J. D. Hagman (Ed.). (1897). *Transfer of learning contemporary research and application*. New York: Academic Press, p. 185.

[45]Baudhvin, E. (1987). The design of industrial and flight simulations. In S. M. Cormier & J. D. Hagman (Ed.), *Transfer of learning: Contemporary research and application*. New York: Academic Press, p. 235.

[46]Brown, A. L. (1989). Analogical learning and transfer: What develops? In S. Vogniadou, & A. Ortony (Eds.), *Similarity and analogy reasoning* (pp. 369–412). Hillsdale, NJ: Erlbaum.

[47]Gladstone, R. (1989). Teaching for transfer versus formal discipline. *American Psychologist*, Aug., 1159.

[48]Gage, N. L., & Berliner, D. C. (1983). *Educational psychology*. London: Houghton-Mifflin, p. 308.

[49]Allport, G. W. (1960). *Personality: A psychological interpretation*. New York: Henry Holt. [Original work published 1937]

[50]Ellis, H. C. (1965). *The transfer of learning*. New York: MacMillan Company, p. 64.

[51]Rychlak, J. F., Nguyen, D. T., & Schneider, W. E. (1974). Formal discipline revisited: Affective assessment and nonspecific transfer. *Educational Psychology*, 66, 139–151.

[52]Fong, G. T., Krantz, D. H., & Nisbett, R. E. (1986). The effects of statistical training on thinking about everyday problems. *Cognitive Psychology*, 18, 253–292.

[53]Lehman, D. R., Lempert, R. O., & Nesbett, R. E. (1988). The effects of graduate training on reasoning: Formal discipline and thinking about everyday life events. *American Psychologist*, 43, 431–442.

[54]Klaczynski, P. A. (1993). Reasoning schema effects on adolescent rule acquisition and transfer. *Journal of Educational Psychology*, 85, 679–692; see also Klaczynski, P. A., & Laipple, J. S. (1993). Role of content domain, logic transfer, and IQ in rule acquisition and transfer. *Journal of Experimental Psychology*, 19(3), 653–672.

[55]Singley, M. K., & Anderson, J. R. (1989). *The transfer of cognitive skill*. Cambridge, MA: Harvard University Press, p. 229.

# What Makes Transfer of Learning Work

# Knowledge Base and Transfer: On the Usefulness of Useless Knowledge

*Learning often cannot be translated into a generic form until there has been enough mastery of the specifics of the situation to permit the discovery of lower order regularities which can then be recombined into higher-order, more generic coding systems.*

—JEROME BRUNER, *Going beyond the Information Given*[1]

In recent years, acquiring a large knowledge base has been basically ignored in education, replaced by a focus on programs that teach learning strategies, heuristics, and general thinking skills, with a minimal knowledge base required. In short, the focus is on short-cuts to learning. The problem is there are no short-cuts.

Many learning theories are based on laboratory research designed to be either concerned with areas that students are unfamiliar with or, for purposes of research convenience, that ignore knowledge base. But to talk of knowledge base is to talk of transfer, for transfer depends on knowledge base. This is as true for young children as it is for adults. To say that students must acquire a large store of knowledge to effectively engage in transfer may appear commonsensical and too obvious to mention. Yet, this is what the present chapter is all about. If you ask anyone in—or outside—of education whether they think knowledge base is important, the answer will be, "yes, of course." But the answer is mostly an automatic one with little specific understanding of the profound implications for transfer. In addition, a closer scrutiny typically reveals that the "yes, of course," refers to a minimal knowledge base. Like answering questionnaires, there is a discrepancy between answers and actual behaviors.

The past 99 years of research on transfer shows clearly that general transfer does not occur in most educational and work situations. I suggest that this is largely because we have not paid sufficient attention to the role of knowledge in learning to think. The (a) quantity of knowledge one possesses and (b) the way it is organized, I refer to as knowledge base. I define knowledge base quite broadly, to include knowledge acquired by reading, personal experience, careful listening, and astute observing. A knowledge base also includes thinking, for when you think you add to this base.

Accordingly, it's crucial to understand why and in what way a large knowledge base is important for us to become proficient in transfer. I consider knowledge base the absolute requirement not only for transfer but for thinking and reasoning.[2] As one researcher has concluded, "it appears that some of what predicts good everyday reasoning is the breath and depth of the knowledge base."[3] Contrary to most current educational thinking, I believe the research shows that knowledge base is the primary ingredient and absolute requirement for transfer. And lots of it.

The trend in education has been to gain quick fixes with the use of what are thought to be general problem-solving strategies and thinking techniques. This trend has come from a misunderstanding of the ingredients involved in expert problem solving. Historically, experts have been thought to possess special thinking strategies that novices don't have that allowed the experts to solve problems. They don't. There is virtually no evidence showing that experts have access to general problem-solving techniques that novices lack. For general transfer beyond a specific area, still more knowledge is necessary. For transfer to occur, learning must be transformed into a general or generic form, and for this to happen requires a considerable knowledge base. As Jerome Bruner pointed out years ago,

> Learning often cannot be translated into a generic form until there has been enough mastery of the specifics of the situation to permit the discovery of lower order regularities which can then be recombined into higher-order, more generic coding system.[4]

In this chapter I will present the general knowledge-base conditions necessary for optimal transfer to occur and explain its importance. Transfer of learning requires more than quick-fix strategies.

As counterintuitive as it may sound, learners must have a knowledge base in a subject in order to even know enough to ask questions about it. It is generally thought that in the absence of knowledge about a subject, questions would be unending. How many times have teachers asked a new group of students, "what questions do you have, before we start," only to wait patiently before a group of blank stares. This is not just a matter of shyness, as Naomi Miyake and Donald Norman demonstrate in a telling piece entitled, "To Ask a Question, One Must Know Enough to Know What Is Not Known." As they point out, "although at first glance, one might expect novices to be filled with questions, there are strong theoretical reasons not to expect this."[5] For example, what significant questions could you ask about the implications of Planck's constant?[6] Thus without a sufficient knowledge base, novices do not have a framework within which to formulate adequate questions.

Possessing a large knowledge base enables a learner to think about the subject in depth. McKeachie notes, "I try to teach my students to use 'deep processing.' But if a student knows nothing about a field, it is not possible to go very deep. The conceptual structures are not there."[7] Making a similar observation about teaching, Carl Bereiter says, "what is typically viewed as a failure of knowledge to transfer is actually a failure to teach the conceptual knowledge in the first place."[8] Voss stresses that, "When learning is viewed as transfer, the primary factor influencing learning is the knowledge the individual brings into and uses in the particular learning situation."[9] Frederiksen remarks that although there are some problems, for example, puzzles, that require only a restricted knowledge base, "there is no substitute for having the requisite knowledge if one is to solve a problem. For some kinds of problems, such as engineering the knowledge base is very large."[10] Indeed.

I have known experts in many fields. The proficient and creative ones have always had an extensive knowledge base. I might note that this knowledge base does not necessarily come from a classroom or other formal learning situation. In reading about great innovators, this becomes clear. Stanford Ovshinsky, the inventor of the amorphous metal semiconductor says,

> You must have a knowledge of technical subjects, but that does not necessarily mean a formal education. After all, I worked in the field of medicine, was published in medical journals, and I had nothing but a high school and trade school education. However, I am continually learning and educating myself.[11]

The knowledge that one possesses affects the type of mental models that one can construct as well as the type of problems that can even be recognized, let alone solved.

Jacob Rabinow, the electrical engineer and renowned inventor and holder of many U.S. patents, also noted,

> An inventor has to be well trained. You're not going to combine ideas if you have none to start with. An amateur can invent very well, but he will invent old junk because he doesn't know what's new. That is one of the tragedies of these self-styled inventors who come to us at the Bureau of Standards with an idea. They're nice people, but they have no training. It's as if they want to write but have never read a book.[12]

Wilson Greatbatch, also an engineer and renowned inventor says,

> I firmly believe that a broad background is helpful when it comes to inventing. I give credit for much of what I've been able to do to Cornell University, where I did my undergraduate work, and to the breadth of coursework they gave me in engineering. I had much more chemistry and physics and math than anyone would ever need in order to do just electrical engineering.[13]

Although the old adage "more is better" doesn't often apply, it does apply to knowledge base.

Meaningful learning, then, is dependent upon a base of relevant prior knowledge. Thus, as Christine M. Tan notes, "students who are very low in prior knowledge cannot benefit from cognitive strategy instruction. Students who adopt a surface passive approach probably do not have the critical mass of facts necessary for them to use any cognitive strategies."[14] Not only is transfer directly responsible for physical invention, psychological invention is directly responsible for mental transfer. Knowledge base is not only important in fields like engineering but in the creative arts as well. There are those, however—both students and faculty—who believe they can perform great acts of creativity by sheer force of their intellect. Some even avoid acquiring knowledge, believing that it may spoil the purity of their individual creations. This is nonsense, of course. The overwhelming majority of us mortals don't function on the basis of a disembodied intellect. To think well requires something to think about—and again, lots of it.

At this point, I would like to note that just having a knowledge base is not enough. Information by itself does little; it needs to be entered into a prepared cognitive system (see chapter 7). Knowledge often consists of a mass of rotely memorized subject matter that's not understood deeply enough to enable a student to think critically about a subject. There are situations, too, where an extremely knowledgeable person can be so well informed about an area that she or he becomes inflexible and is not able to conceive or to consider alternatives. Thus it should be understood that when I use the term knowledge base, I generally refer to an appropriately prepared system of knowledge. Think about it for a moment: if simply entering knowledge into our mental apparatus was sufficient, people who have photographic memories would be brilliant and creative. They're not. At least not any more than the rest of us. This is a simple but paradigmatic example.

There have been two basic reasons for not requiring students to master an extensive knowledge base. The first is that a large knowledge base is thought to be psychologically overloading. The second is that a large knowledge base often complicates controlled laboratory research. Unfortunately both reasons are often true. The transfer implications are nevertheless severe. Robert Glaser has observed that in programs emphasizing general thinking skills,

> An avoidance of the complexity of subject-matter information is typical. The practical reason offered is that teachers and students would find this difficult to manage and inhibiting of the thinking processes that need to be practiced and acquired. The significant aspect is that little direct connection is made with thinking and problem solving in the course of learning cumulative domains of knowledge.[15]

In a later publication, Glaser laments that developmental psychologists—à la Piaget—have devoted little attention to changes in children's knowledge base.[16] Piaget's stage theory has come under severe criticism in recent years and has been all but abandoned by many developmental psychologists, who now conclude that the young child doesn't think all that differently from adults; they are not as illogical and concrete in their thinking as we once thought.

Piaget's stage theory is increasingly interpreted in alternative ways. For example, it seems that children are simply more like novices as opposed to experts; their cognitive shifts are not due to maturation so much as a changing knowledge base.[17] Increasingly recognized is that knowledge of specific content domains isn't only a crucial dimension of cognitive development, but that changes in this knowledge base may be responsible for cognitive shifts previously attributed to acquiring learning strategies and to the natural emergence of Piagetian-type developmental stages. Echoing similar observations, cognitive psychology researchers Gick and Holyoak, note

> Only recently has the learner's background knowledge been considered in relationship to transfer of knowledge. Perhaps this neglect is due to researchers' excessive use of artificial materials, for which little prior knowledge was relevant, in both category-learning and problem-solving tasks. More recent work has made use of more naturalistic materials; accordingly, the role of prior knowledge has become a more central concern.[18]

Without a large and valid knowledge base, the use of isolated transfer strategies are not likely to be transferred to situations outside the instructional context. This is largely the case because without an extensive knowledge base, there is nothing to connect isolated strategies together. As I indicated earlier, although teaching specific strategies is a viable approach, for some situations there are just too many strategies and we don't know when or to what extent or under what conditions any given strategy will work.

Learning strategies and heuristics, or rules and procedures for thinking, have evolved out of an emphasis on *process* teaching in education, on the one hand, and findings from computer programming technology, on the other hand. To many proponents of process teaching, a teacher doesn't even need to have expertise in the area being taught; all that is required are skills at directing the students to learn on their own. I once taught with a colleague who maintained that he could teach any subject because he had expertise in instructional *process*. Certainly knowledge of how to teach is important. But knowledge of the subject is even more important. Current research clearly shows that to teach effectively teachers must understand the structure of the discipline or areas being taught.

We have modeled learning and instruction on a misconception of how computers work, thinking that algorithmic-type rules, procedures, and heuristic principles are all that's required to do good mental computation (i.e., thinking). What are called artificial intelligence (AI) or "expert systems" refers to computer problem-solving systems. For some time now the emphasis on algorithms (i.e., a set of rules or sequence of steps designed for programming a computer to solve a problem) has switched to requiring knowledge base. As Patricia Langley and Herb Simon make clear, "During the decade from the mid 60s to mid 70s, attention in AI turned to professional-level performance in complex task domains. It was discovered, or rediscovered, that expert performance requires knowledge—large amounts of it."[19] It is somewhat of an irony that at a time when computer program designers of so-called expert systems have shifted away from a strategies approach to solving problems to a knowledge-based paradigm, education continues to model itself on an outdated AI technology.

There are medical diagnostic computer programs with the expertise of the most highly regarded physicians. Some programs even surpass physician diagnoses. These programs are not distinguished by their procedures, their special heuristics, or their analytical strategies, but by their large stores of knowledge about medicine, human biology, and chemistry. Such an AI system

> exhibits intelligent understanding and action at a high level of competence primarily because of the specific knowledge that it can bring to bear . . . that the reasoning processes of intelligent systems are generally weak and are not the primary source of power.[20]

Knowledge base is. Further, cognitive "procedures" are increasingly recognized as depending much more on knowledge base than previously thought. For example, John Anderson and his colleagues were forced to revise their computational (AI) view of how mental procedures are developed by re-emphasizing the central role of knowledge base.[21]

Until recently, developmental psychologists focused almost no attention on children's knowledge base in explaining changes in their thinking and reasoning. As noted above, this was because changes in children's thinking were viewed as essentially a maturational process that developed in orderly natural stages. For example, it was thought—and still is by many psychologists—that children under about 5 years of age are not proficient at transfer. Indeed, findings from analogy test questions of the sort: A:B:C:D (e.g., light is to dark as day is to night) seem to clearly support the lack of transfer in young children. But the ground-breaking research of Ann Brown and her colleagues has shown that the lack of transfer by young children is not so much due to their developmental stage as to a lack of an appropriate knowledge base.[22] Brown's research with children can be seen as a model for the importance of knowledge base in general. Her research clearly demonstrates highly competent analogical reasoning in young children as long as they possess the relevant knowledge base required for understanding the relations used in the analogy.

Children, like novices or non-experts, have historically been viewed as being "perceptually bound." Perceptually bound means one is tied to the superficial concrete characteristics of phenomena. As a consequence, it's often thought that children are not able to engage in inference; in short, they are not able to transfer their knowledge. Their knowledge is said to be encapsulated or welded to the specific context or situation in which it was learned. Further, the claim has been that transfer of learning depends largely on the degree of perceptual similarity that exists among objects, ideas, or events. This view dates back at least to the psychologist Edward Thorndike's very influential theory that transfer depends on identical elements among items. The concept of functional fixedness (discussed in chapter 2), where a rock may not be seen as a hammer when a nail needs to be driven, can be explained as the consequence of being perceptually bound. Brown's research has repeatedly shown that only when children lack an adequate knowledge base, including theoretical knowledge (see chapter 9) do they rely on the surface features of identical elements and become perceptually bound—indeed, as we adults do.

## KINDS OF KNOWLEDGE AND WHAT THEY DO

Typically, cognitive and instructional scientists describe four basic kinds of knowledge: (a) declarative knowledge, (b) procedural knowledge, (c) strategic knowledge, and (d) conditional knowledge. I will add a fifth kind, not typically mentioned: (e) theoretical knowledge. It is my view, knowledge base is defined by all five of these kinds of knowledge. People who possess—to varying degrees—all five kinds of knowledge are proficient at transfer. There are other publications covering procedural, strategic, and—to a lesser extent—conditional knowledge, so I do not discuss them in detail but only briefly define them. Instead, I focus on declarative knowledge. (Theoretical knowledge is discussed in chapter 9.)

*Procedural knowledge* is how-to knowledge; though we can identify a Buick, we may not know how to drive one. *Strategic knowledge* is knowledge of our mental processes, such as how we learn and remember; it's the self-monitoring of our progress in the act of learning. *Conditional knowledge* is knowledge of when to apply our knowledge in context-appropriate ways: we don't behave in the same way in all situations. *Theoretical knowledge* is our understanding of deep level relationships, of cause and effect, and other explanatory connections about phenomena.

*Declarative knowledge* is knowledge of or about something. We either do or do not know what a Buick is. Though it's often difficult in practice to separate the five kinds of knowledge, in my view declarative knowledge—knowledge of or about something—is the most crucial for transfer. I say this because (a) declarative knowledge provides us with the preconditions necessary for the other four kinds of knowledge; (b) it often includes or directly generates the other four; (c) declarative knowledge frequently provides a general framework for assimilating more detailed new knowledge; (d) it often facilitates the elaboration of newly acquired knowledge; and (e) it frequently provides useful *analogs* (or mental models) to help in the understanding of new knowledge.

Singley and Anderson, although known for their cognitive work on procedural knowledge, nevertheless assert, "Indeed, one could argue that the defining feature of declarative knowledge is that it serves as the basis for transfer to multiple tasks . . . [and represents] somewhat of an antidote to the encapsulation of knowledge."[23] Knowledge base also affects our use of strategies in a number of ways. It often contains information that makes the use of a strategy unnecessary. Frequently, material learned by relying on an already existing knowledge base stimulates strategies to incorporate other material that is not congruent with prior knowledge. In fact, many strategies can only be effectively applied by people who possess a considerable declarative knowledge base.

One of the functions of a knowledge base is not just learning what needs to be learned but filtering out what should not be learned. Ann Brown and others have noted that a learner cannot be flexible if he or she has little knowledge available; flexibility requires possessing a considerable amount of knowledge. Students with a moderate level of general knowledge about mathematical procedures are able to effectively "screen out" distracting and irrelevant content- or context-specific details in mathematical word problems. Students who are only trained in procedures cannot. In other words, strategy use and selection is often knowledge driven.[24]

Ceci and Ruiz note that

> what makes some knowledge easier to transfer than other types is not the abstractness of its conceptual structure but rather the combination of an invitation to transfer that's contained in the original learning, coupled with an elaborated knowledge representation that is sufficiently well developed that most problems are representations of parts of it.[25]

The psychological research also clearly demonstrates that valid intuitive knowledge is made possible by a large knowledge base.[26] This knowledge base is deeply processed on a nonconscious level and results in the perception of patterns. Declarative knowledge, then, is more likely to produce far transfer than the other kinds of knowledge (with the exception of theoretical knowledge, which in most cases includes or is a kind of declarative knowledge).

Yet another implication of knowledge base is that the similarity of two objects or events is not fixed—contrary to the identical elements theory of transfer—but will change with alterations in our knowledge base. Finally, knowledge base, particularly theoretical knowledge, constrains inappropriate transfer (e.g., seeing a whale as a fish) (see chapter 9). Young children and novices are famous for inappropriate transfer. Without an appropriate knowledge base we can end up with "runaway" transfers.

## THE USEFULNESS OF USELESS KNOWLEDGE

Typically, we want only knowledge that's immediately useful. To achieve general transfer, however, often requires much more than immediately useful knowledge. It requires learning that may be considered useless knowledge. I remember as a freshman in college reading in an edited book an essay entitled, On the Usefulness of Useless Knowledge.[27] The essay was written by Abraham Flexner, a physician, well-known educator, and one-time director of the Institute for Advanced Studies at Princeton. In his essay Flexner cited examples of knowledge that appeared to have absolutely no use, but that years later someone saw as something other than what it appeared to be; the person was therefore able to transfer the "useless" knowledge to other areas, which later had major applied importance. For example, the mathematical equations of James Clerk Maxwell (1831–1879), the Scottish physicist who formulated the relationship between magnetism and electricity, were thought to be useless at the time he formulated them. The detection of Maxwell's theoretical "electromagnetic waves" came only much later when they were discovered by Heinrich Hertz (1857–1894), the German physicist.

Moreover, the work of both Maxwell and Hertz was thought to be relatively useless until Guglielmo Marconi (1874–1937), the Italian engineer and inventor, applied this useless knowledge and invented wireless telegraphy. The same can be said of the English scientist Michael Faraday (1791–1867), who, with little formal education, discovered the induction of "electric" current from magnets. Without all of the above "useless" knowledge, I would not be writing these words—as I'm now doing—on my word processor after sunset. Moreover, the essay on useless knowledge has been tucked away in the back of my mind for years. I have never used that chapter in my teaching or writings; until now it was a "useless" piece of information that I had stored away.

Other examples of "useless" knowledge can be cited. Historically, mathematics is perhaps the field that best exemplifies the discovery of what may appear to be useless knowledge. Non-Euclidian geometry, invented by Carl Friedrich Gauss (1777–1855), the German mathematician, physicist, and astronomer, was originally considered useless. In fact Albert Einstein's (1879–1955) relativity theory could not have been formulated without it. Likewise, Group Theory in mathematics was considered useless, but is now the basis of the quantum theory of spectroscopy. Such examples of seemingly useless knowledge are not rare. More recently in mathematics, knot theory was a system for describing and classifying knots. It was thought to be a quite useless kind of mathematical game for theorists to wile away their time; it remained so until someone transferred this theoretical knowledge to another field: Knot theory is currently important in the biochemical analysis of explaining how jumbled strands of DNA in the nuclei of living cells divide without becoming entangled. Someone saw knots as being like jumbled strands of DNA.

When early in his career Abraham Pais, a theoretical physicist, discovered the k-meson particle, it was thought to have no useful application. Today, however, meson particles are used to treat cancer because they can be beamed at cancerous cells without burning the tissue around them. Pais points out that what at first looked like useless knowledge, "turned out in the past to have practical applications. Electronics, transistors, television, radio—all are based on discoveries made by people who are just interested in conceptual questions."[28] In other words by people not interested in the usefulness of the knowledge.

Stanford Ovshinsky, the renowned inventor, says, "For the most part, my inventions come from seemingly unrelated information."[29] Wilson Greatbatch, electrical engineer and inventor of the first implantable heart pacemaker, recounts how he came by his idea. While in school, he held many part-time jobs, one of which was at Cornell University's animal behavior laboratory. While he was working there, two brain surgeons came to perform experimental surgery on animals. The surgeons, like Greatbatch, brought their lunch to work so Greatbatch and the surgeons sat in the sun and talked. During these lunches, he learned about a disease called heart block, the remedy for which he was later to invent: the implantable pacemaker. The technologies, however, were not available for him to invent what he eventually invented. At the time, then, these talks and the information that came from them were useless knowledge. But they remained in his knowledge base until needed. Let me further describe the usefulness of useless knowledge with a telling illustration from the world of fine art.

Possessing an extensive knowledge base does not just apply to science and engineering. As an example of the importance of his father's training, Nat Wyeth, the engineer and inventor of the plastic soda bottle, son of N. C. Wyeth, brother of Andrew, and uncle of Jaime, all famous artists, describes a particular painting that his brother Andrew painted of General Lafayette's headquarters near Chadds Ford, Pennsylvania, the Wyeth homestead. I would like to quote Nat's description.

> It's a beautiful, old building, built before the Revolutionary War, and in his picture was a huge sycamore tree coming up from behind the building with all its beautiful branches. You could see part of the trunk coming up over the roof line. When I first saw the painting, he wasn't quite finished with it. He showed a lot of drawings of the trunk and the gnarled roots going into the ground, and I said, "Gee whiz, where's that in the picture?" "It's not in the picture," he said. And I looked at him. "Nat," he said, "for me to get the feeling that I want in that tree, the part of that tree that's showing, I've got to understand and know very thoroughly how that tree is anchored to the ground in back of that house." It never showed in the picture. But he could draw the part of the tree above the house with a lot more authenticity because he knew exactly the way that thing was anchored in the ground. To me, this was all very indicative of what my father trained into us in whatever we were doing: to understand what we were doing.[30]

The point here is that all of the apparently useless or irrelevant knowledge of how the tree was anchored into the ground, since this knowledge was not directly used in the painting, was in fact useful. In the *same* way, says Nat, the engineer must have a very fundamental training and understanding of the laws of physics before he or she can use them. "This is particularly important," he says, "when you're using your skills in fields or areas where you're really exploring for the first time. We have enough to do and enough problems without moving in false directions because we haven't learned the basics in engineering." The same holds true for the role of knowledge in transferring our learning.

What we typically view as useful knowledge is knowledge that we consider not only to be relevant but *immediately* relevant. The question is, however, what is meant by relevance? We might ask this question by framing it in a journalistic format: relevant for "who, what, why, when, and where." The terms *useful* and *relevance* are relative to goals, context, and to time. As we saw above, today's useless knowledge may be tomorrow's crucial piece of information. As a society we all too often value only what appears relevant now, the immediate "bottom line" to what we are learning. But deep learning that leads · to transfer requires "useless" and "irrelevant" knowledge (relative to a here-and-now context and time frame). This is not only true for the kinds of "big transfers" cited above but for simpler everyday learning as well.

## IRRELEVANT KNOWLEDGE: THE COUNTERINTUITIVE NATURE OF INSTRUCTING FOR TRANSFER

A subset of what I call useless knowledge is irrelevant knowledge. Unlike useless knowledge, irrelevant knowledge is considered useful, but just not relevant to one's immediate subject or problem. What is required for achieving transfer, however, is often irrelevant knowledge. What we think is necessary for achieving transfer is often counterintuitive, that is, counter to what intuition or common sense would lead one to expect. Accordingly, some kinds of knowledge are considered irrelevant when in fact they are not. For example, many of us who teach often consider it counterproductive to present *incorrect* examples of a concept to students.[31] Common sense seems to tell us that if we want a student to learn a concept or action that we should precisely teach the concept or action and not irrelevant or extraneous pieces of knowledge. Frequently, however, irrelevant knowledge is directly relevant to the process of learning and transfer. Irrelevant knowledge can be seen as a variant of useless knowledge. Knowledge viewed as relevant for something may not be seen as relevant for a given transfer situation.

Years ago, an interesting experiment was conducted that illustrates the relevance of irrelevant knowledge. Marvin Herbert and Charles Harsh designed an experiment on modeling in which two groups of cats were to learn the tasks of string pulling and door opening simply by observing the performances of other cats.[32] One group of cats observed only the final errorless performances, whereas the other group observed the early trials of the cats learning. As a consequence, the latter group of cats observed the mistakes that were made during the learning as well as the correct performances. The result was that the observing cats learned to solve the problems more quickly than the cats who learned only from their direct experience, thus clearly illustrating the effects of observational learning. The important finding, however, was that the cats who observed the errors (read: irrelevant knowledge) made by other cats during learning transferred their learning more readily than those who observed only the correct responses.

The observation of the errorless performances were missing the critical choice points or alternatives during learning. They were missing what is often considered irrelevant knowledge. The observation of a final skilled performance does not provide information needed to choose between concepts. Now, lest we think these findings only pertain to lower animals, other early research with humans has resulted in familiar findings.[33] Another experiment with seventh-grade students from three school districts investigated learning adverb concepts by including and removing negative instances.[34] Results indicated that knowledge of negative instances was a vital part of concept acquisition.

Other researchers have noted the problem of experts modeling their refined skills to students. As in the cat experiment above, students who learn a concept or a principle in the absence of irrelevant cues typically have more difficulty in applying the concept or principle to a similar situation that involves irrelevant cues than does a student who learned the material in the presence of irrelevant cues. Thus, simplified situations, such as verbal presentations or simple diagrams, do not typically involve irrelevant cues and, hence, may provide inefficient teaching situations. Again, we have known this for some time. As another early author observes, a learning situation with all its irrelevant cues is "significantly better in facilitating transfer" than is a situation which has had many of its irrelevant cues removed.[35] Here we have some of the elements that I suggest distinguish training from education: instruction given without "irrelevant" knowledge is best characterized as *training*, not education.

The implications for transfer in many fields is striking, especially in clinical/vocational fields where students learn by observing experts. For example, in medical—and most other—clinical education programs it is common practice for students learning a skill such as diagnosing to observe and imitate the highly selective (that is, minus the irrelevant cues) information-processing strategies of the expert physicians whom they accompany on ward rounds.[36] However, the findings presented here suggest that such short-cut learning experiences inhibit the acquisition of the etiological factors underlying the diagnosis by excluding a wide range of original relevant data that were important to the expert physician's current skill at diagnosing.[37] Further, an item of information that may be irrelevant for diagnosing one case may nevertheless be quite relevant in other diagnoses. The expert physician (who already possesses a rich knowledge base of possible causes of a disease) can afford to consider such immediate information in the interests of diagnostic efficiency. There are other problems, too, for acquiring transfer from professional practice situations (shown in chapters 9 and 10). It seems that knowledge from many apparently diverse situations share similar structures that may summate into generic learning. The more we know, the better.

## EXPERTISE AND KNOWLEDGE

Until recently, it was generally thought that what made experts different from novices was not primarily their knowledge base but rather the mental strategies for seeing into and solving problems. But research has now found experts in most fields are differentiated from novices not by their strategies but by their rich stores of knowledge. In his review of the research on expert and amateur chess players, Robert Glaser found

> no strategy differences. All players tended to consider the same number of moves. They also looked ahead about the same number of moves as they tried to evaluate each move, and they used similar strategies to guide this search. In contrast to other players, experts simply recognized the best move and gave it first consideration; they evaluated the other moves only as a way of double checking themselves.[38]

Later summaries of the literature on experts find "no convincing evidence that experts really differ in their cognitive processes. . . . All the other research did not succeed convincingly in specifying different cognitive strategies and capacities of experts."[39] It is now well known that expert chess players utilize an enormous amount of knowledge of chess patterns. Chess players must spend thousands of hours in acquiring a large knowledge base, by playing chess, reading books and magazines on chess, and carefully studying thousands of chess positions (see chapter 10).

Now, there are two kinds of expertise. One is routine expertise, the other adaptive expertise. Each kind is based upon the amount of knowledge acquired and how it is used. Routine expertise rests on a restricted knowledge base in a particular area; adaptive expertise, on the other hand, is based on a more extensive knowledge base. Adaptive experts utilize procedures flexibly, can modify them based on feedback demands, and can invent new procedures to deal with novel problems and situations. To use an *analogy*, someone who implements a recipe quickly and accurately can be called a routine expert, whereas an adaptive expert would be able to substitute ingredients in the recipe if necessary and modify it for different requirements. In general, *training* leads to routine expertise, whereas knowledge-based *deep learning* leads to adaptive expertise and to creativity. Accordingly, routine expertise leads to narrow transfer within an area; adaptive expertise leads to broad transfer extending beyond an area. By comparison, children are a kind of routine expert, and adults a kind of adaptive expert.

Competent problem solvers (experts) not only have an appropriate knowledge base available in their long-term memory, they also have the ability to access and use that knowledge. The essential difference between experts and novices is not simply knowledge base but how that knowledge base is organized. Again, Glaser has found that "the evidence indicates that what humans actually do as they learn and acquire experience is to build up an extremely large store of structured knowledge."[40] This structured knowledge enables them to "see into" a problem more quickly than a novice. "What differentiates an expert problem solver from a non-expert" says Glaser, "is not the use of different or more powerful heuristics, but an initial representation that allows the expert to succeed in pursuing the better path to solution without considering all the others."[41] Thus we can see once again that an extensive knowledge base allows the expert to either not be sidetracked by irrelevant aspects linked to a problem, or to see what may be considered irrelevant knowledge as in fact directly relevant. It is perhaps noteworthy to point out that Glaser's early expertise was as a behavioral psychologist doing research in measurement theory, human performance, and as an advocate of programmed instruction and teaching machines.

Studies indicate that the way we process information is greatly enhanced by experience with new information. Research suggests that experts form immediate representations of problems that systematically cue their knowledge, whereas novices do not have such efficient access to their knowledge.[42] The implication is that when experts look at a complicated situation, they form mental representations composed of a few patterns or chunks and other hierarchically organized mental structures.

There are other important differences, too, between those with lots of knowledge and those with little. As I have already pointed out, high-knowledge individuals are able to identify problems and issues more precisely and more quickly than are low-knowledge individuals. Further, this difference enables them to more precisely encode and store information. As a consequence, access to and retrieval of pertinent information is more efficient. High knowledge individuals have a much greater knowledge of contingent, irrelevant, and contextual relationships and are more adept at using or discarding this knowledge.[43] Thus, Glaser concludes, "Our interpretation is that the problem-solving difficulty of novices can be attributed largely to the inadequacies of their knowledge bases and not to limitations in their processing capabilities such as the inability to use problem-solving heuristics."[44] But other consequences issuing from a large knowledge base have implications for transfer.

A knowledge base develops our ability to perceive patterns in the environment. Years ago, Jerome Bruner recognized that

> much of what we classify as learning, recognition, and problem solving consists of being able to identify recurrent regularities in the environment. What makes such a task a problem is that the recurrent regularities—be they turns in a maze, elements in a temporal pattern, or a pattern in successive events—may either be masked by factors that are irrelevant to the regularity, or the regularity itself may be of such complexity that it exceeds the memory span that an observer brings to the task.[45]

Since Bruner, others have also recognized that "a very important component of the knowledge-base is a fast-action pattern-recognition system . . . that greatly reduces processing load . . . [and] . . . these patterns serve the purpose of retrieval aids for desirable courses of action."[46] Others also conclude that

> the expert is not merely an unindexed compendium of facts, however. Instead, large numbers of patterns serve as an index to guide the expert in a fraction of a second to relevant parts of the knowledge store. This knowledge includes sets of rich schemata that can guide a problem's interpretation and solution and add crucial pieces of information. This capacity to use pattern-indexed schemata is probably a large part of what we call physical intuition.[47]

Finally, people high in knowledge base exhibit superior memory and encoding procedures for retrieval and transfer than do those low in knowledge base. At first glance, the commonsense explanation might be that those with a good memory are able to amass and retain a larger knowledge base than those with poorer memories. But this is not the correct explanation. Somewhat counterintuitively, acquiring a large knowledge base is not the consequence of a superior memory. Rather, superior memory is the consequence of having a large knowledge base. Having a large knowledge base provides more frameworks and related connections, and enables information to be remembered, maintained, and retrieved. For example, studies have shown that master chess players could not remember a randomly generated chess board set-up any better than chess players of lesser ability.

Lauren Resnick, though an advocate of learning strategies, suggests "that learning depends heavily on what people already know poses a fundamental problem for instruction. Without special intervention, the knowledge rich would grow greatly in knowledge, the knowledge poor very little."[48]

It seems that as with monetary capital, intellectual capital feeds on itself: The rich grow richer and the poor grow poorer. Resnick also suggests a remedy for knowledge deficits called "bootstrapping." She says, "It may be helpful to recast the traditional instructional question of how to convey information as a problem of cognitive bootstrapping—beginning a climb without firmly established prior knowledge, yet behaving as if one had the knowledge."[49] Learning strategies presumably provide the remedy. As we have seen, however, learning strategies have yet to yield any significant profit. Making believe that one has intellectual capital doesn't seem to work any more than making believe one has real capital.

## CONCLUSION

In the classic, formal-discipline view of education, knowledge base was always considered important, but it was largely an intuitive principle. Now, however, there is considerable hard evidence pointing not only to the importance of knowledge base but to its cognitive advantages as well. The two camps, the knowledge-base camp—sometimes referred to as the Knowledge

Mafia[50]—and the learning/thinking strategy camp—which I refer to as the cookbook camp—remain largely divided.

We still have a way to go to understand all that a knowledge base does. As James Voss noted years ago, "The extent to which knowledge of one domain may be useful in learning new information of another domain is, of course, an open question; we do not know how specific or how general transfer effects really are."[51] He goes on to point out that we need to know more about how the vague hypothetical construct "schema" works. More importantly for transfer, he says, "when the schema notion becomes sufficiently unpacked, we may find that we have highly specific transfer which is found frequently with high-knowledge individuals because of their varied experiences."[52] Although we are beginning to unpack the hypothetical construct of "schema," we still need to know more about what knowledge base does. We need to know, for example, the differences between the knowledge required for well-structured problems and domains, such as mathematics and physics, as opposed to ill-structured areas, such as literary analysis, psychology, and political theory.

Contrary to popular expectation, despite the importance of knowledge base, for most people there appears to be little if any transfer from one domain to another, quite different domain. We often expect that there should be transfer. This expectation, however, is based on false assumptions about the nature of intelligence; it is also based on what is called the "halo effect" (The halo effect is when some one is highly regarded, we often tend to consider their opinions in other areas to be valid ones). For example, we hold physicists and physicians in high regard. But knowledge of medicine or skill in problem solving in physics does not necessarily transfer to moral, philosophical, political, or economic problems. A given individual may, of course, acquire such knowledge across a number of domains.

As addressed in chapters 9 and 10, a knowledge-base crisis exists in many professional fields, and in our schools as well. In many professional fields and programs, practitioners tend neither to engage in nor to read or utilize relevant research-based knowledge about their fields. One final caveat: over the years, I have observed that some people need a large knowledge base to accomplish a little, whereas others need only a little knowledge base to accomplish a lot. What's the difference between these two types? Part of the answer may be motivation (see chapter 7) or a transfer ability that is hardwired into our nervous systems (see chapter 11). But we do not need to be hardwired in an extraordinary sense to engage in transfer.

## Notes

[1] Bruner, J. S. (1973). Going beyond the information given. In J. Anglin (Ed.), *Going beyond the information given: Studies in the psychology of knowing* (pp. 218–238). New York: W. W. Norton, p. 232.

[2]See Suzuki, H. (1994). The centrality of analogy in knowledge acquisition in instructional contexts. *Human Development*, 37(4), pp. 207–219, p. 208.

[3]Galotti, K. M. (1989). Approaches to studying formal and everyday reasoning. *Psychological Bulletin*, 105, 331–351, p. 338.

[4]Bruner, J. S. (1973). Going beyond the information given. In J. Anglin (Ed.), *Going beyond the information given: Studies in the psychology of knowing* (pp. 218–238). New York: W. W. Norton.

[5]Miyake, N., & Norman, D. A. (1979). To ask a question, one must know enough to know what is not known. *Journal of Verbal Learning and Verbal Behavior*, 18, 357–364, p. 357.

[6]German physicist Max Planck (1858–1947) won a Nobel Prize in 1918 for his discoveries in connection with quantum theory. *Planck's constant* refers to the proportional energy of a photon to the frequency of that photon (a photon is a quantum of electromagnetic energy, generally described as a discrete particle having zero mass, no electric charge, and an indefinitely extended life).

[7]McKeachie, W. J. (1987). The new look in instructional psychology: Teaching strategies for learning and thinking. In E. De Corte, H. Lodewijks, R. Parmentier, & P. Span (Eds.), *Learning and instruction* (vol. I, pp. 443–456). Oxford: Pergamon Press, p. 453.

[8]Bereiter, C. (1995). A dispositional view of transfer. In A. McKeough, J. Lupart, & A. Marini (Eds.), *Teaching for transfer: Fostering generalization in learning* (pp. 21–34). Mahwah, NJ: Lawrence Erlbaum Associates, p. 28.

[9]Voss, J. F. (1977). Cognition and instruction: Toward a cognitive theory of learning. In A. M. Lesgold, J. W. Pellegrino, S. D. Fokkema, & R. Glaser (Eds.), *Cognitive psychology and instruction* (pp. 13–26). New York: Plenum Press, p. 19.

[10]Frederiksen, N. (1984). Implications of cognitive theory for instruction in problem solving. *Review of Educational Research*, 54, 363–407, p. 378.

[11]Brown, K. (1988). *Inventors at work: Interviews with 16 notable American inventors*. Redmond, WA: Microsoft Press, p. 158.

[12]Ibid, p. 208.

[13]Ibid, p. 130.

[14]Tan, C. M. (1992). An evaluation of the use of continuous assessment in the teaching of physiology. *Higher Education*, 23, 255–272, p. 263.

[15]Glaser, R. (1984). Education and thinking: The role of knowledge. *American Psychologist*, 39, 93–104, p. 96.

[16]Glaser, R. (1987). Learning theory and theories of knowledge. In E. De Corte, H. Lodewijks, R. Parmentier, & P. Span (Eds.), *Learning and instruction* (vol. I, pp. 397–413). Oxford: Pergamon Press, p. 402.

[17]See for example, Guberman, S. R., & Greenfield, P. M. (1991). Learning and transfer in everyday cognition. *Cognitive Development*, 6, 233–260; Carey, S. (1986). Cognitive science and science education. *American Psychologist*, 41(10), 1123–1130.

[18]Gick, M. L., & Holyoak, K. J. (1987). The cognitive basis of knowledge transfer. In S. M. Cormier & J. D. Hagman (Eds.), *Transfer of learning contemporary research and application* (pp. 9–45). New York: Academic Press, p. 37.

[19]Langley, P., & Simon, H. A. (1981). The central role of learning in cognition. In J. R. Anderson (Ed.), *Cognitive skills and their acquisition* (pp. 362–380). Hillsdale, NJ: Erlbaum, p. 363.

[20]Feigenbaum, E. A. (1989). What hath Simon wrought? In D. Klahr & K. Kotovsky (Eds.), *Complex information processing: The impact of Herbert A. Simon* (pp. 165–182). Hillsdale, NJ: Lawrence Erlbaum, p. 179.

[21]Anderson, J. R., & Fincham, J. M. (1994). Acquisition of procedural skills from examples. *Journal of Experimental Psychology: Learning, Memory, & Cognition*, 20(6), 1322–1340.

[22]Brown, A. L., Kane, M. J., & Long, C. (1989). Analogical transfer in young children: Analogies as tools for communication and exposition. *Applied Cognitive Psychology*, 3, 275–293.

[23]Singley, M. K., & Anderson, J. R. (1989). *The transfer of cognitive skill*. Cambridge, MA: Harvard University Press, p. 220.

[24]Suzuki, H. (1994). The centrality of analogy in knowledge acquisition in instructional contexts. *Human Development*, 37(4), 207–219.

[25]Ceci, S. J., & Ruiz, A. (1993). Transfer, abstractness, and intelligence. In D. K. Detterman & R. J. Sternberg (Eds.), *Transfer on trial: Intelligence, cognition, and instruction* (pp. 168–191). Norwood, NJ: Ablex.

[26]Brewer, W. F. (1989). The activation and acquisition of knowledge. In S. Vosniadou & A. Anthony (Eds.), *Similarity and analogical reasoning* (pp. 532–545). New York: Cambridge University Press.

[27]Flexner, A. (1961). On the usefulness of useless knowledge. In L. G. Locke, W. Gibson, & G. Arms (Eds.), *Toward liberal education* (pp. 443–452). New York: Holt, Rinehart and Winston.

[28]*Fortune*. (1990). Today's leaders look to tomorrow. *Fortune* (March 26th), p. 78.

[29]Brown, K. (1968). *Inventors at work: Interviews with 16 notable American inventors.* Redmond, WA: Microsoft Press, p. 163.

[30]Ibid, p. 375.

[31]Lasley, T. J., Williams, S. J., & Hart, P. M. (1991). Nonexamples: Why teachers don't use them and why teacher educators should. *Mid-Western Educational Researcher*, 4, 2–6.

[32]Herbert, M. J., & Harsh, C. M. (1944). Observational learning by cats. *Journal of Comparative Psychology*, 37, 81–95.

[33]Overing, R. L. R., & Travers, R. M. W. (1967). Variation in the amount of irrelevant cues in training and test conditions and the effect upon transfer. *Journal of Educational Psychology*, 58, 62–68.

[34]Tennyson, R. D. (1973). Effect of negative instances in concept acquisition using a verbal-learning task. *Journal of Educational Psychology*, 64(2), 247–260.

[35]Ibid.

[36]Bransford, J. D., Franks, J. J., Vye, N. J., & Sherwood, R. D. (1989). New approaches to instruction: Because wisdom can't be told. In S. Vosniadou & A. Anthony (Eds.), *Similarity and analogical reasoning* (pp. 470–497). New York: Cambridge University Press, p. 484.

[37]See, for example, Overing, R. L. R., & Travers, R. M. W. (1967). Variation in the amount of irrelevant cues in training and test conditions and the effect upon transfer. *Journal of Educational Psychology*, 58, 62–68, p. 62.

[38]Glaser, R. (1987). Learning theory and theories of knowledge. In E. De Corte, H. Lodewijks, R. Parmentier, & P. Span (Eds.), *Learning and instruction* (vol. I, pp. 397–413). Oxford: Pergamon Press, p. 400.

[39]Rehm, J. T., & Volker, G. (1990). *Intuitive predictions and professional forecasts: Cognitive processes and social consequences.* New York: Pergamon Press, p. 101.

[40]Glaser, R. (1987). Learning theory and theories of knowledge. IN E. De Corte, H. Lodewijks, R. Parmentier, & P. Span (Eds.), *Learning and instruction* (vol. I, pp. 397–413). Oxford: Pergamon Press, p. 400.

[41]Ibid, p. 401.

[42]See for example, Resnick, L. B. (1989). Preface. In L. B. Resnick (Ed.), *Knowing, learning and instruction: Essays in honor of Robert Glaser.* Hillsdale, NJ: Lawrence Erlbaum, p. xiv.

[43]Voss, J. F. (1977). Cognition and instruction: Toward a cognitive theory of learning. In A. M. Lesgold, J. W. Pellegrino, S. D. Fokkema, & R. Glaser (Eds.), *Cognitive psychology and instruction* (pp. 13–26). New York: Plenum Press, p. 15.

[44]Glaser, R. (1984). Education and thinking: The role of knowledge. *American Psychologist*, 39, 93–104, p. 98.

[45]Bruner, J. S. (1973). Going beyond the information given. In J. Anglin (Ed.), *Going beyond the information given: Studies in the psychology of knowing* (pp. 218–238). New York: W. W. Norton, p. 198.

[46]Frederiksen, N. (1984). Implications of cognitive theory for instruction in problem solving. *Review of Educational Research*, 54, 363–407, p. 370.

[47]Larkin, J., McDermott, J., Simon, D. P., & Simon, J. A. (1980). Expert and novice performance in solving physics problems. *Science*, 208, p. 1342.

[48]Resnick, L. B. (1989). Introduction. In L. B. Resnick (Ed.), *Knowing, learning, and instruction: Essays in honor of Robert Glaser.* Hillsdale, NJ: Lawrence Erlbaum, p. 3–4.

[49]Ibid, p. 4.

[50]Brewer, W. F. (1989). The activation and acquisition of knowledge. In S. Vosniadou & A. Anthony (Eds.), *Similarity and analogical reasoning* (pp. 532–545). New York: Cambridge University Press, p. 535.

[51]Voss, J. F. (1977). Cognition and instruction: Toward a cognitive theory of learning. In A. M. Lesgold, J. W. Pellegrino, S. D. Fokkema, & R. Glaser (Eds.), *Cognitive psychology and instruction* (pp. 13–26). New York: Plenum Press, p. 19.

[52]Voss, J. F. (1987). Learning and transfer in subject-matter learning: A problem-solving model. *International Journal of Educational Research, 11*, 607–622, p. 619.

# The Spirit of Transfer
# and Personality: Motivation,
# Meaning, and Emotion

*Generalization itself will not tell the whole story. To insure transfer, therefore, the atti-
tude in question must be raised to the plane of an ideal and given an emotional tone.*

—JOHN R. RYAN, *Transfer of Training*[1]

To say that students must be motivated to learn or that motivation is important to education is to state the most obvious of educational clichés. Yet, this
chapter emphasizes that often what appears to be the most obvious is what
we, in fact, don't clearly see or understand except on a most general level. In
recent years, personality and dispositional characteristics of learners have
been largely ignored in education. Nevertheless, if you ask anyone inside—
or outside—of education if they think attitude, motivation, temperament,
and character are something they try to foster in their teaching, the answer
will be a resounding *yes.* But this largely automatic answer typically resonates
with a hollow ring. In an article in the *American Psychological Association Monitor,*
Susan Moses observes that

> Despite a decade of earnest educational restructuring across the country, all the na-
> tional statistics still paint the same picture of students' lackluster academic perfor-
> mance. At least in part, that's because 1980's-style education reform often ignored
> issues of student effort and motivation. . . . Many students settle for mediocre per-
> formance because little is expected from them, experts agreed. Schools admittedly of-
> fer few carrots for high achievers.[2]

More specifically in terms of transfer, Rita Richey in her book, *Designing Instruction for the Adult Learner,* notes that "the question of the role of learner attitudes . . . is rarely addressed in the literature."[3] I might add that this is especially true in relation to transfer. In taking a dispositional approach to
transferring knowledge in science learning, Carl Bereiter says that in order for

a principle like gravitation to become fully effective, it needs to be incorporated into the way a learner perceives and comprehends the world. That the earth is spherical, for example, should operate automatically and unconsciously. In a striking turn of phrase that I wish I had thought of, Bereiter notes, "An adult in the modern world should not have to *remember* that the world is round."[4] He concludes that transfer of a concept or principle is only achieved when it's incorporated so thoroughly into one's cognitive system that it becomes a part of one's personality.

In this chapter I suggest that significant and general transfer is primarily the consequence of personality and other dispositional characteristics such as attitude, motivation, and feeling. In short, I will suggest that general transfer is the consequence of what I refer to as the spirit of transfer, not simply—nor even significantly—to educational methods, learner strategies, or teaching techniques. Again this is not revelatory. As the epigraph to this chapter shows, the role of emotion in learning was recognized in 1951 to be specifically important for transfer. In fact, the role of emotion is as ancient as the very first reflections on learning. Sometimes in history important ideas either get lost, are considered invalid, or are thought to be passé. This has been especially true of the relationship between "personality" characteristics and transfer, which has occurred at least twice in history, first in relation to learning and then in direct relation to transfer. The former can be traced to ancient Greece, the latter to more contemporary times. In this chapter I address the second occasion it was lost, as well as the affective aspect of the first time it was lost.

In 1937 the renowned psychologist Gordon Allport[5] recognized the relationship of personality characteristics and transfer, but his views have since been largely lost or ignored. In this chapter I will resurrect Allport's ideas on the relationship between personality and transfer in support of my approach to general transfer. Virtually all contemporary discussion on instruction and transfer concerns techniques, strategies, skills, and methods of instruction. These discussions appear to be hard-nosed, no-nonsense approaches to education. They are not. Although instructional technologies are important, from my years of teaching experience and my review of the significant transfer research, I have become convinced that without the transfer "spirit," there is precious little transfer. I consciously use the word *precious*; transfer research shows that whatever transfer may be generated by technique, strategy, and method is typically the lowest level of transfer. Moreover, an emphasis on strategies and techniques are extremely costly, with a cost–benefit ratio typically way out of proportion to their significance. So what is the transfer spirit and how does it work?

## THE SPIRIT OF TRANSFER

The spirit of transfer refers to a personality attribute; more importantly it is a learner's state of being, not just a set of situational learning strategies or instructional implants. Though *spirit*—as opposed to *skill*—may seem at first glance a "soft" term, it is in fact a hard-nosed concept. As I intend to show in this chapter, the transfer spirit is a psychological, emotional, and motivational disposition toward deep learning. The transfer spirit, however, is not simply another term for motivation, for the term *motivation* has come to refer to short-run, task-specific activities. The transfer spirit is more inclusive than that.

I specifically selected the term *spirit* because it means so much more than motivation. A dictionary definition of spirit typically includes (a) an animating principle of life, (b) a vital essence, (c) an attitude or dispositional principle that pervades thought, (d) as stirring or prompting one to action, (e) the soul or heart as the seat of feelings, (f) a vigorous, courageous, or optimistic attitude, (g) a dominant tendency or character, (h) the essence or active principle of a substance. Spirit, as one might suspect, also has a spiritual dimension that originates in what the well-known humanistic psychologist, Abraham Maslow, called a natural and primitive *need to know*.

We have only to look at the history of science and invention to clearly see that the great scientists and innovators were deeply and emotionally moved to achieve what they did. Some were moved by religion, some by fame, some by money. For some, the quest bordered on obsession. Sir Isaac Newton (1642–1727) the British scientist and mathematician known for his theory of gravitation and who invented differential calculus was an avid alchemist. Both he and Johannes Kepler (1571–1630), the German astronomer and mathematician, were motivated out of deep religious convictions to discover the perfect law and form of God's design among the celestial bodies. Johannes Gutenberg (1397–1468) who (arguably) invented movable type, was motivated to invent the printing press by his desire to mass produce the Christian Bible. Now, I'm not suggesting we all should or need to become obsessed—religiously or otherwise. Rather, I am simply pointing out the deep spirit that typically characterizes those who are expert at transfer. The spirit of transfer is not merely a mental module; it's a motivated, affective personality matrix.

Calling spirit different names, some educational theorists recognized the necessity of a more fundamental motivation for learning and transfer. The need for a deep-seated *disposition* to transfer is recognized, for example, in the cottage industry of teaching critical thinking. In a minority report of an otherwise majority approach to teaching critical thinking, which maintains a skills or cookbook orientation to teaching with techniques and strategies, Carl Brell recognizes that

> a concept of critical thinking as transfer . . . calls attention to the fact that teaching for transfer is less a matter of transmitting knowledge, skills, strategies, and principles of thinking (though it is that, too) than it is of fostering in students from the start an inquiring disposition, by which I mean a "readiness" to consider the bearing of apparently discrete frames of reference on one another and toward the construction of a more integrated world view.[6]

In an optimal sense, the transfer spirit envelopes the whole person.

Wilbert McKeachie, well known in educational research, also recognizes the significance of motivation for transfer. Referring to the development of achievement and other aspects of motivation for learning, he says, "we might be facilitating the development of important transferable human characteristics that would, in turn, increase the likelihood of transfer of cognitive skills."[7] David McClelland and his associates have been studying the need for achievement for over twenty years. He defines achievement motivation as an urge to improve or a desire to excel and as a drive to persist in attaining those goals.[8] McClelland estimates that only about 10% of the population is high in need for achievement.

The well-known researcher, Laura Resnick, also holds a similar view, maintaining, "There is good reason to believe that a central aspect of developing higher order cognitive abilities in students is a matter of shaping this kind of disposition to critical thought."[9] In his doctoral dissertation, David Mittelholtz found that prediction for long-term retention of material was best predicted for students who had a "deep processing" motive for studying, that is, students who were motivated to understand the material.[10] More recently, Peter Gamlin has stressed

> that the learner must acquire a general strategic orientation to acquiring knowledge, developing a sense of the general nature of the problem, the big picture, so as to determine what counts as relevant information in problematic or unfamiliar situations.

He concludes by saying, "I argue that *this is the key to transfer* [italics added]."[11]

A spirit for transfer infuses information with meaning; for it's meaning that transforms *information* into *transferable knowledge*. Historically, mainstream cognitive science has not dealt with such seemingly humanistic or "soft" variables as emotion and motivation, maintaining that such variables could be accounted for in entirely cognitive, nonmotivational, and nonaffective terms, and therefore there is no need to assume their existence.[12] Although cognitive psychologists are concerned with goals, in an article in *Psychological Science*, Deci says that "goal theory is only a partial theory of human motivation: It does not speak to the content of motivation."[13] Recently, however, researchers are rethinking this historical neglect of the role of emotion in learning. In an interesting article titled, "The Case for Motivated Reasoning,"[14] Ziva Kunda suggests that many of the so-called soft variables cannot in fact be accounted for in nonmotivational terms. Indeed, not accounting for such variables requires making a number of auxiliary and hypothetical assumptions, many of which have little empirical support. Kunda concludes that given the current state of knowledge, a motivational account may be a more parsimonious and coherent account than a purely computational cognitive one. Although psychologists and educators talk about motivation as an important variable, more often than not the term motivation falls far short of a total personality characteristic. Motivation is typically seen as a kind of energizing or drive module.

## PERSONALITY, MEANING, AND ENCODING
## FOR TRANSFER

Gordon Willard Allport (1897–1967) recognized the close relationship between learning and personality. As early as 1937, he maintained that "any law of learning is at the same time a law of the development of personality."[15] More specifically he saw that "one of the outstanding problems in the psychology of learning is transfer of training and, as might be expected, it turns out that this same problem is equally important for the theoretical psychology of personality."[16] This was a momentous insight.

Part of the reason for connecting transfer and personality was Allport's observation that for the majority of us "generalization of conduct does not extend as far as most people suppose, with the result that conduct for the large masses of people remains unorganized, a rather loose bundle of unrelated and dissociated habits."[17] For example, we compartmentalize different aspects of our "selves." We often fail not only to connect our knowledge of the external world, but our internal world as well. We may be a wonderful parent and friend, but a tyrannical and mean boss.

Indeed, Allport maintained, "The solution to the problem of personality organization will depend to a large degree upon the solution found for the problem of transfer."[18] Critiquing the traditional identical elements theory of learning and speaking about the then modern "character education" movement, Allport pointed out that it had been greatly influenced by the belief that no child can be taught virtue except "by doing specific things in specific situations."[19] In other words, abstract universals can't be taught. Few have understood, as did Allport, the far-reaching implications of transfer and personality theory.

Allport's insight into the nature of similarity relations à la identical elements theory was prophetic. Only recently are some educational theorists and cognitive researchers acknowledging that "similarity relations" are often determined by psychological characteristics, not just by external objective criteria. Allport recognized that similarity is

> conditioned by temperament and previous learning; it is certainly lawful enough if regarded from the point of view of the individual's life-history. Instead of lawless it would be more accurate to say that similarity is personal. And just because it is personal, the transfer value of any item in the school curriculum cannot be standardized or predicted. Neither for school children nor for adults are similarities uniform.[20]

Because similarity is essentially the subjective counterpart of equivalence, says Allport,

> it plays a corresponding role in the structural arrangement of personality. To an artistic person, a sunset, a landscape, a sonnet, a threshing machine, a derelict in the sands, may all be similar in that to him they all mean beauty.[21]

In another example, he says suppose,

one is studying the personality of a "super-patriot." One quickly discovers that to him many different items of experience are equivalent in the response they provoke: a red flag, a volume by Marx, a teacher's union, the peace efforts of a Yale professor, or the formation of a neighborhood co-operative. One and all they arouse the communist phobia. The equivalence of these items can be explained only by assuming that there is an underlying disposition of some sort, whose threshold of arousal is low and capable of being crossed by this whole diverse range of stimuli.[22]

Allport also contends that the similarity operation is thus difficult to predict. Further, he maintains that objective and concrete similarity relations do not automatically cause transfer; *rather only under the guidance of general concepts* and "volitional dispositions are they effective."[23] All this sounds rather logical and makes theoretical sense, but is there any hard evidence?

At about the time Allport was writing, an experiment on the transfer of affect or emotion was being conducted by Lorge.[24] Students were presented with the following statement: "I hold that a little rebellion, now and then, is a good thing, and as necessary in the political world as storms are in the physical." The experimenter first attributed the statement to Thomas Jefferson, then to Lenin. Lorge found that students agreed with the statement when it was thought to be attributed to Thomas Jefferson, but disagreed with it when it was thought to be attributed to Lenin. He argued that the positive affect or emotion associated with Jefferson transferred to the message, rendering it a positive statement, whereas the negative affect associated with Lenin was transferred to the statement with the opposite effect, rendering it a negative statement. More recent research also supports transfer of affect in a variety of contexts.[25] The transfer of affect seems to work better, however, for material that people are relatively unfamiliar with and, conversely, less well when people are familiar with the attitude material.

Some years ago, the well-known educational researcher and practitioner David Ausubel and his associates designed a test to measure the tendency to generalize or particularize. It seems that there are two basic personality styles called generalizers and particularizers. Ausubel describes these cognitive styles as follows:

> The implications of the generalizing–particularizing cognitive style dimension for meaningful learning were established when the hypothesis was confirmed that generalizers would transform presented information, while particularizers would select presented informational elements verbatim in substantiating their conclusions in a decision-making task. It was concluded that generalizers tend to approach potentially meaningful material with a meaningful learning set to utilize information in supporting a decision while particularizers tend to approach potentially meaningful material with a rote learning set to utilize information in supporting a decision.[26]

Ausubel observes that the somewhat paradoxical finding that generalizers retain more verbatim items than particularizers can be explained by hypothesizing that generalizers retain facts meaningfully for purposes of long-term memory storage, whereas particularizers tend to store them rotely. It is the generalizers that engage in significant transfer.

It has been suggested that, provided it's meaningful, prior content or learner's knowledge base functions similarly to Ausubel's notion of an advanced organizer.[27] An advanced organizer is a passage introducing the to-be-learned material that contains conceptual background material presented at a higher level of generality, abstraction, or inclusiveness than the material to be learned. An advanced organizer is like a topic sentence. Unfortunately, much of Ausubel's research is seldom cited by those actively engaged in instructional research. As one author has noted, this is

> very likely because his views are at odds with the prevailing climate of opinion. The lack of attention to this research is a shame because it seems possible that Ausubel's experiments are showing a kind of non-specific transfer never before revealed with complex verbal tasks.[28]

In addition to the more global personality disposition and style, traits like persistence, locus of control, confidence, anxiety, fear of failure, other emotional issues have also been found to influence learning and transfer. The "hard-nosed" question is, then, how do such personality characteristics work to produce transfer? Although we don't know everything about how personality characteristics work in learning and transfer, we do know some of the mechanisms. Research clearly shows that the manner in which information is encoded or stored determines—or at least strongly influences—how it is retrieved.

If knowledge is encoded as isolated bits of information, then this is the way it will most likely be retrieved; if knowledge is encoded for a test or exam, then this is the way it will be retrieved; if it's encoded for connections to other information, then this, too, is how it will be retrieved. If knowledge is encoded for transfer, then it will be retrieved for transfer. Among other variables, personality characteristics influence the encoding process. It is the personal meaning that information holds for us that affects the way we encode, retrieve, and relate information. Personal meaning somehow facilitates transfer by "tagging" information as either relevant or nonrelevant to current and new situations. Harald Hoffding also recognized the importance of feelings and ideals to learning:

> The strongest feeling is that with which men embrace their ideal or practical aims; this feeling leads to search for the means to realize the aims, *and so lays the foundation of a firm connection between a whole set of ideas* [italics added]. This leads to the consideration of the real unity of consciousness and its importance for the continuance and healthiness of mental life.[29]

In a chapter on how students learn from examples, Michelene Chi concludes, "When students fail to generalize from examples, perhaps we should attribute the failure not to the characteristics of the examples, but rather, to the disposition of the learners." In order to optimize learning, she continues, "the students must actively construct an interpretation of each action in the context of the principles introduced in the text."[30] So as a person encodeth, so shall a person retrieveth.

## FEELING AND TRANSFER: WHAT'S FEELING
## GOT TO DO WITH IT?

Like meaning, feelings somehow influence the way we encode, retrieve, relate, and transfer information. Recognizing the role of affect (the term psychologists use for feeling) and motivation to the access problem of transfer, Roy Pea, says "Critical to the access problem are *affective* and *motivational* factors that are ill-understood. How students feel about their capabilities in learning tasks can drastically affect their interest not only in knowledge transfer but in learning itself."[31] Historically, feeling or affect, in cognitive science and in education, has had a limited and quite controversial history.[32]

The great Swiss psychologist, Jean Piaget, best known for his work on the cognitive development of children (but who did not consider himself to be a child psychologist but rather a genetic epistemologist concerned with cognitive processes and how knowledge is acquired), has commented that one of the most significant concerns of the social and behavioral sciences is "trying to characterize affective life in relation to cognitive functions [in so far as they relate to structure] and especially of defining their interrelation in the actual functioning of behavior."[33] More recently, however, notes, Richard Davidson, "emotion research has come of age."[34]

The debate over the relationship between feeling and cognition was reexamined a few years ago by two well-known psychologists, Robert Zajonc and Richard Lazarus.[35] Zajonc maintained that emotion and cognition are basically separate processing systems, whereas Lazarus maintained that they are essentially one system. Like most cognitive psychologists, Zajonc appears to identify cognition with rationality. He recognizes that affect is primary and occurs phylogenetically early and points to this fact as evidence that it would have evolved its own processing system long before the inception of language and other higher cerebral functions. There are good arguments on both sides of the issue. Despite these occasional skirmishes, however, mainstream computational cognitive psychology still doesn't deal with the consequences of feeling on cognition.

Part of the problem of cognitive science not dealing with emotion may be semantic, as the terms *feeling* and *emotion* are typically used interchangeably. But Paul Ricoeur, the philosopher of language, suggests that the two terms refer to distinct phenomena. *Emotion*, he says, is a first-order experience. Presumably it's "noncognitive"; emotion is what we usually think of when we think of irrational or at least arational, or a more or less strictly physiological event. This is what cognitive scientists usually think of when we refer to emotional responses. *Feeling*, on the other hand, according to Ricoeur, is a second order "*intentional* structure."[36] Feeling as opposed to emotion, then, is not merely an inner physiological state but an internal "precognitive" structure, a kind of "intuition" or preconscious perception, as it were. Emotion and feeling might be seen as analogous to the distinction made by psychologists who study perception. Sensation is simply the registering of stimuli; perception is the interpretation of the sensation. Apparently, in this view, emotion is analogous to sensation, whereas feeling is analogous to perception.

More recently, a fascinating general-audience book by Daniel Goleman entitled, *Emotional Intelligence: Why It Can Matter More Than I.Q.*, has placed the issue of emotion in mental and behavioral achievement in the public consciousness. Goleman marshaled the research of the past 10 years or so on the brain, which shows the importance of emotion for our cognitive functioning,[37] though Goleman doesn't relate this data to transfer. Building on Howard Gardner's theory of multiple intelligences, and the neurological findings of Joseph LeDoux (see chapter 11), Goleman shows how harnessing our emotions can lead to success, even if we don't possess an especially high level of intelligence; conversely, studies show clearly that possessing a high I.Q. does not guarantee us success either in our personal lives or in our business affairs.

Similarly, Ronald Wideman and Herbert Owston lamented,

> The fragmented information and skills that students are supposed to master are often lacking in enough personal meaning to lead students to make the cognitive efforts necessary to learn and develop.[38]

On a neurophysiological level, emotion and cognition may well be "separate" systems, whatever that means in the realm of neurological processes. To ask whether affect and cognition are separate, one would of necessity have to determine on what developmental level they are separate. Whatever the case, I will not presume to solve this problem here. I have suggested elsewhere that it is quite feasible that on some neurophysiological level of processing affect and cognition are separate, while on other levels they become fused, and on still higher levels of abstraction they become "functionally autonomous" (to resurrect a term used by Allport in other contexts).[39]

The fact is, the more meaning that learning has for us, the more complex are our conceptualizations. In turn, the deeper our understanding, the greater are our transfer possibilities. This is especially true in ill-defined problem-solving situations as opposed to the typically well-defined problems presented in laboratories and classrooms. David Ausubel, in his classic paper titled, "The Facilitation of Meaningful Verbal Learning in the Classroom," says that

> meaningful learning takes place if the learning task is related in a nonarbitrary and nonverbatim fashion to the learner's existing structure of knowledge. This presupposes (1) that the learner manifests a meaningful learning set, that is, a disposition to relate the new learning task nonarbitrarily and substantively to what he already knows, and (2) that the learning task is potentially meaningful to him, namely, relatable to his structure of knowledge on a nonarbitrary and nonverbatim basis.[40]

Meaning, then, consists in the number of internal connections a piece of information has in our existing knowledge base. Again, Roy Pea correctly recognizes the importance of feeling especially for the accessing versus the availability of knowledge. He points out that

> a distinction has been drawn between one's *access* to and the *availability* of knowledge and skills during a problem situation. Critical to the access problem are *affective* and *motivational* factors that are ill-understood. How students feel about their capabilities in learning tasks can drastically affect their interest not only in knowledge transfer but in learning itself. How is the disposition to engage in persistent memory search for transfer-relevant knowledge in a problem situation influenced by self-efficacy, fear of failure, anxiety, intolerance of mistakes, or other emotional blocks?[41]

In the *Journal of Personality and Social Psychology* Isen and Daubmen found that positive affect does influence how our cognitive material is categorized or grouped together. More specifically, they found that weak examples of a category are more likely to be rated as being a member of a particular category, and that colors are more likely to be sorted into more inclusive categories by people who are experiencing positive affect (i.e., feeling happy). In addition, happy people tend to make more diverse associations to words. Thus, under conditions of positive affect, we are more likely to see the relatedness and interconnections among events, and perhaps even to process the material in a more integrated way.[42]

But lest we think this increased cognitive functioning is only with positive affect, these researchers also found that in two of their four studies negative affect appeared to influence categorization in the same way that positive affect did, though to a lesser degree. Those experiencing negative affect were slightly more likely to assign higher ratings to poor exemplars of a category and tended to group more colors together than those in a control group. Though these findings did not reach accepted levels of statistical significance, they are suggestive. One interpretation offered for the findings that happy people tend to be more efficient (and also more distractible) is that the learned material may somehow be multiply encoded and retrievable as a function of positive affect. In other words, when we experience positive affect we may have increased access to multiple cues and apply more extensive encoding and retrieval processes to the material.

In part, a more efficient and productive cognitive processing may take place because positive affect cues a wider variety of material along with a more complex cognitive context, leading to more diverse interpretative, encoding, and retrieval processes. Another possibility is that under an affective tone, learned material may be grouped together or seen as similar because of a similar emotional impact of the material. It may also be that affect does not influence the cognitive structure or relations between cognitive elements directly, but only affects certain processes that may be responsible for effects. For example, affect may work through inducing a general arousal or drive level. From the perspective of a more recent connectionist neural net model of the brain, affect may create a spreading activation process throughout the neural network and thereby increase our connections (see chapter 11). Whatever the specific mechanisms are, it seems clear that feelings influence the cognitive processes responsible for transfer.

In *Learning in Medical School: A Model for the Clinical Professions*,[43] John Biggs points out that most everyday learning derives from a felt need to learn what is important at the time. For example, a medical practitioner examining a patient has an immediate need for specific information on anatomy, physiology, pharmacology, and so on. A student in a classroom studying these same subjects typically has no such immediate affective need. Regardless of how sincere a student's intentions and plans may be, such classroom (cognitive) knowledge tends not to provide sufficient motivation for learning, except in learners who have intrinsic motivation.

Biggs divides learning into three basic types—surface, achieving, and deep—based on motivation or felt need. The surface approach to learning is based on extrinsic motivation where the student sees learning as simply a means towards some other end such as obtaining a better job. The goal or strategy of surface learning is to limit and focus on the concrete and literal aspects of learning such as the actual words used, rather than on meaning. The components of the learning are seen as unrelated to each other or to other tasks. Affectively, the surface approach student does not seek or see the personal meaning a task might have and has little or no feeling attached to it. At best, this approach is effective for the recall of unrelated detail.

The achieving approach to learning is based on a kind of extrinsic motivation resulting from achieving and attaining high grades. The related strategy is a "study skills" approach to organizing one's time, by covering the material systematically and efficiently. Such a student sees high grades as the important end product. The deep approach to learning, on the other hand, is based on a *felt* interest in the subject matter. The strategy or goal is to maximize understanding and to see the learning as interesting and personally involving, with the focus on meaning rather than on the literal and immediate aspects. The components of the material are integrated with each other and with other tasks. Such a student reads widely, discusses the learning with others, and mentally explores learning, theorizing about it and forming hypotheses about how it relates to other known or interesting material. Affectively, the student feels close to the material.

According to Biggs, the surface and deep approaches are in many ways mutually exclusive, with the achieving approach linked to either surface or deep. When these approaches are related to learning outcomes, Biggs found that in the essays of 24 students ranging in level from undergraduate to postgraduate, no surface "writers ever produced essays that had a more complex internal structure than a linear narration of detail, while deep writers without exception produced essays with a coherent and integrated structure that was appropriate to the question."[44] Similar results have been found in the learning of history, of literary studies, and in the learning of computing science tasks. To relate Bigg's three approaches to transfer, obviously the surface approach is not conducive to transfer; the achieving approach may lead to near transfer but it is the deep approach with its affective motivational base that can lead to significant and general transfer.

Even in the development of automatic skills and procedures, meaningful learning is crucial. As Singley and Anderson point out regarding their computational theory of procedural transfer,

> The content of a production rule is based upon the underlying content of the declarative knowledge from which it is compiled. If the underlying declarative knowledge reflects a shallow or even rote understanding of some procedure, then the resulting production rules will have that same character.[45]

It seems that even learning ritualized behavior is dependent on meaning and feeling. Indeed, contrary to the identical elements theory of transfer, Eich concludes that "converging evidence . . . suggests that how well information transfers from one environment to another depends on how similar the environments *feel* [italics added] rather than on how similar they look."[46]

## TRANSFER AND THE ANCIENT NOTION
## OF THE "GOOD MAN"

The research cited so far suggests that transfer is integrally related to feeling or affect, and that significant transfer derives from deep dispositional characteristics of the learner. Transfer, then, has implications not only for processing information, but for the development of personality. We seldom speak today about the relationship between personality and learning, because learning is generally not seen as fundamentally dependent on individual character traits. Congruent with our technological society, learning is considered something that can be taught with appropriate techniques or that can be grafted on to learners with special teaching methods or curricular design. This view has not always been the prevailing view. As noted in the opening of this chapter, ideas often get lost in history or are considered passé. In any but the most perfunctory way, the idea that learning is fundamentally influenced by core personality characteristics has been all but lost, or at least relegated to the dusty archives of educational theory, or is considered important only to those who are viewed as rigid traditionalists or political conservatives.

In the early part of the 1900s, there was a social movement called the moral education movement. It was concerned with instructing for moral character. With few exceptions, which include those who think that their own specific religious beliefs should be infused into educational curriculums, the idea of moral character being connected to learning is, at best, currently viewed as a non sequitur, or at worse, as repugnant, if not downright undemocratic. I generally concur that teaching a specific morality—as we popularly understand it—has no place in the classroom. But herein lies the rub. What do we mean by moral education?

One of the current exceptions to a nonmoral stance in education is found in a faction of the critical thinking movement. In an edited book on critical thinking, Johnson asks,

> What is the relationship between critical thinking and character? In order to think critically, must one have a certain moral character or set of traits? If so, which ones? If so, where are the border-lines between critical thinking and morality, and between critical thinking and moral theory?[47]

I can't imagine any cognitive psychologist (at least of the computational brand) suggesting that proficiency in thinking depends on one's moral outlook. At best, to suggest such a connection would be considered a non sequitur. In any case, the moral character view in some factions of the critical thinking movement maintains that "good" thinking depends on "good" character. Is this in fact true? Or is this moral approach a fossil out of the past?

Whether, and to what extent, this moral outlook on the educational process issues from specific religious bases, I won't speculate. The point is, however, that a moral or character theory of learning and thinking does not need to be generated out of popular religious convictions. In any event, history shows that the idea of "good character" being important to knowing and learning is neither original to the 1900s, nor to Christianity. In the Western tradition, the idea goes back to ancient Greece well before the birth of Christianity. Perhaps beginning with Socrates (469–399 B.C.), Plato (427–347 B.C.), the Roman statesman, orator, and philosopher Marcus Tullius Cicero (106–43 B.C.), it was thought that to be a good public speaker (i.e., a rhetor or rhetorician) required that the rhetor be a "good man." At first glance the new emphasis on morality and education may seem to be just a new twist on this ancient moral approach to education. And for some, it may indeed be. This is not my intent, however. Although the question of the role of morality in education is a serious one, I do not address it here. Rather I want to look at the idea of "the good rhetor as the good man" and see if it has any contemporary meaning and validity from a cognitive and transfer perspective.

The ancient idea of "the good man as the good rhetor" has never been cognitively explained, and is seldom referred to today outside of a small cadre of scholars and historians of ancient rhetorical theory. I would like to suggest, however, that the ancient notion of the "good man" is nearly synonymous with what I am calling the spirit of transfer, and indeed is both a cause and consequence of transfer. Reading Plato's account of the "good man" reads almost identically to the definition of "spirit" outlined above: (1) an animating principle of life, (b) a vital essence, (c) an attitude or dispositional principle that pervades thought, (d) as stirring or prompting one to action, (e) the soul or heart as the seat of feelings, (f) a vigorous, courageous, or optimistic attitude,

(g) a dominant tendency or character, (h) the essence or active principle of a substance.

The idea of the "Good man as the good rhetor" was developed prior to Aristotle's invention of rhetorical techniques. After Aristotle, rhetors could "artificially" learn an explicit, conscious, and consistent system of thinking and persuasion. According to Charles Baldwin, the teaching of rhetoric during the Roman Empire became decadent. As it became so, he says, it was "to pervert this principle as to make all training subordinate to technical skill in rhetoric; and indeed the principle has this danger of making the whole man serve rhetoric, instead of making rhetoric bring out the whole man."[48] The good rhetor was concerned with seeking Truth, the bad rhetor with persuasion and argumentation. The Italian philosopher and rhetorician Giambattista Vico describes his view of a stage in human political history when

> As the popular states became corrupt, so also did the philosophies. They descended to skepticism. Learned fools fell into calumniating the truth. Thence arose a *false eloquence* [italics in original], ready to uphold either of the opposed sides of a case indifferently.[49]

And of his own book, *The New Science*, he says, "This Science carries inseparably with it the study of piety, and that he who is not pious cannot be truly wise."[50] Eloquence and piety are characteristics of the "good rhetor."

Most modern scholars versed in the Western classical tradition make reference in one way or another to this moral issue of the good man. Allan Bloom's *The Closing of the American Mind* is a tractatus derived from his training in this classical tradition of the "good man as the good rhetor." Is Bloom's book perhaps the last nostalgic gasp of a dying age, with Bloom—at the time of its writing—one of its few surviving indigenous people? What is a modern reader to make of this Platonic moralizing? Is it just a "conservative" agenda? If so, why then do we find one of the leaders of the "radical" postmodernism movement, the French philosopher Jacques Derrida, writing that "There is therefore a good and bad writing: *the good and natural is the divine inscription in the heart and the soul; the perverse and artful is technique.* [italics added]."[51] Shades of ancient Ciceronian rhetoric railing against the rhetoric cookbooks of his time. Other contemporary writers have voiced similar views.

Similarly, in discussing a narrow skills-based approach to learning and understanding literature and social conversation, W. A. Hart (cited in chapter 1) also maintains that a person with a "paltry and impudent" nature will never write anything but paltry criticism. To be a good critic, in the sense of being someone who can read properly, he says, "You need to be more than a skilled operator or an expert. You need to be someone to whom literature speaks . . . [and] . . . literature only speaks to those in whom it can find an echo."[52] Continuing his analysis of a skills approach, he says, having something to say in a conversation is not just a matter of skill, it "is a matter of being someone, someone, that is, with his own unique outlook on things."[53] Finally, he cites the great Austrian-born British linguistic philosopher, Ludwig Wittgenstein (1889–1951), who reportedly lamented, "I wish I were a better man and had a better mind: the two are really the same thing."[54] Wittgenstein was no touchy-feelie humanist philosopher. He wrote such hard-nosed things as the *Tractatus Logico-Philosophicus*.

So, what could the ancient notion of (a) the "good man as the good rhetor," (b) Wittgenstein's idea that being a better man meant having a better mind, (c) Hoffding's suggestion that having a feeling for an idea leads to mental connections and thus to a healthy mental life, and (d) Allport's notions of personality, feeling, and transfer, mean, I mean, cognitively? First, we may generally equate the "good rhetor" with deep learning and the "bad rhetor" with surface learning. The "good man" then, is the person who "firmly believes" in what he or she is doing, who is in a state of strong emotion and "feeling," which, as we have seen, leads to a more complex encoding of their learning. Thus, everything she or he sees and thinks is encoded in an integrated cognitive way into the personality and emerges in an integrated form.

The "bad rhetor" on the other hand, is the rhetor who lacks the energizing power of a strong affectively loaded belief system necessary for creating the emotional matrix responsible for encoding systemic transfer connections that consistently and coherently link all ideas and learning within its sphere of influence. But, still, how does this happen, cognitively? I suggest it happens because the "bad rhetor's" cognitive structure—that is lacking an emotional matrix of strong belief and feeling—is less complete and more fragmented; it doesn't have a core schema from which the entire argument is integrally developed. I have suggested elsewhere that the increased cognitive connections that come out of such a core schema are due to analogical transfers.[55] The terms in a good rhetor's vocabulary are like links in a chain developing from a single schematic cognitive matrix, resulting in an integrated rhetorical pattern. Recent research suggests that emotion is "a *self organizing, integrative state* [italics added] that is coherent across several different response systems."[56] Further, this appears to be a relatively stable personality style related to our cortical hemispheres and not just to our lower, more primitive, brain structures. (See chapters 11 and 12.)

Ultimately, then, the good rhetor is one who is able to persuade an audience. How does this happen? Kenneth Burke, the great literary critic, says that "once you grasp the trend of the form it invites participation regardless of the subject matter. Formally you find yourself swinging along with the succession."[57] In short, the audience grasps the deep pattern that initiates their own set of connections. From this perspective, a rhetoric (or a learning) built on technique, and lacking a strong emotional commitment to the subject, will not have the integral transfer linkages of one predicated on a strong emotional belief and systemic affective matrix. In the language of Plato, such a rhetoric will not reach down into the "soul." From a cognitive and transfer perspective, then, the "good man" is one who, based on strong affect, possesses an integrated cognitive structure encoded and woven from a complex of transfer linkages. To assess whether a person will be good at transfer, then, one should be judged not by the number of their strategic skills, nor by their specific moral outlook, but by the affective structure and knowledge content of their character.

One implication of this cognitive explanation of the "good rhetor as the good man" is that, unlike in the classical view, there is no reason why a "bad man" (i.e., immoral man) cannot also be a "good rhetor." The crucial variable is not the "good" or the "moral" as some of the ancients apparently thought, but the strong belief in what one is thinking. This is what the ancients apparently didn't see. Few would deny, for example, that Hitler's rhetoric persuaded many people and that therefore he was in fact a good rhetor, though certainly not the "good man" of the ancients and of today. Indeed there have been no shortage of leaders in history that we consider immoral or not good people, yet almost by definition—being leaders—they were good orators.

## ON TRANSFER AND WISDOM

How this "good" character is acquired and made second nature, however, is not completely known. Ann Brown and Joseph Campione in a different context note that the nature of the "internalization mechanism is more than somewhat mystical, and we are a long way from knowing how to "turn it on" on command."[58] One way to assist in creating conditions for the spirit of transfer is to develop what Roy Pea has referred to as a "culture of transfer." From his research, he concludes that rather than the common belief that individuals are "intrinsically motivated" or to seek out the characteristics of a computer software game that ostensibly makes learning intrinsically motivating, he suggests a sociocultural orientation to transfer. A sociocultural approach, he says, "implies that such affective and motivational influences on knowledge transfer are best studied in the cultural systems that give rise to them rather than as traits of individuals"[59] (I address the sociocultural approach to transfer in more detail in chapter 8).

At best, liberal arts students come into classes expecting that if they memorize enough information that it will turn into knowledge. It doesn't. Career or vocationally oriented students come into classes simply wanting quick lists of "how-to's." These, too, don't work. With such personality dispositions, learning is like a computer with a large knowledge base but with no underlying program to systematically operate on that knowledge. Without a program (i.e., the spirit of transfer) the information remains inert. Both Allport and Ausubel have been largely ignored because, going against the Zeitgeist, they understood that teaching skills and techniques are not the methods that are going to increase learning and transfer. I hope this book will convince teachers, school administrators, parents, but most of all convince the learner, that the deep learning that leads to transfer is not an "add on," but a function of the entire personality as well as the environment of the learner.

A seasoned spirit of transfer with its integrated cognitive structure implies a fundamental sense of order and proportion, which in turn implies a kind of wisdom. If there is a relationship between transferability and wisdom, can this wisdom be transferred? In an article published in 1940 from the *Harvard Alumni Bulletin* entitled, "Because Wisdom Can't Be Told," Charles Gragg cites French writer, Honoré de Balzac (1799–1850):

> So he had grown rich at last, and thought to transmit to his only son all the cut-and-dried experience which he himself had purchased at the price of his lost illusions; a noble last illusion of age.[60]

What Balzac laments here is that knowledge and experience cannot be transferred to the next generation. Like Gragg and Balzac, Freud (1856–1939), too, understood the issue of transfer. I recall that one of Freud's favorite quotes was from Goethe's *Faust*, where Mephistopheles says, "After all, the best of what you know may not be told to boys."[61] But the prior question is whether transfer is related to wisdom. To answer this we need to have an understanding of what wisdom is.

According to Howard Gardner,[62] wisdom may involve a considerable amount of common sense and originality in one or more areas, conjoined with a seasoned "metaphorizing" or analogizing capacity, which in my terms spell t-r-a-n-s-f-e-r. The wise individual, says Gardner, can draw upon these abilities appropriately and make wise evaluations of situations. This is what we expect, he says, from older individuals who have a wide range of experiences in their earlier life and can now apply them to present circumstances. Implicitly embedded in Gardner's view of wisdom is the ability to "appropriately" transfer past experience to present circumstances.

I would add to Gardner's account of wisdom that profound levels of wisdom require a broad knowledge base—including life experience—plus the spirit of transfer and the ability to create transfer linkages within these data and experiences. Lacking the knowledge base that wisdom and deep learning requires, cookbooks are doomed to failure. Cookbook and strategy approaches to transfer are like trying to pass on wisdom to the next generation, and attempts to do so perhaps reflects a lack of wisdom. Let us hope not.

## CONCLUSION

Although we may not know exactly how this "good" character or spirit of transfer is acquired, internalized, and made second nature, the ancient Greeks did recognize that being a part of the community—of a *Polis*, as they referred to it—was an important ingredient. Modern research has rediscovered the importance of a community for influencing transfer. It is to the issue of cultures of transfer that I now turn.

## Notes

[1]Ryan, J. J. (1951). Transfer of training: Subject matter. In R. Pintner, J. Ryan, P. West, A. Aleck, L. Crow, & S. Smith (Eds.), *Educational Psychology* (pp. 92–104). New York: Barnes and Noble, p. 89.

[2]Moses, S. (1991). Motivation neglected in educational reform. *American Psychological Association Monitor*, 22, 1, p. 34.

[3]Richey, R. (1992). *Designing Instruction for the adult learner: Systemic training, theory and practice*. New York: Kogan Page, p. 163.

[4]Bereiter, C. (1995). A dispositional view of transfer. In A. McKeough, J. Lupart, & A. Marini (Eds.), *Teaching for transfer: Fostering generalization in learning* (pp. 21–34). Mahwah, NJ: Lawrence Erlbaum Associates, p. 24.

[5]Allport, G. W. (1960). *Personality: A psychological interpretation*. New York: Henry Holt. [Original work published 1937]

[6]Brell, C. D. Jr. (1990). Critical thinking as transfer: The reconstructive integration of otherwise discrete interpretations of experience. *Educational Theory*, 40, 53–68, p. 54.

[7]McKeachie, W. J. (1987). Cognitive skills and their transfer: Discussion. *International Journal of Educational Research*, 11, 707–712.

[8]McClelland, D. (1976). Entrepreneurship and management in the years ahead. In C. A. Bramlette, Jr. (Ed.), *The individual and the future of organizations* (pp. 12–29). Atlanta, GA: Georgia State University Press.

[9]Resnick, L. B. (1987). Instruction and the cultivation of thinking. In E. De Corte, H. Lodewijks, R. Parmentier, & P. Span. (Eds.), *Learning and instruction* (vol. I, pp. 415–441). Oxford: Pergamon Press, p. 433.

[10]Mittelholtz, D. J. (1988). *The effects of essay tests on long-term retention of course material*. Doctoral Dissertation, Educational Psychology, University of Iowa; Lohman, D. F. (1992). Encouraging the development of fluid abilities in gifted students. In N. Colangelo, S. G. Assouline, & D. L. Ambroson (Eds.), *Talent development: Proceedings from the 1991 Henry B. and Jocelyn Wallace national research symposium on talent development* (pp. 143–162). New York: Trillium Press.

[11]Gamlin, P. J. (1990). Strategy instruction: Issues for the transfer of knowledge. *Canadian Journal of Special Education*, 6(2), 145.

[12]Casey, G., & Moran, A. (1989). The computational metaphor and cognitive psychology. *The Irish Journal of Psychology*, 10, 143–161; Kunda, Z. (1990). The case for motivated reasoning. *Psychological Bulletin*, 108, 480–498.

[13]Deci, E. (1992). On the nature and functions of motivation theories. *Psychological Science*, 3(3), 167–171, p. 170.

[14]Kunda, Z. (1990). The case for motivational reasoning. *Psychological Bulletin*, 108, 480–498.

[15]Allport, G. W. (1960). *Personality: A psychological interpretation*. New York: Henry Holt, p. 151. [Original work published 1937]

[16]Ibid. As I noted in chapter 5, Allport did not mean "training" in the narrow contemporary sense of the term; he meant *learning*. In 1937 the phrases *transfer of training* and *transfer of learning* were often used interchangeably.

[17]Ibid.

[18]Ibid.

[19]Ibid.

[20]Ibid.

[21]Ibid.

[22]Ibid. It is interesting to note the perhaps prophetic nature of Allport's observations on transfer to the subsequent 1950s McCarthyism. U.S. Senator Joseph McCarthy achieved national

prominence and power with his sensational senatorial hearings that involved widespread un-substantiated accusations against many he saw as Communists. McCarthy saw signs of their communist affiliation everywhere. It is perhaps also interesting to relate this to the current superpatriot militia movement. Any theory of transfer must equally explain the positive as well as the negative transfer outcomes.

[23]Ibid.

[24]Lorge, I. (1936). Prestige, suggestion, and attitudes. *Journal of Social Psychology*, 7, 386–402.

[25]Cacioppo, J. T., Marshall-Goodell, B. S., Tassinary, L. G., & Petty, R. E. (1992). Rudimentary de-terminants of attitudes: Classical conditioning is more effective when prior knowledge about the attitude stimulus is low than high. *Journal of Experimental Social Psychology*, 28, 207–233.

[26]Ausubel, D. P. (1977). The facilitation of meaningful verbal learning in the classroom. *Educational Psychologist*, 12, 162–178, p. 170.

[27]Brooks, L. W., & Dansereau, D. F. (1987). Transfer of information: An instructional perspective. In S. Cormier & M. Hagman (Eds.), *Transfer of Learning: Contemporary research and applications* (pp. 121–149). New York: Academic Press, p. 136.

[28]Cited in Ausubel, D. P. (1977). The facilitation of meaningful verbal learning in the classroom. *Educational Psychologist*, 12, 162–178, p. 174.

[29]Hoffding, H. (1893). *Outlines of psychology*. Macmillan: New York, pp. 160–161.

[30]Chi, M. T. H. (1989). Learning from examples Via self-explanations. In L. B. Resnick (Eds.), *Knowing, learning, and instruction: Essays in honor of Robert Glaser* (pp. 251–282). Hillsdale, NJ: Lawrence Erlbaum, p. 265.

[31]Pea, R. D. (1987). Socializing the knowledge transfer problem. *International Journal of Educational Research*, 11, 639–663, p. 650.

[32]See, for example, Abelson, R. P. (1963). Computer simulation of hot cognitions. In S. Tomkins & S. Mesnick (Eds.), *Computer simulation of personality*. New York: Wiley, p. 39.

[33]Piaget, J. (1973). The affective unconscious and the cognitive unconscious. *Journal of the American Psychoanalytic Association*, 21, 249–261.

[34]Davidson, R. J. (1992). New developments in the scientific study of emotion: An introduction to the special edition. *Psychological Science*, 3, 21–22, p. 21.

[35]Lazarus, R. (1982). Thoughts on the relations between emotion and cognition. *American Psychologist*, 37, 1019–1024; Zajonc, R. B. (1980). Feeling and thinking: Preferences need no in-ferences. *American Psychologist*, 35, 151–175.

[36]Ricoeur, P. (1977). *The rule of metaphor: Multi-disciplinary studies of the creation of meaning in language*. (R. Czerny, Trans.). Toronto: University of Toronto Press, p. 154.

[37]Goleman, D. (1995). *Emotional intelligence: Why it can matter more than I.Q.* New York: Bantam Books. The evidence Goleman gathers on the importance of emotion to learning is impressive and adds considerable credence to my thesis on the importance of emotion to transfer.

[38]Wideman, H. H., & Owston,R. D. (1993). Knowledge base construction as a pedagogical activity. *Journal of Educational Computing Research*, 9, 165–196, p. 166.

[39]Haskell, R. E. (1989). Analogical transforms: A cognitive theory of the origin and development of equivalence transformation. Part I & II. *Metaphor and Symbolic Activity*, 4, 247–259.

[40]Ausubel, D. P. (1977). The facilitation of meaningful verbal learning in the classroom. *Educational Psychologist*, 12, 162–178, p. 163.

[41]Pea, R. D. (1987). Socializing the knowledge transfer problem. *International Journal of Educational Research*, 11, 639–663, p. 650.

[42]Isen, A. M., & Daubman, K. A. (1984). The influence of affect on categorization. *Journal of Personality and Social Psychology*, 47, 1206–1217.

[43]Biggs, J. (1989). Institutional learning and the integration of knowledge. In J. I. Balla, M. Gib-son, & A. M. Chang (Eds.), *Learning in medical school: A model for the clinical professions*. Hong Kong: Hong Kong University Press.

[44]Ibid, p. 25.

[45]Singley, M. K., & Anderson, J. R. (1989). *The transfer of cognitive skill*. Cambridge, MA: Harvard University Press, p. 228.

[46]Eich, E. (1995). Mood as a mediator of place dependent memory. *Journal of Experimental Psychology: General*, 124, 293–308, p. 293.

[47]Johnson, R. H. (1992). The problem of defining critical thinking. In S. P. Norris (Ed.), *The generalizability of critical thinking: Multiple perspectives on an educational idea* (pp. 38–53). New York: Columbia University, p. 42.

[48]Baldwin, C. S. (1959). *Ancient rhetoric and poetics.* (Gloucester, MA: Peter Smith Pub., p. 40.

[49]Vico, G. (1948). *The new science.* |Abridged| (T. G. Bergin & M. H. Fisch, Trans.). Ithaca, NY: Cornell University Press, p. 379. |Original work published 1744|

[50]Ibid, p. 384.

[51]Derrida, J. (1974). *Of grammatology.* (G. C. Spivak, Trans.). Baltimore, MD: Johns Hopkins University Press, p. 17.

[52]Hart, W. A. (1978). Against skills. *Oxford Review of Education*, 4, 205–216, p. 208.

[53]Ibid, p. 209.

[54]Ibid, p. 214.

[55]See Haskell, R. E., & Hauser, G. (1978). Rhetorical structure: Truth and method in Weaver's epistemology. *Quarterly Journal of Speech*, 64, 233–245. Richard Weaver is considered to be one of the great conservative scholars of rhetoric. See Weaver, R. (1948). *Ideas have consequences.* Chicago: University of Chicago Press.

[56]Davidson, R. J. (1992). Emotion and affective style: Hemispheric substrates. *Psychological Science*, 3, 39–42.

[57]Burke, K. (1969). *A rhetoric of motives.* Berkeley: University of California Press, p. 58.

[58] Brown, A. L., & Campione, J. C. (1982). Modifying intelligence or modifying cognitive skills: More than a semantic quibble. In D. K. Detterman & R. J. Sternberg (Eds.), *How and how much can intelligence be increased* (pp. 215–230). Norwood, NJ: Ablex Publishing, p. 225.

[59]Pea, R. D. (1987). Socializing the knowledge transfer problem. *International Journal of Educational Research*, 11, 639–663, p. 650.

[60]Gragg, C. (1940). Because wisdom can't be told. *Harvard Alumni Bulletin* (Oct), 78–84.

[61]Freud, S. (1954). *The interpretation of dreams.* (First English edition.) ( J. Strachey Trans.). London: George Allen & Unwin Ltd., p. 142. |Original work published 1900|

[62]Gardner, H. (1983). *Frames of mind: The theory of multiple intelligences.* New York: Basic Books.

# CHAPTER 8

# Cultures and Contexts of Transfer: Social Origins and Support Systems

*Promoting knowledge transfer in education will depend on more effective arrangement of environments for bridging knowledge utilization across contexts within a culture.*

—Roy Pea, *Socializing the Knowledge Transfer Problem*[1]

Let me begin with a story from my small group dynamics course. The 10–15 students learn about group dynamics by functioning as a group through extensive verbal interaction. With one exception, middle-class white students comprised the group. The one exception was a bright Cherokee woman from a reservation in Oklahoma. Whenever she spoke, most of the group rolled their eyes—nonverbally saying, "Oh, here she goes again." The group was reacting to her constant story telling during group conversation, which bored many group members. Understanding why she told stories, I intervened at an appropriate time and asked the group to analyze and discuss this dynamic. The group's first response was that they didn't see what all these stories had to do with interpersonal communication and group dynamics. At my request, the Cherokee student told the group that in her culture a great deal of teaching, learning, and relating was done through stories; if the group looked closely at the stories, they would see them as metaphors and analogies about the group and its interaction. Even knowing this, the group had a difficult time "translating" these stories into something they could understand, so they worked out a compromise. Both learned a great deal about the other. This example has many implications for cultures and contexts of transfer.

First, this story points out how different cultures may come into conflict: intercultural norms and different cultural cognitive styles interfere with learning, communication, and the transfer of meaning. Second, even though the Cherokee student was generally aware of these differences, as she admitted later in the discussion, it was not culturally acceptable for her to initiate a discussion about the problem white students were having with her story telling. From her set of cultural norms, the responsibility was the professors'—being the "elder" in the group. More specifically, in terms of transfer the stores she told were, for the white students, metaphors or *like* parables that had to be translated or interpreted. For the Cherokee student, the stories were—in effect—not metaphors at all, but literal. This is an important aspect of transfer: what requires transfer or is considered metaphorical for one person may not be metaphorical or require transfer for another.

## THE SOCIAL BASES OF TRANSFER

I noted previously a consistent finding in the transfer literature that learning tends to be welded to the context in which it is learned. In this chapter I outline the contexts and social situations in which transfer often operates: learning contexts and cultural settings. The encapsulation of learning in a specific cultural situation becomes the broader paradigm for different transfer contexts. In fact, specific different contexts of learning can be considered learning cultures writ small, so to speak. Learning contexts versus cultures of transfer are somewhat arbitrary distinctions, except at their extremes. A learning situation viewed holistically as an integrated set of norms, cues, and other factors that influence transfer is called a *learning culture* (or sometimes an anti-learning culture—see below). When viewed as a number of relatively isolated norms and cues, it's called a *learning context*. Depending on how we assess the significance of the *similarity* between situations, there are theoretically an infinite number of transfer contexts and cultures.

The mechanisms of transfer as well as the transfer spirit (see chapter 7) are shaped by the social, organizational, and group systems within which they take place. This has not been widely recognized. It is counterproductive to view transfer as simply the product of possessing or developing higher order thinking procedures. Transfer also has a social and cultural dimension. Though context and social factors are recognized as important for learning, their implications have generally not been applied to understanding transfer.

Western society in general, and U.S. psychologists in particular, have a long tradition of seeing the individual as separate and distinct from the collective (anthropological), societal (sociological), and group (team) contexts of learning, despite the fact that for nearly one hundred years we have known that just being in the presence of others facilitates individual performance.[2] In what has become a classic in social psychology, Norman Triplett in 1898 experimentally demonstrated that when we are in the presence of others, we perform better.[3] The traditional abstracted view of the individual has unfortunately been transferred to the understanding of learning and transfer. We need, however, to understand transfer as a cultural, social, group, and team product; transfer is in large measure a collective process. We carry these reference groups around in our heads. It is this collective process that I'll refer to as a culture of transfer, adopting Roy Pea's term.

I am defining culture of transfer in a general sense, to include all social and group influences on transfer. By a culture of transfer, I mean not only a system of support for individuals to apply or transfer their knowledge, but a learning system as well. A culture of transfer approach can be viewed as a systems perspective on learning.[4] In this chapter, I can only outline the structure of the idea of cultures of transfer. Though there is a vast body of educational studies by anthropologists on the influence of culture on learning, most of this material needs to be reanalyzed and specifically applied to transfer.

If we adopt the view that learning is situated, contextually and culturally, that transfer is social in a fundamental way, then we understand also that learning occurs in the context of people engaging in social activities. At a minimum, social and work situations shape a person's sense of achievement, competence, self-image, and their sense of standards. Wilbert McKeachie recognized that if we can learn how to develop these individual characteristics through social activities, "we might be facilitating the development of important transferable human characteristics that would, in turn, increase the likelihood of transfer of cognitive skills."[5] Once we see that individuals behaviors, their thought processes, and their mental models are profoundly shaped by social situations, it follows logically that transfer of learning must be understood as a sociocultural process.

Moreover, the meaning and significance of these activities derive from the roles defined by those activities. Goals, too, are defined socially. The social situation often determines what elements of a situation are important to attend to and which ones are not.[6] In addition, conversations with others during activities that influence the attention given to ideas provide valuable learning cues for retrieval and relating of information. In short, the social situation creates a universe of meaning for us that shapes our learning, transfer, and even our memory. Indeed, memory is largely a collective process. Its locus is the interpersonal interaction among people engaging in activities and in recollections. In fact, some memory, like reminiscing, only takes place within a context of social interaction. We frequently only remember personal things when they are socially meaningful.[7] As an example, it's well known that most people recall exactly where they were and what they were doing on November 22, 1963; the date the U.S. President John F. Kennedy was assassinated.

Those who are on the forefront of viewing transfer as a social process recognize that knowledge "is not an invariant property of an individual, something that he or she has in any situation. Instead, "knowing is a property that is relative to situations, an ability to interact with things and other people in various ways."[8] James Greeno, Joyce Moore, and David Smith engage in transfer themselves in explaining this view of transfer. They note that physicists know that motion is not a property of a moving object; rather, their description of a moving object is in terms of speed, direction, and its acceleration depends on a frame of reference. To say that the frame of reference influences motion, is in fact, is quite misleading. They go on to point out that

> the property that we refer to as motion is a relation between an object and a frame of reference, and it makes no sense to try to characterize motion except with reference to a frame. Similarly, it may not suffice to say that cognition is influenced by contexts. In the view of situated cognition, we need to characterize knowing, reasoning, understanding and so on as relations between cognitive agents and situations, and it is not meaningful to try to characterize what someone knows apart from situations in which the person engages in cognitive activity.[9]

The authors go on to point out that what is now called situated learning is not new. Situated learning is a contemporary version of educational theorists like the American philosopher and educator John Dewey (1859–1952), the Russian psychologist Lev Semyonovich Vygotsky (1896–1934), and other interfactional psychologists.

In chapter 5, I outlined four historical models of the mind relating to transfer: (a) a rationalist, (b) an empiricist, (c) the sociohistorical, and (d) the ecological. Each of these models influences how we teach and do research on transfer. Although this book is based on all four of these models of mind, cultures of transfer relate most directly to the sociohistorical view. The sociohistorical view assumes that transfer processes reside not so much in an individual mind but in the social world; as such, the focus is essentially on transfer structures that exist within social activities, not in the individual mind. Accordingly, for most people, transfer is influenced by their participation in social or work activities where the very structures that form, facilitate, and cue transfer are found.

The sociohistorical model directs our attention to what in effect are learning "cultures" or learning communities. As educators and life-long learners, the social aspects of our learning in the 21st century will be a demanding one. As one report concluded,

> American educators face great challenges in the years ahead. There are demands on educators to produce higher levels of literacy and numeracy skills in line with the high-tech future projected for our children. Simultaneously, educators will have to deal with the unprecedented degree of diversity that our heterogeneous population presents to the practicing classroom teacher.[10]

Thus, in a 21st-century world of increasing diversity and global interaction, it is imperative to understand how context and culture determines transfer.

## CONTEXT AND TRANSFER

Learning always takes place in a particular context. Children are an excellent example of the effects of cultures and contexts of transfer. Roy Pea observes that a spectacular amount of learning and transfer occur within the first 5 years of a child's life. This is when children rapidly acquire concepts, language, motor skills, spatial, and social skills—and they do this with little explicit or formal intervention. During this period they learn and master massive amounts of information with little obvious effort, and little of the agony later experienced in the formal classroom. Often they do so despite a lack of formal knowledge, few available conscious learning strategies, and considerable limitations on their working memory. How does this happen?

It happens because during their first 5 years children learn within culturally meaningful ongoing contexts in which they receive immediate feedback on the effects—successes or failures—of their actions. Second, their learning is often mediated by their parents and peers, who not only serve as models for imitative learning, but who facilitate learning by providing structures and connections among their experiences. This clearly delineates the relevant information in situations and establishes continuity among their different contexts of social interaction.

There is long-standing research in psychology that can be applied (i.e., transferred) here to understand the encapsulation of learning in a particular context. We have known for some time that learning is cued by the place or environment in which it occurred. Appropriately enough, this is called place learning. In place learning, cues from the environment facilitate the recall of the learning. In the absence of such cues, information may not be retrieved. A poignant example of place learning from therapy with children will illustrate the power of context. Children undergoing therapy for speech conditions were required to monitor their speech (a learning strategy) under two conditions. The first condition was in the clinic setting only, the second in conditions both inside and outside the clinic. Learning acquired by the children within the clinic setting only showed no transfer outside the clinic. Their learning was encapsulated or welded to the clinic context. However, children required to monitor their speech outside the clinic setting showed transfer in a variety of situations.[11] The similarity here for learning in different settings is clear.

Research on what is called state-dependent learning can also be transferred to an understanding of context affects on transfer. At the extreme end of the state-dependent "continuum," organisms that learn under a specific physiological state are able to recall or use their learning only when they are in the physiological state in which they learned the material. For example, rats taught to negotiate a maze while intoxicated with alcohol are unable to negotiate the maze in a sober state. At first glance we might think that the alcohol interfered with the learning or didn't allow the learning to be consolidated into long-term memory. However, when the same rats are again intoxicated, they are once more able to run the maze.[12] A similar state-dependent condition may explain why most of us have trouble recalling dreams. Because dreaming occurs in a specific physiological state we have trouble remembering (transferring) the dream to our waking state.

Yet a further everyday example of the power of context is not recognizing someone if she or he is seen in an unexpected context. For example, walking down the Champs Elysées in Paris on your way to the Arc de Triomphe, you might not expect to see an old friend and so not recognize him or her when looking right at them. In the same way context influences transfer. Research on context learning has led psychologists to understand learning and cognition, then, as *situated learning.*

More specifically, situated learning refers to the physical and psychological features of the context in which learning occurs. What this means is that "knowledge—perhaps better called knowing—is not an invariant property of an individual, something that he or she has in any situation. Instead, knowing is a property that is relative to situations, an ability to interact with things and other people in various ways."[13] Research on how experts solve problems shows that they rely on a variety of cues in finding solutions that are provided by the environment.

For instance, it is recognized that the context of learning school mathematics and the context of everyday applications of the mathematics are quite different. Everyday contexts of activity are organized according to the social, personal, physical, and other resources available to us as well as the cues of interacting with a familiar environment. One of the downsides of formal instruction is that it radically disconnects learning from these contextual cues. School contexts tend to organize information according to concepts and principles of the academic discipline with the goal of providing the learner with a logically coherent conceptual structure. For example, school mathematics tends to relate multiplication of fractions to multiplication of whole numbers and the concept of fractions, and contrasts multiplication with addition of fractions. These abstract mathematical relationships are often not salient in the workplace because there are no cues to the relevant information.[14] Significant transfer seldom takes place. The well-known instructional researcher Laura Resnick notes, "The process of learning is aided when there are many opportunities to observe others engaging in such thinking activities. Finally, such dispositions require sustained long term cultivation and do not emerge from short term quick-fix interventions."[15] We still do not know all the relevant factors that influence context and transfer. Learning a computer program in one context, for example, may not result in its transfer to a different context. On the other hand, social and interpersonal skills are highly context dependent and variable. Because we do not have all the information, however, does not mean we cannot act on the knowledge we do have about the importance of context and transfer.

Perhaps the largest breach of context concerns learning in the classroom versus the everyday world. It is in students' everyday world that they are expected to apply (transfer?) what they have learned in the classroom. This is as true for K–12 as it is for adult learners. Two cognitive psychologists, Mary Gick and Keith Holyoak conclude "some of the most spectacular and widely decried failures of transfer—failures to apply knowledge learned in school to practical problems encountered in everyday life—may largely reflect the fact that material taught in school is often *disconnected* [italics added] from any clear goal and hence lacks a primary *cue* [italics added] for retrieval in potentially relevant problem contexts."[16] Students who can figure the area of a rectangle in a math class may not be able to figure how much floor covering is needed for a room at home. Conversely, many students who have to measure and multiply for cooking a large number of meals at home cannot measure and multiply in school. But this transfer breach is not news. Noting this breach, Nathaniel Gage and David Berliner suggest that student failure to cross this breach is, "because transfer across dissimilar contexts requires so much effort, so much mindfulness, it is often avoided."[17]

Learning in the workplace is a subset of learning contexts in general.[18] As the number of coordinated training programs between corporations and schools increase, accountability and transfer to the work environment becomes increasingly important. The work setting provides a context for transfer. Though the business training literature is increasingly using the term *work* or *organizational culture*, I will generally use the term *context* when discussing transfer in relation to work settings and the term *culture* when discussing more anthropological factors. In part, a work context consists of roles, norms, cues, procedural knowledge, goals, reinforcement patterns, modeling behaviors and attitudes, meanings, and specific kinds of information that are part of the activities we engage in, as well as a host of other contextual factors that are an integral cognitive part of our carrying out a relevant task. These factors influence which features of a situation are important to us and play a major cognitive part in determining which features we will attend to. These variables are constantly learned and applied through our direct observation and verbal communication with others. Context not only influences psychological orientations, it also shapes our responses to the physical workplace.[19] The question is, why should the simple application of knowledge seem to require such effort? Such effort is certainly not inherent in the subject matter.

Simulations are designed to duplicate as closely as possible the contexts of real work environments; for example, physical fidelity of industrial simulators and other mock work situations like training restaurants, hairdressing salons, and car maintenance facilities. Despite the attempt to create a training environment with many "identical elements" to real work situations, such attempts are substitutes at best in terms of the cues provided by the real social and cultural context of the workplace. Mounting evidence challenges the traditional view of transfer applied to high-fidelity (i.e., ones with as many identical elements to the workplace as possible) industrial simulators. Ever since 1901 when Edward Thorndike put forth his identical elements view of transfer, it has been believed that transfer is best facilitated by creating simulators that resemble as closely as possible the real situation. From a situated learning perspective, however, close physical fidelity of simulators per se does not contribute to high positive transfer but rather the presence or re-trieval of cues from the situation. Thus simulators low in fidelity should be effective in facilitating transfer as long as they provide the trainee with es-sential cuing relationships.

In her article, "Designing Instruction for the Adult Learner," Rita Richey contends that

> transfer is influenced by general behavior modeling of management and co-workers alike. In addition, far transfer is predicted by those environmental characteristics re-lated to the physical working conditions and aspects of employee empowerment, both of which are factors unrelated to the surface training.[20]

As important as contextual or environmental factors are, we need more re-search before we can specify precisely how they work. Two business training researchers, Timothy Baldwin and Kevin Ford, note that

> the "strong" support for the importance of environmental characteristics to transfer is based solely on correlational studies in which causality can not be inferred. What is needed is the identification of key work–environment variables and the operational-ization of these variables. For example, while research suggests that supervisory sup-port is an important component affecting transfer, there is little attempt to understand the supervisory behaviors that lead to perceptions of support by trainees.[21]

Although there is little doubt that setting influences transfer, one of the prob-lems concerning cultures and contexts of transfer is that they tend to be con-ceptualized in a holistic manner and it is therefore difficult to exactly specify how they influence transfer.

## CULTURES OF TRANSFER

Research on cultures of diversity, whether in gender, ethnic, or work contexts, would greatly improve our understanding and implementation of transfer. As one author recognizes, "We need to ask what would make one social context different from another to the extent that it might constitute a challenge to the transfer of skills."[22] What we need is greater understanding about cultures from a culture-of-transfer perspective, in which transfer is considered an interpret-ed concept based on sociocultural factors or properties of the group rather than being defined objectively or technically. Most current cognitive theories of transfer beg the real question; transfer is seen as an objective given, part of the theorist's construction of the problem situation. Roy Pea explains,

> Elements perceived by the thinker as common between the current and prior situa-tion are not given in the nature of things but read in terms of the thinker's culturally-influenced categorisation of problem types as judged against a set of conventions re-flecting the values of the culture to which the learner belongs.[23]

Our social and cultural standards provide us with cognitive schemas for ac-cessing and judging transfer appropriateness.

A culture-of-transfer approach is in stark contrast to the dominant common elements theory of transfer advocated by Edward Thorndike, which prevails even today in most educational theory. So-called common elements that a learner perceives between a current and a prior situation are thus not given in the nature of things but "read as" being on the basis of learners culturally influenced categories.

A culture of transfer may be as large as a society, an organization, or as small as a classroom. A culture of transfer does not even have to be based on physical proximity. You don't have to physically interact to experience the effects of a culture of transfer, for a group or culture is not necessarily defined by the physical proximity of its membership. Many scientists and scholars, for example, are solitary animals, but they have an abstracted culture of transfer and support. Historically, scientists and scholars communicate and feel support in the privacy of their own minds while reading professional journals, newsletters, and books. More recently, they also receive support by participating in teleconferences, bulletin boards on the Internet, and with fax machines. The point is, the phrase "cultures of transfer" can take on many forms and facilitate transfer in many ways. As a social psychologist, I am only too aware that we carry our reference groups around in our heads. We can't escape the influence of the social on our individual behavior and cognitive structures.

Howard Gardner points out that given the consistent differences found on intelligence tests showing females scoring somewhat lower on spatial ability, it is reasonable to assume that Eskimo males might perform better on spatial tasks than Eskimo females. In fact, skilled performances on spatial tasks are found among Eskimo females as well, demonstrating that the sex differences in spatial abilities reported regularly in our Western culture can either be overcome in certain environments or that biases in our own environments are producing only apparent spatial ability differences in females. Gardner notes that at least 60% of Eskimo children score as high on tests of spatial ability as the top 10% of Caucasian children.[24] Moreover, this increased ability generalizes not only to tests of conceptual ability but to tests measuring visual details. It can thus be useful to consider gender as a separate culture with its unique evolutionary characteristics, cultural norms, influences, and different ways of knowing that affect transfer.

That cultures transmit norms that influence student learning is not new to anthropologists who study education; understanding how cultures specifically influence and shape transfer is new. The anthropological research that does exist needs to be gleaned for its specific relevance to transfer. Thus new research into the educational anthropology of transfer is needed. I can do neither of these here. I can, however, begin to point the way. For example, in terms of the culture of the educational setting and its social norms, we know it can either encourage or discourage motivation to learn and to transfer. Classic in organizational and industrial psychology is the "rate buster" phenomenon. Rate busting refers to a person in a work situation who is much more productive than his or her fellow workers. Because the high rate of productivity makes the other workers look inferior, they bring measures to bear on the person to reduce their productivity. In group dynamics, we refer to these measures as group pressure. Like many who teach, for years I have observed this industrial "rate busting" phenomenon in the classroom. Since I emphasize transfer of learning in my classroom, it is not uncommon to see students bringing measures to bear on any student who offers "too many" examples of transfer in class discussions.

People and organizations often develop myths about themselves that are perpetuated by the group culture. For example, despite children in the United States scoring far lower in mathematics than children in China and Japan, U.S. children and their parents tend to regard themselves as above average or superior in mathematics, while the superior Asian students don't regard themselves as highly. The same research found that American students derogate the importance of hard work in achieving a skill. When asked what they considered most important for doing well in mathematics, over 60% of the Chinese and Japanese students said studying hard, while less than 25% of the U.S. students said studying hard is important.[25] The implications here are clear, especially from the evidence I'll present in the next chapter on the importance of practice and drill for achieving transfer.

Thus group norms set up expectations that become fulfilled. A comprehensive review of the research shows, for example, that Asian-American children work harder than Caucasian children do, engaging in over 40% more homework. Moreover, part of the reason seems to be that although American parents tend to accept a child's weak areas, choosing to concentrate on their strengths and ignoring the weaknesses, Asian parents tend to encourage their children to practice harder and longer.[26]

Israel Scheffler, in an interesting book entitled, *In Praise of Cognitive Emotions and Other Essays on the Philosophy of Education*, recognizes that

> what one culture opens as a possibility for learning may be closed to another. This is an aspect of what might be termed the relativity of potential. Appreciation of such relativity should serve to draw the policy maker's attention to his or her presuppositions as to cultural context.[27]

Although Scheffler refers to cultures in the social sense, it applies to all other cultures and contexts of transfer. For example, in terms of student teachers transferring what they have learned, once they enter the full-time culture of a school, transfer may meet with resistance. Studies have shown

> that a number of factors lead to the reversal of what is learned in a student's academic training, once a student enters teaching. The "norms" of the school, the techniques of colleagues, even the pupils themselves may all play a role in reversing the techniques taught in an academic program.[28]

If teacher education programs are to avoid this antitransfer effect, they are going to have to design programs that innoculate students to the effects of such antitransfer norms.

Moreover, as Frank Pratzner pointed out years ago,

The development of transferable skills and transfer skills probably cannot be accomplished effectively if they are the objectives, special interest, or special ability of only one or two teachers or courses in a school The project's contention is that their effective development can only be accomplished if they are pervasive and deliberate objectives for an entire school program.[29]

In short, promoting transfer requires a systems approach.

Merlin Wittrock pointed out that intuitive cultural "theories" of physical phenomena influence teaching and learning in the science classroom. We know, for example, that different cultures transmit different conceptions of the physics of heat. According to Wittrock, the caloric view (a calorie is the unit of heat equal to the amount of heat required to raise the temperature of 1 kilogram of water by 1°C at 1 atmosphere pressure) of heat flow is common among children in the United States, Canada, France, and England.[30] By contrast, a scientifically more advanced conception of heat, a kinetic or at least a prekinetic view is common among many Sotho children in Africa who haven't been specifically taught a kinetic theory of heat.[31]

One very important cultural influence on transfer is language, which exerts a powerful influence on transfer. It is through the language of a group or culture that we encode our concepts and categories. Steven Guberman and Patricia Greenfield wrote that "children master their culture's theory of the connections between contexts as they master their language."[32] Understanding how people from different groups and cultures classify things in the environment is important for transfer, which is often dependent on how we classify our environment. In turn our classification systems determine how we make inferences and thus how we transfer. When we say something is typical, we mean that it is a kind of prototype; that it shares many *similar* features with whatever is being discussed. But various cultures have different conceptions of what is similar, and therefore cultures classify things differently. For example, when talking about birds, what is considered typical by American subjects decreases from robin to pigeon to parrot to ostrich. A robin, too, is perceived as more typical than a swan to North Americans, but a swan is more typical than a robin to the average Chinese.

When classifying sources of meat, a Westerner's core concept includes cows. This would obviously not be true for many people in India. Instead, because cows are sacred, for them the cow belongs to the concept of religion. In India, imagine the answer to the analogy question, *pig is to bacon as cow is to hamburger*. Each context may change our classification system. For example, a raccoon and a snake are much less similar when judged in a general or biological context than when judged within the context or a scheme for pets. Research has unequivocally demonstrated that the structure of a category is variable, depending on the population, individual, or context.

Some cultures and groups have more built-in mechanisms of support for learning than do others. In her study, "Strategy Acquisition and Transfer among American and German Children," Martha Carr and her colleagues found that German children were more strategic on certain tasks than were the U.S. children.[33] The cross-national differences were associated with strategy instruction in the home. The German parents reported more instruction of strategies with their children than did U.S. parents.

On a basic level, cultures determine what language we use and how we use it; they determine what metaphors and analogies we use and the feeling cues for selecting them. On another level, language is often troublesome in terms of transfer—with clear implications for globalization and multiculturalism. At a recent international training and development conference near Los Angeles, California, I shared a luncheon table with a Latin American woman. As I explained what transfer of learning was all about, she quickly transferred my explanation to her own consulting business. She had been recently asked by a well-known international consulting firm to retranslate their training material into Spanish. The problem was that the first translation had merely translated the material literally. The example she used was the current pithy phrase often used in popular culture, "walk the talk," meaning that a trainer or manager should demonstrate their instructions by active demonstration of them themselves. It seems that this phrase cannot be literally transferred or translated into Spanish. If literally translated, it ends up being gibberish. Moreover, she said, "walk the talk" won't transfer into any equivalent pithy phrase. Some phrases simply can't be meaningfully transferred from one culture to another.

## CAMPUS CULTURE AND TRANSFER

The culture I know best is the college campus. If there is a single culture of transfer that should be the model *par excellence* for other cultures of transfer, it should be the school environment. Typically, however, it's not the case. Ironic as it may seem, college campuses do not typically create a culture of transfer. Even most classrooms are not structured for transfer. Students in most academic settings have no culture of support to facilitate transfer.

By and large, on many campuses student life is counterproductive to transfer. Concentration on and conversation about pop culture and athletics is often a primary preoccupation of students. Indeed on many college campuses athletic supporters do not support the high level of learning required in courses. At worse, many college campuses are little more than playgrounds for atavistic behaviors that are reminiscent of Freud's Primal Horde, and campus life in many dormitories little more than islands right out of William Golding's *Lord of the Flies*. At best, campus culture serves as a prolongation of adolescence and pop culture norms and knowledge base, a kind of McDonald's Land for fast and effort-free learning.

Am I exaggerating? Yes, of course—but not by much. My criticism of typical campus life is not an indictment of students enjoying themselves, nor is it a bid for eliminating an environment of experimentation, or as a learning laboratory for developing social skills. Nor is the goal of my criticism to denigrate spending time learning athletic skills and team work. I am a believer in the ancient Greek Olympian tradition of educating the body as well as the mind (despite the fact that there is virtually not a shred of evidence to support the widespread belief that sports "builds character"). Nor do I intend to make socially withdrawn scholars out of students. My goal is the promotion of transfer. Unless students live in learning environments that provide support structures and models that communicate a value system for learning and transfer, it will not occur, as it indeed has not widely occurred in the past. The U.S. social environment, the cultural "campus" of the adult, nontraditional learner is not much different.

From a culture-of-transfer perspective, transfer is in large measure the consequence of a learning "system," of educational structures, of social and individual rewards, and of models of transfer. Mainstream academic instruction, with its emphasis on (a) the individual, (b) internal mental processes, and (c) instructional methods that seldom extend learning beyond the small group learning environment has virtually ignored the social or cultural context or social support components to learning. In contrast, learners in corporate environments have a built-in context of transfer application and support: their work environment. Even by default, the very structure of the workplace is a support system, a culture of transfer to some degree. It is a support system because learning is (a) a valued goal (i.e., the job), (b) it is meaningfully evaluated (i.e., job performance), (c) it is rewarded, (d) it is a paycheck, (e) it is action based (i.e., application activities), and (f) it involves social interaction with other workers around common and related work activities.

A culture-of-transfer approach is exemplified most systematically by business training consultants Mary Broad and John Newstrom in their book, *Transfer of Training*. They approach transfer almost exclusively as a managerial and organizational problem.[34] Although academic educational settings have been concerned almost exclusively with the cognitive aspects of individual learning and ignored transfer support systems, business training has generally ignored individual cognitive aspects of individual learning, and has been concerned with transfer support systems. As one trainer remarked, "They speak of . . . modifying the culture to support new skills, preparing participants' managers to reinforce new behavior, and designing follow-up programs and measures. Such practices are crucial for training to have impact, but somewhere along the way they leave out a key player: the employee being trained."[35] Both aspects of transfer are needed. Perhaps business could learn something from education and education from business training.

As I indicated above, there are some college campuses that are actively involved in the social and group aspects of learning, with the implicit goal of transfer. My colleague, Dr. John Lemons and his associates have designed what is called a "learning community."[36] When he was appointed Chair of the Life Sciences Department, Lemons initiated a year-long learning community for first-year students. The goal is to provide students with a culture of learning that promotes not only learning and the application of that learning, but to facilitate integrated interdisciplinary connections between and among different perspectives and disciplines. Students receive 19 credits for introductory biology, environmental issues, literature, nature and biology, and English composition, along with a one-credit course called introduction to learning community. The courses are not taught, however, as individual courses; they are integrated into a series of modules that, in effect, constitute one big, year-long course that is team taught by professors from the various disciplines represented in the learning community. Students take the modules together as a group, and various group discussions and experiences are designed to increase student involvement and active participation in the learning process.

These learning communities can be seen as cultures of transfer, at least theoretically. I say theoretically, as sufficient evidence is not yet in on their effectiveness in terms of learning or transfer, though the national evaluation of learning communities has been ongoing for some time.[37] The preliminary evidence from the outcome evaluations, however, is that learning communities have shown promise. All else being equal—in theory at least—transfer is made from the basic design of learning communities. At least theoretically, learning communities have the "Right Stuff."

As noted in the introduction and in chapter 1, the ultimate culture of transfer is societal. We either value transfer or discourage it—either actively, or by default. The U.S. culture has not and is not supportive of transfer. As I outlined in chapter 1, the public attitude in the United States toward education is and has been, at best, ambivalent, and at worst, anti-intellectual, as the eminent historian Richard Hofstadter's (1916–1970) classic work, *Anti-intellectualism in American Life*, made painfully clear.[38] But the transfer problem in our larger culture goes beyond just psychological climate. It extends to the very living conditions of everyday life.

From the rigorous international research of Richard Jaeger, director of the Center for Educational Research and Evaluation at the University of North Carolina, Greensboro, it is clear that the problem of transfer lies not just with our psychological climate or our schools. In large measure, the problem seems to rest in our economic and family structure. From his comparative international research, Jaeger finds that the typical U.S. educational villains include ineffective teachers, too large classes, too few hours spent in school, and insufficient educational resources. But these are not the main reasons why U.S. students score lower than students in many other countries. Although these factors are important, according to Jaeger, the largest factors that correlate with these cross-cultural differences in student scores are poverty and the instability of the family structure. U.S. high school students come more often from single-parent homes, work more hours at a job, and do less homework than comparable students in other countries.[39] This is not a "conservative-agenda" analysis; it's just the way the data fall out. These findings do not indicate optimal conditions for a culture of transfer.

## CONCLUSION

It is clear, then, that cultures and contexts are powerful shapers of transfer. Of course, not all transfer is contextually and culturally generated. We would not want to react in the opposite direction to the personal view of transfer. In fact, shifting the focus and definition of transfer to the contextual and cultural levels can be seen as not addressing the problem of transfer at all. As Guberman and Greenfield note, "This shift of focus does not so much solve the transfer problem as it dissolves it."[40] The problem of transfer does not lend itself well to single-perspective theories.

## Notes

[1]Pea, R. D. (1987). Socializing the knowledge transfer problem. *International Journal of Educational Research*, 11, 639–663, p. 648.

[2]See, for example, Sampson, E. E. (1989). The challenge of social change for psychology: Globalization and psychology's theory of the person. *American Psychologist*, 44(6), 914–921; Sampson, E. E. (1988). The debate on individualism: Indigenous psychologies of the individual and their role in personal and societal functioning. *American Psychologist*, 43(1), 15–22.

[3]Triplett, N. (1898). Dynamogenic factors in pacemaking and competition. *American Journal of Psychology*, 9, 507–533.

[4]See, for example, Jordan, C. (1985). Translating culture: From ethnographic information to educational program. *Anthropology and Education Quarterly*, 16(2), 105–123; Laboratory of Comparative Human Cognition (1986). Contributions of cross-cultural research of educational practice. *American Psychologist*, 41(10), 1049–1058.

[5]McKeachie, W. J. (1987). Cognitive skills and their transfer: Discussion. *International Journal of Educational Research*, 11, 707–712, p. 170.

[6]See, for example, Greeno, J. G., Moore, J. L., & Smith, D. R. (1993). Transfer of situated learning. In D. K. Detterman & R. J. Sternberg (Eds.), *Transfer on trial: Intelligence, cognition, and instruction* (pp. 99–167). Norwood, NJ: Ablex; Lave, J. (1991). *Situated learning: Legitimate peripheral participation*. New York: Cambridge University Press.

[7]Neisser, U. (Ed.). (1982). *Memory observed: Remembering in natural contexts*. San Francisco: W. H. Freeman.

[8]Greeno, J. G., Moore, J. L., & Smith, D. R. (1993). Transfer of situated learning. IN D. K. Detterman & R. J. Sternberg (Eds.), *Transfer on trial: Intelligence, cognition, and instruction* (pp. 99–167). Norwood, NJ: Ablex, p. 99.

[9]Ibid.

[10]Laboratory of Comparative Human Cognition (1986). Contributions of cross-cultural research of educational practice. *American Psychologist*, 41(10), 1049–1058, p. 1057.

[11]See Koegel, R. L., Koegel, L. K., Van Voy, K., & Costello, I. J. (1988). Within-clinic versus outside-of-clinic self-monitoring of articulation to promote generalization. *Journal of Speech and Hearing Disorders*, 53(4), 392–399, p. 392.

[12]See Fischer, R. (1976). On the remembrance of things present: The state-bound and stage-bound nature of consciousness. *Man-Environment Systems*, 6(3), 131–136; Weingartner, H., Adelfris, W., Eich, J. E., & Murphy, D. L. (1983). Encoding specificity in alcohol state-dependent learning. *Journal of Experimental Psychology: Human Learning and Memory*, 2, 83–87.

[13]See Greeno, J. G., Moore, J. L., & Smith, D. R. (1993). Transfer of situated learning. In D. K. Detterman & R. J. Sternberg (Eds.), *Transfer on trial: Intelligence, cognition, and instruction* (pp. 99–167). Norwood, NJ: Ablex, p. 99.

[14]Lave, J. (1991). *Situated learning: Legitimate peripheral participation*. New York: Cambridge University Press; Lave, J. (1977). Tailor-made experiments and evaluating the intellectual consequences of apprenticeship training. *The Quarterly Newsletter of The Institute of Comparative Human Development*, 1, 1–3.

[15]Resnick, L. B. (1987). Instruction and the cultivation of thinking. In E. De Corte, H. Lodewijks, R. Parmentier, & P. Span (Eds.), *Learning and instruction* (vol. I, pp. 415–441). Oxford: Pergamon Press, p. 433.

[16]Gick, M. L., & Holyoak, K. J. (1987). The cognitive basis of knowledge transfer. In S. M. Cormier & J. D. Hagman (Eds.), *Transfer of learning contemporary research and application* (pp. 9–45). New York: Academic Press, p. 31.

[17]Gage, N. L., & Berliner, D. C. (1929). *Educational psychology* (5th ed.). Boston, MA: Houghton Mifflin, p. 321.

[18]See, for example, Hatano, G. (1982). Cognitive consequences of practice in culture specific procedural skills. *The Quarterly Newsletter of the Laboratory of Comparative Human Cognition*, 4(1), 15–18.

[19]See Billett, S. (1992). Towards a theory of workplace learning. *Studies in Continuing Education*, 14(2), 143–155; Cormier, S. M. (1987). The structural processes underlying transfer of training. In S. M. Cormier & J. D. Hagman (Eds.), *Transfer of learning: Contemporary research and application* (pp. 151–181). New York: Academic Press.

[20]Richey, R. (1992). *Designing instruction for the adult learner: Systemic training, theory and practice*. London: Kogan, p. 168.

[21]Baldwin, T. T., & Ford, J. K. (1988). Transfer of training: A review and directions for future research. *Personnel Psychology*, 41, 61–105, p. 85.

[22]Bridges, D. (1993). Transferable skills: A philosophical perspective. *Studies in Higher Education*, 18(1), 43–51, p. 49.

[23]Pea, R. D. (1987). Socializing the knowledge transfer problem. *International Journal of Educational Research*, 11, 639–663, p. 639.

[24]See Gardner, H. (1983). *Frames of mind: The theory of multiple intelligences*. New York: Basic Books.

[25]Cited in Dawes, R. M. (1949). *House of cards: Psychology and psychotherapy built on myth*. New York: Free Press.

[26]Cited in Goleman, D. (1995). *Emotional intelligence: Why it can matter more than I.Q*. New York: Bantam Books.

[27]Scheffler, I. (1991). *In praise of cognitive emotions and other essays on the philosophy of education*. New York: Routledge, p. 108.

[28]Ibid, p. 79.

[29]Pratzner, F. C. (1978). *Occupational adaptability and transferable skills*. (Information Series No. 129). Columbus, OH: National Center for Research in Vocational Education, p. 2.

[30]Wittrock, M. C. (1985). Learning science by generating new conceptions from old ideas. In L. H. T. West & A. L. Pines (Eds.), *Cognitive structure and conceptual change* (pp. 259–266). New York: Academic Press.

[31]See Barsalou, L. W. (1989). Intraconcept similarity and its implications for interconcept similarity. In S. Vosniadou & A. Anthony (Eds.), *Similarity and analogical reasoning* (pp. 76–121). New York: Cambridge University Press, p. 251.

[32]Guberman, S. R., & Greenfield, P. M. (1991). Learning and transfer in everyday cognition, *Cognitive Development*, 6, 233–260, p. 252.

[33]Carr, M., Kurtz, B. E., Schneider, W., Turner, L. A., & Borkowski, J. G. (1989). Strategy acquisition and transfer among American and German children: Environmental influences on metacognitive development. *Developmental Psychology, 25*, 765–771, p. 769.

[34]Broad, M. L., & Newstrom, J. (1992). *Transfer of training: Action-packed strategies to ensure high payoff from training investments.* New York: Addison-Wesley; See also Analoui, F. (1993). *Training and transfer of learning.* Brookfield, MA: Avebury.

[35]Friedman, B. (1990). Six ways to make it work at work. *Training & Development Journal, 44*, 17–19, p. 17.

[36]Morgan, P., Lemons, J., Carter, J., Grumbling, O., & Saboski, E. (1993). A scientific learning community at the University of New England: Interdisciplinary approaches to introductory biology. *Journal of College Science Teaching, 22*, 171–177.

[37]See Washington Center Evaluation Committee. (1995). *Assessment in and of collaborative learning: A handbook of strategies (pilot version).* Washington, DC: Washington Center for Improving the Quality of Undergraduate Education.

[38]Hofstadter, R. (1962). *Anti-intellectualism in American life.* New York: Random House.

[39]Jaeger, R. (1992). World class standards, choice, and privatization: Weak measurement serving presumptive policy. *Phi Delta Kappan,* October, 118–128.

[40]Guberman, S. R., & Greenfield, P. M. (1991). Learning and transfer in everyday cognition. *Cognitive Development, 6*, 233–260, p. 252.

# 9

# When Theory Fails:
# The Importance of a Learner's
# Theoretical Knowledge
# for Transfer

*What may look like profound developmental differences in the basis of conceptualiza-*
*tion, or in the type of reasoning available to the child, may actually be a reflection of*
*the status of young children's core theories.*

—ANN BROWN, *Analogical Learning and Transfer: What Develops?*[1]

I approach this chapter with a Kierkegaardian fear and trembling.[2] Any time
theory enters into discussions, students—and even many faculty's—eyes
glaze over. This reaction, however, is the very reason why we find so little
transfer thinking. In chapter 6, I outlined the importance of the different kinds
of knowledge. Although that chapter was mainly about declarative knowledge, this chapter is about theoretical knowledge. But I am not concerned
about a theory *of* transfer, but about theories that learners carry (and don't
carry) around in their heads that affect transfer. Even small children require
theoretical knowledge if they are to engage in transfer. Ann Brown's work with
children (see below) clearly shows that young children fail to transfer only
when they lack theoretical knowledge.

Contrary to popular conception, "theory" is no more abstract than is most
of our everyday thinking. Theory is not Ivory Tower philosophical speculation
about the Seven Proofs for the Existence of God, nor about the ancient
Scholastic speculation about how many angels can dance on the head of a pin.
Theory is as natural as everyday thinking itself. In fact, *it is* everyday thinking.
Theory is simply forming a hypotheses (roughly, guesses) about something,
testing those hypotheses, then taking the individual results of those tests and
putting them together into a logically coherent and consistent explanation.

Not only is transfer dependent on theoretical knowledge, but theory is dependent on transfer. "Science is in the business of discovering ordered structure in dynamic systems," says Walter Weimer, "and it attempts to exhibit the *invariant* [italics added] properties of such complex systems. Natural science has become a search for invariants."[3] (See chapters 11 and 12.) As we have seen, transfer and invariance relations (similarity relations) are pragmatically indistinguishable. Good theoretical understanding of an area, then, is crucial for achieving transfer.

Lacking theory, there are, in fact, no facts. Theory creates facts. A fact is the end product of a theory. As Weimer correctly observes, "What we learn to see in 'facts' are similarity relationships: we learn to see instances as instances of thing-kinds, and we learn how thing-kinds are structurally related."[4] To reiterate, a theory is merely a logical and ordered explanation of a set of observations based on tested evidence. We are all scientists, armed with theoretical knowledge. Certainly most of our knowledge is not as extensive or as precisely and rigorously tested as is the scientist's, but we are theoreticians nevertheless. In fact, our everyday understanding of people is almost entirely theoretical. Because we cannot get inside people's feelings and thoughts, we understand people by theorizing (i.e., inferring from their behaviors), *comparing* people to ourselves and weaving plausible connections (theory) between the everyday evidence we have of them (see chapter 4). To say that we are not theoretical, then, is in fact to say that we are not aware of our theories and how they determine how we think and act. The problem is that everyday theory is typically bad theory.

For many of the same reasons that I consider declarative knowledge to be of cardinal importance (see chapter 6), I consider theoretical knowledge to be of equal importance. People typically want only weak forms of declarative knowledge (i.e., "just the facts," and procedural "how-to" knowledge). Facts and how-to knowledge are thought to be concrete, whereas theory is thought to be abstract and speculative. A so-called "fact," however ,is not all that concrete, nor is a theory all that speculative. Having just facts and how-to knowledge is helpful but not enough. If, as research findings indicate, theoretical knowledge is understood and applied by children in order to learn and transfer, it can certainly be used by anyone.

Science advances by the use of theoretical knowledge. Jerome Bruner most succinctly describes what a theory does. He says,

> A theory, of course, is something we invent. If it is a good theory . . . it should permit us to go beyond the present data both respectively and prospectively. We go backward—turn around on our own schemata and order data that previously seemed unrelated to each other. Old loose ends now become part of a new pattern.[5]

In the evolution of chemistry out of alchemy, only when theoretical laws and principles were developed did chemical knowledge advance rapidly. This is equally true for other professional forms of knowledge as well as for our understanding of everyday events.

Learning, and the way we develop concepts also advances by the use of theory. Indeed, science can be used as a *model* (i.e., transferred) for individual learning and concept formation. Robert Glaser, in a chapter entitled, "Learning Theory and Theories of Knowledge," says, "People restructure their knowledge in the course of learning in a way that is *analogous* [italics added] to conceptual changes in the history of science."[6] Learners bring their own concepts to learning. Instruction then fosters an evolution from these untutored "theories" to more sophisticated theories and conceptualizations. The development of individual learning, then, is *like* the development of science concepts and theories. That is, the development of theoretical knowledge is to science as conceptual development is to individuals.

The more complicated and high-tech our personal worlds become, the more we need a good (valid) theoretical knowledge base to compete and survive. The choice, then, is not between having theoretical knowledge or not having theoretical knowledge. The choice is between (a) being aware of our theories so that we can use them, and (b) or not being aware of them, in which case they use us. Most of our theoretical knowledge is implicit; we are not aware of it. Our theories can be like unconscious mental models. Moreover, it is theoretical knowledge, not simple surface perception—and this is the essence of what this chapter is all about—that tells us and children *that a whale is not a fish*. It's theoretical knowledge that tells us that even though something is in the water, has fins, swims like a fish, and looks just like a fish, that it's not a fish. The apprehension of simple perceptual facts incorrectly informs us that a porpoise is a fish. After all, it lives in the water, has fins, and swims. But our theoretical knowledge of biology and evolutionary theory inform us differently.

In an important, yet common way, children provide us with a *model* for understanding the importance of theoretical constraints. Before they acquire theoretical knowledge, children are famous for runaway transfer or *overgeneralization*. For example, until they absorb theoretical knowledge, all four-legged animals are seen as kitties or doggies (depending on what pet they first have). Theory is our hedge against randomly accessing reality; it guides us to a intended reality and allows us to recognize it. As a consequence, we need balancing feedback. Theoretical knowledge creates the constraints or *balancing feedback*, it's our hedge against a runaway system of thinking.

Theoretical knowledge provides us, simultaneously, with (a) a rule to guide our transfer, and (b) a framework to constrain runaway transfer. Theory directs us (consciously or unconsciously) to look in this place and not in that place. Theory thus acts as an efficiency manager. Each time we recognize a similarity, or transfer a piece of knowledge, we receive *reinforcing feedback* to seek more. Because similarities exist among all phenomena, if we noted all similarities among all events, we would very quickly be overwhelmed.

Theoretical knowledge, then, is necessary for creating coherence out of a bunch of novel or otherwise disconnected experiences. In addition, theoretical knowledge is more likely to be transferred to new situations. Conversely, isolated rules or concrete strategies learned in particular situations are less likely to be transferred. In an article entitled, "Learning And Transfer In Everyday Cognition", Guberman and Greenfield warn that isolated rules, or concrete strategies learned in particular situations, are also less likely to protect us "against unwarranted interference and generalization. Only when isolated rules are supported by a coherent theoretical framework will transfer be likely."[7] Similarly, from her research with children Ann Brown concludes that

> if that which is to be transferred consists of a coherent theory or a causal explanation that is understood, it is difficult to impede a flexible application of prior knowledge. It is when the application of a previously learned isolated rule or specific solution is required that observers decry a lack of transfer.[8]

Applying strategies to areas of which one has little or no knowledge *is like* applying a scientific technology in a formulaic fashion outside one's area of expertise.

Our perceptions of the world are not just imprinted on our brains; they are shaped by the theory that greets them. Olson put it this way,

> Once taken into a system of verbally formulated links, the stimulus in question becomes not a mere signal, but an item of *generalized information* [italics added] and all subsequent reactions depend more on the system it is taken into than on its physical properties.[9]

Contrary to popular belief, theory is clearly primary over facts; indeed, theory creates facts. A concept, too, is a theory, a kind of mini-theory, a general idea derived or inferred from specifics. For example, the concept of dog or canine requires relational knowledge. A canine is an animal that belongs to the biological family Canidae, which in part is defined by having pointed, conical teeth located between the incisors and the first bicuspids. Concepts, unlike individual facts, concrete skills, or simple procedures are based on theoretical knowledge and are themselves theories. *To say that you are not theoretical, then, is in fact to say that you don't think at all.*

## WHEN THEORY FAILS: CHILDREN
## AND THEORETICAL KNOWLEDGE

The research on how children learn is a powerful general (i.e., transfer) model for understanding adult learning and transfer. This fact is not generally recognized because it has been assumed that children think and learn quite differently from adults. This assumption is largely based on the work of the well-known Swiss psychologist, Jean Piaget. Piaget maintained that there are natural cognitive stages of development through which children progress. Each stage is characterized by certain qualitatively different kinds of thinking that change as they mature. According to Piaget, moving from one stage to another is characterized by a qualitative "shift" in thinking. For example, in the early stages of cognitive development, it is thought that children are unable to engage in analogical reasoning or transfer.[10] In recent years, however, many developmental psychologists have abandoned much of Piaget's scheme.

Research on analogical transfer has shown that indeed very young children are able to engage in analogical transfer. As one of these researchers, Ann Brown, notes, "It has been claimed that below 5 years of age, transfer rarely occurs, and it is a widely held belief that the younger the learner the less likely is transfer."[11] Children have been thought to be what is called "perceptually bound." The perceptually bound hypothesis claims that children are bound to the concrete physical appearance of objects and therefore are unable to engage in appropriate analogical transfer until they are older and have moved into the appropriate stage of cognitive development. According to Brown's research (and others), rather than there being a qualitative shift from being perceptually bound to theoretically based, young children's conceptual systems are integrated with theoretical knowledge from the earliest age—children's theories are just not as well developed as adults'. Brown goes on to note that "in the absence of the requisite knowledge, it is difficult to imagine any other basis for partitioning than appearance, whether one is an adult or a child."[12] But children know more than we give them credit for.

Indeed, children know more than we have suspected, and they are not as dependent on concrete similarity features among objects as we once thought. Brown's research shows that 4-year-olds who are told that a human has a spleen, nevertheless believe that a worm is more likely to possess a spleen than is a mechanical monkey, even though they judge a mechanical monkey more *perceptually* similar to a human than a worm. Theoretical knowledge enables a child to know that a whale is not a fish. Thus, Brown says,

> It would seem that young children do transfer their knowledge and can do so on deeper bases than mere appearance matches. What determines the extent of their knowledge projections is not some developmental constraint on the inductive process itself but a constraint on the type of knowledge to be transferred and its status within their emergent conceptual theories.[13]

Although it is true that children rely on concrete surface similarity, they only do so when they lack theoretical knowledge, or as Ann Brown puts it, "when theory fails." So do we adults.

An interesting study by Anne Hickling and Susan Gelman entitled, *"How Does Your Garden Grow? Early Conceptualization of Seeds and Their Place in Plant Growth Cycle,"*[14] clearly shows the possession and use of theoretical knowledge by young children. The authors studied 80 4-year-olds for their understanding of the growth of plant seeds. Overall, the children demonstrated an impressive understanding of seeds and their function in the growth cycle. By age 4½ years, the children realized that natural causal mechanisms and not other causes (e.g., human intervention) was responsible for growth. They also have an appreciation of the unique relation of seeds to the plant domain, and demonstrate a developing grasp of the cyclical nature growth. The authors conclude that the preschoolers hold theory-like understandings of plants similar to those that they have of humans and lower animals.

Brown and her colleagues have maintained that it is important to distinguish among different kinds of knowledge in terms of their breadth and depth. She distinguishes (a) arbitrary knowledge (e.g., canaries are yellow), (b) locally meaningful knowledge (e.g., birds that eat seeds have thick beaks), (c) principled knowledge (evolution leads to birds' having appropriate beaks for their food), and (d) broad theory-based knowledge (birds are animate). In her work with young children she has found that as their knowledge moves from arbitrary knowledge to theoretical knowledge, the amount of transfer increases dramatically. Research with children is a powerful model for the requirements of effective adult learning. If we know what kinds of knowledge there are by classifying them, we can seek out the kind of knowledge we need for a given task. Tasks vary by the kind of knowledge required. Categories based on the various kinds of knowledge create order and structure that help us to transfer our knowledge.

Although Brown's research largely contraindicates the strict developmental shift model of Piagetian-type cognitive stages, she does acknowledge that young children do not perform as well as older children on a variety of transfer tasks. She suggests, however, that what may be developing in the older child is not so much a cognitive shift into a new developmental stage but a general ability to use metacognitive strategies (e.g., searching for underlying structures without being told). As I suggested in chapter 6, even young children's knowledge about the world, especially processes involved in their theoretical knowledge base, has a powerful effect on learning and transfer when age-appropriate tasks and questions are used. The more we know about these processes, the more we will understand the mental mechanisms that promote transfer as well as learning.

## THEORY, TRANSFER, AND THE LEARNING OF SCIENCE

As we have seen, not only adults but children carry theories around in their heads, and these theories operate either explicitly or implicitly. The problem is, however, that these theories are all too often erroneous. Implicitly erroneous theories influence learning and have serious consequences for teaching and transfer. Studies have shown that the erroneous theories about scientific phenomena that students come into the classroom with block their learning of science. Studies consistently demonstrate that naïve or beginning physics and biology students hold fundamentally erroneous theories about these subjects that negatively influence their learning and transfer.[15]

Worse yet, observes Tan, "many students are unable to autonomously collect the relevant bits and pieces of information from their textbooks, lectures and laboratory experiments and create a coherent representation of the relationships."[16] One reason why students are unable to integrate the information taught in their classes and laboratories is that science textbooks tend to be informationally based rather than conceptually or theoretically based. As Tan laments, a "large number of students are unable to effectively use basic science theory in diagnostic problem-solving."[17] Accordingly, Tan suggests that a restructuring of textbook knowledge is needed in order to make theoretical knowledge practically useful.

As an example of erroneous theoretical knowledge among science students, it is widely believed that "heat molecules flow" and that a physical vacuum "sucks" matter into it.[18] In space travel movies, for example, when the spaceship is punctured by a meteorite or a hatch door is accidentally opened and the occupants fly out into space, many students believe that they are sucked out by the vacuum of space. They are not, of course sucked out, they are blown out into space. These commonsense and intuitive, but erroneous, analogical notions appear to be satisfactory in explaining some everyday experiences. Implicit and intuitive theories are not limited to students. Indeed, the great French chemist Antoine Lavoisier (1743–1794) gave an explanation of heat that sounded very much like the intuitive notion that "heat molecules flow." The classic case of Ignaz Semmelweis's (1818–1865) theory that invisible microbes (germs) caused disease and infected patients during surgery was an elegant, simple, and parsimonious theory that most scientists and surgeons of his day intuitively thought was a ludicrous idea because it didn't fit their intuitive ideas and erroneous theories. How similarly strange some modern-day scientific theories must seem to students who hold intuitively appealing, but incorrect, everyday theories in their heads.

Such findings have consequences for teaching and instructing for transfer. Normally we assume that students either know nothing about a subject matter or that they possess some correct knowledge about the domain to be learned. But as we have seen, this assumption is not an appropriate one. What we must know before we can teach, especially for transfer, is what incorrect theories students have in their heads. Findings suggest that it's not effective to simply teach the correct scientific body of knowledge and theories, because the scientific body of data are entering a cognitive system resistant to accommodating the new information. For transfer to occur, instruction must take into account the cognitive system it's attempting to influence. (See the concluding Coda.)

Students' everyday knowledge and intuitive conceptions about a subject matter often act like antibodies, surrounding and trying to eject a "foreign invader" (i.e., knowledge). I find this to be especially true in teaching psychology. Despite the research in physics and natural science showing that students come into classes with erroneous "theories," I suspect it doesn't begin to reach the proportions it does in psychology. We live in a psychologically oriented society, with pop psychology theories on every book and magazine stand, TV, and radio talk show in America. I define pop-psychological knowledge as psychological information that is (a) widely disseminated to the general public, (b) simplified and distorted, (c) has little or no rigorous evidence to support it, but (d) that is accepted as true. By comparison, there really is nothing worthy of the title "pop mathematics" or "pop chemistry." Increasingly I have to spend an inordinate amount of time in my classes counteracting these implicit and pop theories about psychology and human behavior. It is difficult for students to learn new psychological material, not because it is complex, but simply because it is not compatible with what they think they know about psychology. Their everyday theories act like antibodies in their immune system and tend to eject the new material. Their old knowledge interferes with new knowledge. This is the essence of negative transfer.

I have found, for example, that when I present questions on exams with the same structure but different content, thus requiring the same logic to answer the question correctly, as the content of the questions increasingly contradict students' erroneous theories about psychology, they increasingly answer them incorrectly—i.e., very little transfer—despite the fact that I have extensively gone over in class the valid research on the content of the questions. The "foreign" material just does not adhere. From a transfer perspective, then, the first thing those of us who teach must know is what incorrect theories our students have in their heads. To the extent that we do not know what is in their heads, is the extent to which we are probably ineffective as teachers. Consequently, I make it my business to know the pop psychology theories that students bring to my classroom. Knowing this information, I can then confront the erroneous theories and begin to dispel them.

## YET ANOTHER (APPARENT) PARADOX
## AND MYSTERY OF TRANSFER

Having extolled the virtues of theory, there is yet another paradox involved in transfer—or at least a counterintuitive consequence. We might think that people with a high level of theoretical knowledge would be able to transfer in all situations better than people with only concrete knowledge. They can't. At least sometimes they can't. In fact, those who have theoretical knowledge enabling them to engage in general, abstract, and far transfer of that knowledge, may not be able to transfer in simpler, more concrete ways. In a slightly different context, Ann Brown recognizes that "it is important to note that the conditions of learning that lead to higher-order rule abstraction are not necessarily those that lead to broad generalization of specific rules."[19] In short, conceptual knowledge (which is to say theoretical knowledge) may not lead to more concrete forms of transfer. Although this paradox has been recognized and demonstrated by specific researchers, it is not generally a part of the current body of knowledge about transfer.

The instructional implications are significant. For example, students who learned to operate a computer with two different instructional modes subsequently transferred their learning quite differently. Some students were taught concrete procedures, and others were taught conceptual knowledge about operating a computer. Not surprisingly, the students taught with concrete procedures transferred only to very concrete applications. However, the students who learned conceptually, "demonstrated significantly more skill in applying knowledge about computer commands to novel problems but significantly less ability to respond to factual questions about the commands."[20] In other words, students taught with conceptual information were able to engage in far transfer but performed more poorly in near transfer.

Similarly, students who learn to use mathematical skills creatively are often not as able as the student who learns mathematics in a more concrete mode to solve familiar problems. Students taught binomial probability with concepts that are part of their prior knowledge—for example, within a context of batting averages or rain forecasts—performed better on far transfer tasks that were dissimilar from those they were taught with and better with questions that required understanding. In contrast, however, students taught in a formulaic, more mechanical mode, who learned the basic components of the binomial theorem and were given practice at solving specific problems outperformed the students who were conceptually taught simple problems to which the formula could be easily applied.[21] Similarly, other research suggests that if the goal of instruction is "straightforward performance of explicitly taught skills,"[22] then learning instrumental and concrete procedures is just as effective as conceptual learning for both immediate postinstructional performance and for retention of material. However, if the goal of instruction is both near and far transfer, then, again, learning conceptually is superior to simple instrumental learning.[23]

Other research also shows that students who used a deep learning or conceptual approach to material tended to score lower on simple recognition tasks, but to score higher on more complex recognition tasks. Students who lack prior knowledge about a skill tend to do better than those who have prior knowledge of the skill—but only under rote learning conditions. Students who learn reading material in a verbatim or rote fashion do better than students who learned the material in a conceptual fashion on verbatim tests, whereas students who learn the material conceptually are better at applying their knowledge in a more generalized way.[24] The point is that although conceptual or theoretical knowledge is best for engaging in far transfer, it may be disadvantageous for simple concrete application situations.

As I suggested in chapters 6 and 7, how we encode information influences how we are able to retrieve and apply it. This may explain why conceptual or theoretical knowledge may not always transfer to concrete situations. Nancy Sagerman and Richard Mayer conducted research on two groups of students reading science texts. One group read passages for verbatim information and another group read passages for conceptual understanding. The authors found that "the verbatim group showed an advantage only on verbatim questions, and the conceptual group showed a larger advantage on conceptual than on verbatim questions."[25] They conclude by noting that when student readers expect to have to answer verbatim questions, they read passages differently than when they expect to have to answer conceptual questions. In our terms, the students encode the passages differently.

From a quite different theoretical perspective, Mark Singley and John Anderson conclude similarly from their research on learning language:

> We would predict no transfer from a *production* [italics added] system embodiment of English syntax for comprehension to a production system embodiment of English syntax for *generation* [italics added]. Although an abstract characterization of the syntactic knowledge underlying competence is the same in *comprehension* and *generation* [italics added], the knowledge is organized differently in the productions for the two tasks.[26]

It seems that our brain has different modules that deal with different aspects of language: one for understanding language and one for generating language. In further explaining how we encode different material depending on its use, Singley and Anderson describe an organic brain syndrome that clearly illustrates this modular encoding. In brain-damaged people whose linguistic systems of comprehension and generation have been radically disconnected through some type of physical trauma,

> We can observe something that is never observed in the course of normal language development: the ability to generate language in the absence of an ability to comprehend language. In a rare disorder called word deafness, a person with normal hearing cannot understand speech but nonetheless can speak quite fluently.[27]

In yet another rare disorder called *alexia*, or word blindness, a person is able to write but unable to read. Though rare, these brain syndromes provide evidence for the specificity of our encoding of knowledge and its implications for transfer.

Perhaps the example par excellence of theoretical knowledge not translating into specifics is the great coach who is not able to perform the activity as expertly as the person he or she is coaching. As these data illustrate, there are costs associated both with a narrow specific learning and with general conceptual or theoretical learning. An effective education would provide both forms of knowledge. Although for specific concrete situations, sheer rote or concrete information may be superior, in general—if given a forced choice— I would vote for theoretical knowledge and its far transfer.

## PTOLEMAIC THEORY: "POP" THEORY, TRANSFER, AND THE CULT OF EXPERIENCE

We have seen that not only adults but children carry theories around in their heads and these theories are often erroneous. Erroneous theories operate implicitly and have serious consequences for teaching and, more specifically, for transfer. This is also true in many professional practice fields. In fact, there is a knowledge-base crisis in many professions, and in many of our schools as well. This is not just my opinion. It's based on the research findings of others. The research clearly shows, that in many applied fields and programs, professors and practitioners tend neither to engage in nor to read or utilize relevant research-based knowledge about their fields.[28] As I will outline in the next chapter, there is precious little evidence to support the belief that most practitioners "practice" from a valid theoretical knowledge base: Many college, university, and professional school programs designed to train professionals are based on curricula that are difficult to distinguish from the popular book-stand literature, with little or no research basis to what is being taught. From what has been outlined above, assuming that we accept "truth" (with a small "t") the implication for transfer is clear: Valid knowledge is fundamental to productive transfer. In fact, much of the information students and the general public receive belongs more to the category of rumor than to valid knowledge.

I have already noted that in a general sense, all knowledge—factual or otherwise—is theoretical knowledge. What constitutes a fact is determined by an implicit or explicit web of connected knowledge. The concept of schizophrenia, for example, can only be a fact when it is grounded in a Western cultural framework of mental health and our conception of reality. Grounded in a preliterate culture's reality of spirit, gods, and demons, the same behaviors that we term schizophrenia, become signs of possession by spirits or voices from the gods. The knowledge that we acquire, then, constitutes our loose web of theory. But it is not just knowledge that's important, it's how we acquire it. The fundamental basis of education—at least higher education—is that knowledge should be acquired on the basis of sound research methods, not by divination, uninformed opinion, or ideology.

The extent to which our knowledge base does not meet this "truth" requirement determines whether or to what extent the theory in our heads is valid. Unfortunately, much of our working knowledge base is corrupted. To explain this further, I will stick to the field I know the best, psychology, although research suggests that what I am saying about applied areas of psychology is also true of many other fields, especially education. I use psychology as a general model that can be transferred to many other fields.

Much of what the general public and psychological practitioners use as theoretical knowledge can be seen as Ptolemaic knowledge at best. So, what is Ptolemaic knowledge? Claudius Ptolemaeus (A.D. 100–170), known as Ptolemy, was the Alexandrian astronomer, mathematician, and geographer in the second century A.D. who based his astronomy on the belief that the earth stood motionless at the center of the universe with the sun, moon, planets, and stars revolving about it in circular orbits. Ptolemy's system dominated astronomy until the German astronomer and mathematician Johannes Kepler's (1571–1630) heliocentric model of the solar system showed that the earth and planets revolve around the sun. The Ptolemaic system combined complicated circular orbits called epicycles to explain the movement of the planets. The epicycles were ad hoc or after-the-fact add-ons to compensate for celestial events that could not be explained by his theory.

Now, Ptolemy's model of the solar system was based on practical everyday empirical data and personal experiences acquired in a "real-world" setting. In the everyday world, we still experience the "proof" of Ptolemy's model: *We personally observe (perceptually experience) the sun revolving around the earth, first visible in the east and disappearing in the west as it seems to circle the earth.* Much of our everyday theoretical knowledge is thusly Ptolemaic. Now in all fairness, I should point out that Ptolemy's model could predict the movement of the planets quite accurately and was extremely useful for marine navigation at that time. But try transferring this knowledge for plotting a course to the moon—or for any other space travel. If there is one thing that scientific research in all fields has shown is that our personal experience is often a poor basis for developing valid theoretical knowledge that we can use (i.e., transfer) outside of some very concrete and restricted situations.

Indeed, it is well known that our culture is one that proudly proclaims its pragmatic and personal experience approach to life. As a consequence, one of the most difficult concepts to convince students—indeed to most people including many practicing professionals—is the profound limitations of personal experience and knowledge gained from practical settings. I should point out that there is nothing inherently wrong with data gathered from practical settings as long as practical knowledge is subjected to rigorous methodological testing and analysis.[29] Typically it isn't.

Perhaps more than any other field, psychology suffers from a "pop" syndrome. There really is no "pop" equivalent in other fields to pop psychology. What would an equivalent pop math, or pop chemistry, or pop biology be? There is, however, a kind of pop (New Age) medicine and a pop physics. More currently, there is even a kind of pop environmental science. Certainly there are misconceptions about what is true regarding each of these fields by the layperson (undoubtedly including myself). For example, the nondeterministic theory of quantum mechanics is widely touted as the proof of human free will. It isn't.[30]

The expectations that many students bring to class around this cult of experience is often counterproductive to transfer. Typically, they don't want to have these expectations contradicted. I have had individual students complain to the administration when I have critiqued popular clinical findings—twice they have complained in groups. Popular culture and often their clinical faculty agree with them. Many of these faculty are as influenced by popular culture and pop psychology as the students they teach. Indeed, many of these faculty use pop psychology books in their programs and courses and thus pass on this Ptolemaic knowledge. Where would atomic or quantum physics be if its theory simply depended on everyday experience? Where would chemistry be if it simply depended on everyday experience instead of theory? The answer is we would still be practicing alchemy. Try curing diseases with the psychopharmacology of the alchemists.

To illustrate the extreme to which pop theory in psychology influences the classroom, consider the following: I have lectured on a pop psychology issue that students have disagreed with. A few months later, I have had some of those same students come to me and say, "You know, Dr. Haskell, the CBS program 60 *Minutes* just did a piece on X, and they said exactly what you did, so you were right after all." Consider the profound implications of this statement. If the moral of this statement isn't already clear it is this: For many students—both young and old—truth is what comes from popular culture. The pop media is seen as validating scientific research. (Need I point out that it's supposed to be the other way around?)

I briefly note a few examples of pop psychology that are used by many practitioners—both inside and outside of psychology. Many business training and allied health programs are in part based on Abraham Maslow's (1908–1970) hierarchy of needs model of human motivation, in which a higher need, ultimately that for self-actualization of one's potential, can occur only after lower needs are fulfilled. We have known for years that Maslow's so-called theory is not supported by the evidence.[31] In addition, many nursing programs are either based on or make use in their training programs of a model of the stages of death and dying based on the work of the Swiss-American physician Elisabeth Kübler-Ross, which describes five psychological stages (denial, anger, bargaining with a deity for time, grieving, and acceptance) experienced by the dying person. Her model, too, is not supported by the evidence.[32] Although both Maslow and Kübler-Ross's models make for wonderful humanistic philosophy, they have no general basis in fact. Other pop psychology areas include the ever popular Doll Play Therapy, repressed memory syndrome, low self-esteem effects, past lives therapy, satanic ritual child abuse, and biofeedback methods. Each of the above pop psychologies are the consequence of a lack of valid theoretical knowledge.[33] Each is largely based on personal and clinical experience, and each is at best Ptolemaic. There is nearly no end to the list.

If we build scientific theories based on incorrect data, our applied fields and transfer will be ineffective. I belabor this point somewhat because It's crucial. The founding of education on solid research is a prerequisite for clear thinking, for scientific research is a form of rigorous reasoning, and therefore teaches us how to think critically (i.e., analytically). But an increasing number of our educational institutions and professional programs are not adequately preparing students. In 1985 therapist Alan H. Roberts recognized that many clinical psychology graduate training institutions, by not selecting students with aptitudes and interests in scientific reasoning, turn out "muddle-headed" (his term, not mine) students who lack the ability to assess information critically.[34] More recently, Robyn Dawes, a nationally recognized research psychologist, trained as a clinician, laments that the quality of training for clinical psychologists "has deteriorated rapidly in the past several years."[35]

The implication, however, goes beyond education and transfer: pragmatically, multibillions of client dollars, tax payer revenues, insurance premiums, and college tuition charges are being poured into programs that are not founded on research-based knowledge, nor once they are implemented are they evaluated to see whether what they are designed to do works. Consequently, we often don't know if they are delivering what they claim to deliver. Ethically, there are clear implications, too: Is it ethical to charge money for something without knowing if it works? So, how does invalid theoretical knowledge find its way into the classroom?

## MARKETPLACE INSTRUCTION: CYCLICAL POETS

The incorrect theories of pop psychology find their way into the classroom in many ways, each of which interferes with transfer. Again, I will only speak about what I know best: the university classroom. One of the primary ways pop psychology finds its way into the classroom is through the increasing trend in higher education to hire part-time faculty instead of shouldering the cost of full-time positions. Many of these part-time faculty are Ptolemaic practitioners who—as I have indicated above—tend to neither engage in, nor to read valid research. Consequently, they bring into their classrooms all manner of erroneous knowledge—knowledge from their "clinical experience," and so-called theoretical knowledge from a myriad of pop psychology books. Pop instruction is not entirely new, of course. During the fifth century in ancient Greece, there were teachers of rhetoric known as Sophists who were famous for their ingenuity in argumentation. The Sophists were itinerant teachers who received fees for their lectures. They were known for their adroit thinking and skills of persuasion, not for the truth value of their reasoning. They would argue any side of an issue, without concern for truth. Hence the modern term *sophistry* refers to a plausible but fallacious argumentation.

There were also what were termed *cyclic poets*, "simple men who would sing the fables to the common people gathered in a circle around them on festive days." One of the great Latin poets, Horace (Quintus Horatius Flaccus, 65–8

B.C.) "speaks of a 'cyclical poet' as a trivial market place poet."[36] It is no mere analogy to suggest that many of those who teach today function as sophists and cyclic poets, pandering to the sentiments of the modern marketplace. If the programs and practicing professionals who teach and supervise our students lack a valid theoretical knowledge base, how can we expect our students to acquire the appropriate theoretical knowledge to engage in productive transfer? It is to this issue of practice that I now turn.

# Notes

[1]Brown, A. L. (1989). Analogical learning and transfer: What develops? In S. Vosniadou & A. Ortony (Eds.), Similarity and analogical reasoning (pp. 369–412). Hillsdale, NJ: Erlbaum, p. 374.

[2]Danish existential philosopher Soren Kierkegaard (1813–1855) wrote about life's anxieties in Fear and Trembling and Sickness unto Death.

[3]Weimer, W. (1974). Overview of a cognitive conspiracy: Reflections on the volume. In W. Weimer & D. S. Palermo (Eds.), Cognition and the symbolic processes (pp. 415–442). Hillsdale, NJ: Erlbaum, p. 433.

[4]Weimer, W. (1975). The psychology of inference and expectation: Some preliminary remarks. IN G. Maxwell & R. M. Andreson, Jr. (Eds.), Minnesota studies in the philosophy of science: Induction, probability, and confirmation (pp. 430–486). Minneapolis, MN: University of Minnesota Press, p. 475.

[5]Bruner, J. S. (1973). Going beyond the information given. In J. Anglin (Ed.), Beyond the information given: Studies in the psychology of knowing (pp. 218–238). New York: W. W. Norton, p. 221.

[6]Glaser, R. (1987). Learning theory and theories of knowledge. In E. De Corte, H. Lodewijks, R. Parmentier, & P. Span (Eds.), Learning and instruction (vol. I, pp. 397–413). Oxford: Pergamon Press, p. 397.

[7]Guberman, S. R., & Greenfield, P. M. (1991). Learning and transfer in everyday cognition. Cognitive Development, 6, 233–260, p. 248.

[8]Brown, A. L. (1989). Analogical learning and transfer: What develops? In S. Vosniadou & A. Ortony (Eds.), Similarity and analogical reasoning (pp. 369–412). Hillsdale, NJ: Erlbaum, p. 370.

[9]Olson, D. R. (1972). On a theory of instruction: Why different forms of instruction result in similar knowledge. Interchange, 3, 11–24, p. 10.

[10]See for example, Piaget, J. (1954). The construction of reality in the child. New York: Basic Books.

[11]Brown, A. L. (1989). Analogical learning and transfer: What develops? In S. Vosniadou & A. Ortony (Eds.), Similarity and analogical reasoning (pp. 369–412). Hillsdale, NJ: Erlbaum, p. 372.

[12]Brown, A. L. (1989). Analogical learning and transfer: What develops? In S. Vosniadou & A. Ortony (Eds.), Similarity and analogical reasoning (pp. 369–412). Hillsdale, NJ: Erlbaum, p. 372.

[13]Ibid.

[14]Hickling, A. K., & Gelman, S. A. (1995). How does your garden grow? Early conceptualization of seeds and their place in plant growth cycle. Child Development, 66(3), 856–876.

[15]See for example, Wollman, W. (1984). Models and procedures: Teaching for transfer of pendulum knowledge. Journal of Research in Science Teaching, 21(4), 399–415; Sutton, C. (1993). Figuring out a scientific understanding. Journal of Research in Science Teaching, 30, 1215–1227.

[16]Tan, C. M. (1992). An evaluation of the use of continuous assessment in the teaching of physiology. Higher Education, 23, 255–272.

[17]Ibid, p. 255.

[18]See Wittrock, M. C. (1985). Learning science by generating new conceptions from old ideas. In L. H. T. West & A. L. Pines (Eds.), Cognitive structure and conceptual change (pp. 259–266). New York: Academic Press.

[19]Brown, A. L. (1989). Analogical learning and transfer: What develops? In S. Vosniadou & A. Ortony (Eds.), Similarity and analogical reasoning (pp. 369–412). Hillsdale, NJ: Erlbaum, p. 404.

[20]In Clark, R. E., & Voogel, A. (1985). Transfer of training principles for instructional design. *Education communication and technology*, 33(2), 113–123, p. 119.

[21]Cited in Gick, M. L. & Holyoak, K. J. (1987). The cognitive basis of knowledge transfer. In S. M. Cormier & J. D. Hagman (Eds.), *Transfer of learning: Contemporary research and application* (pp. 9–45). New York: Academic Press, p. 38.

[22]Winkles, J. (1986). Achievement, understanding, and transfer in a learning hierarchy. *American Educational Research Journal*, 23(2), 275–288, p. 286.

[23]Mittelholtz, D. J. (1988). *The effects of essay tests on long-term retention of course material*. Unpublished doctoral dissertation, Educational Psychology, University of Iowa, Ames.

[24]Brooks, L. W., & Dansereau, D. F. (1987). Transfer of information: An instructional perspective. In S. M. Cormier (Eds.), *Transfer of learning: Contemporary research and applications* (pp. 121–149). New York: Academic Press.

[25]Sagerman, N., & Mayer, R. E. (1987). Forward transfer of different reading strategies evoked by adjunct questions in science text. *Journal of Educational Psychology*, 79, 189–191.

[26]Singley, M. K., & Anderson, J. R. (1989). *The transfer of cognitive skill*. Cambridge, MA: Harvard University Press, p. 138.

[27]Ibid, p. 140.

[28]Cohen, L. H., Sargent, M. M., & Sechrest, L. B. (1986). Use of psychotherapy research by professional psychologists. *American Psychologist*, 41, 198–206; Dawes, R. M. (1994). *House of cards: Psychology and psychotherapy built on myth*. New York: Free Press; DeAngelis, T. (1988). Gerontologists lament practice-research gap. *American Psychological Association Monitor*, 19(2), p. 9; Drew, C. J., Preator, K., & Buchanan, M. L. (1982). Research and researchers in special education. *Exceptional Education Quarterly*, 2(4), 47–56; Morrow-Bradley, C., & Elliot, R. (1986). Utilization of research by practicing psychologists. *American Psychologist*, 41, 197–188; Seligman, M., Rappaport, J., & Gatz, M. (1987). Clinical research: Endangered species? *American Psychological Association Monitor*, 18(12), p. 4.

[29]The United States has a well-known culture of pragmatism. The basic question a pragmatic culture asks of knowledge is, Is it useful? (Of course what is useful is relative—see chapter 6.) The dominant culture has bastardized the concept of pragmatism. The doctrine of pragmatism was originally developed by the American philosophers Charles S. Peirce (1838–1914), and William James (1842–1910), who held that the meaning of an idea or a proposition was in the observable practical consequences to which the idea would lead.

[30]Using quantum theory to support the notion of free will is much too quick and dirty. It assumes only one of the two interpretations of quantum mechanics. The other interpretation is that the indeterminacy of quantum theory is not describing an ontological state of affairs, but simply an inherent methodological shortcoming in measurement. On this interpretation, the theory would say nothing about free will because the indeterminacy is simply an artifact of the method of measurement. Further even if the first interpretation of quantum theory is true, it would not necessarily be an appropriate transfer to the phenomenological concept of free will. Numerous other problems, notwithstanding, the transfer is not a good one.

[31]See for example, Wahba, M. A., & Bridwell, L. G. (1976). Maslow reconsidered: A review of research on the need hierarchy theory. *Organizational Behavior and Human Performance*, 15, 212–240.

[32]See for example, Kalish, R. A. (1985). Dying: Causes, trajectories, and stages. In R. A. Kalish (Ed.), *Death, grief, and caring relationships*. Pacific Grove, CA: Brooks/Cole.

[33]See Ceci, S. J., & Bruck, M. (1993). The suggestibility of the child witness: An historical review and synthesis. *Psychological Bulletin*, 113, 403–439; Dawes, R. M. (1994). *House of cards: Psychology and psychotherapy built on myth*. New York: Free Press; Loftus, E. F. (1993). The reality of repressed memories. *American Psychologist*, 48, 518–535; Mednick, M. T. (1989). On the politics of psychological constructs: Stop the bandwagon, I want to get off. *American Psychologist*, 44, 1118–1123; Scarr, S. (1985). Constructing psychology: Making facts and fables for our times. *American Psychologist*, 40(5), 499–512; Schacht, T. E. (1985). DSM-III and the politics of truth.

*American Psychologist*, 40(5), 513–521; Victor, J. S. (1993). *Satanic panic: The creation of a contemporary legend*. Chicago, IL: Open Court Press; Wakefield, H., & Underwager, R. (1994). *Return of the Furies: An investigation into recovered memory therapy*. Chicago, IL: Open Court Press.

[34]Robert, A. H. (1985). Biofeedback: Research, training, and clinical roles. *American Psychologist*, 40, 938–941.

[35]Dawes, R. M. (1994). *House of cards: Psychology and psychotherapy built on myth*. New York: Free Press.

[36]Vico, G. (1948). *The new science*. (T. G. Bergin & M. H. Fisch, Trans). Ithaca, NY: Cornell University Press, p. 265.

# The Two Faces of Practice: Transfer and That Old-Time Lesson Drill

*Although we have a reasonable bias for hope that we may find ways to make learning processes more efficient, we should not expect to produce the miracle of effortless learning.*

—LARKIN, MCDERMOTT, SIMON, AND SIMON, *Expert and Novice Performance in Solving Physics Problems*[1]

Like the last chapter, I approach this chapter, too, with some trepidation. If eyes begin to glaze over when "theory" is mentioned, disgusted moaning can typically be heard whenever drill and repetitive practice are mentioned in discussions about education. Nevertheless, practice is just what the transfer research suggests is required to promote transfer. And lots of it. The term practice has two basic meanings. The first is to do or perform something repeatedly in order to acquire or polish a skill; the second is to work at something as in a profession or vocation. I will be addressing both of these meanings in this chapter.

Practice makes perfect, right? Well, sometimes—if done appropriately. For some time now the value of repetition and rote mastery of material has not been considered progressive in educational theory and practice. One of the reasons for the devaluing of practice and repetition was the cultural shift that occurred during the 1960s and 1970s. Since that time, the trend has been to allow the learner individual freedom to express his or her creativity and to instruct students in short-cut learning skills and thinking strategies. This trend to allow the learner near complete freedom was a reaction to "old-time" schooling methods of rote memorization and mindlessly drilling students in their lessons of readin', writin' and 'rithemetic—which, although not perfect, had its usefulness as I will show. It was also a consequence of an escalating cultural value of demanding instant and effortless results. We live in a culture where expectations of instant gratification prevail.

Although giving free reign to learning may feel good, it's most often not an effective approach to instruction—at least not without considerable practice and drill attached to it. We can now see the consequence of this ostensibly progressive approach on the college level. At least half the students can't read, write, or spell adequately and have to be enrolled in remedial courses. In addition, many can't or don't think well and are not the least bit creative. If history is thought to be the day before yesterday, practice is thought to be constituted by repeating an activity a couple of times. This is not welcomed news, I know. But the evidence is in, not only from recent research but from evidence that has been around for quite some time.

We only have to read the life stories of famous artists, athletes, and others who have great expertise to see that practice and drill was central to their success. They didn't become great Olympians or artists by sheer force of creativity, at least for the overwhelming majority of them. In recalling the education and upbringing in his famous artist family, Nat Wyeth (brother of Andrew) the engineer and inventor, relates the emphasis on preparation, knowledge base, and repetitive drill that he and his siblings received. His father, N. C. Wyeth, told him, "Before you can do a really good job at anything, you've got to be well trained in the basics."[2] Knowledge and practice bring understanding. If something is drawn with a sense of understanding, says Nat, you can feel it. His artist brother, Andrew, was taught by his father.

According to Nat, his father told young Andrew "what you do on your own time is alright with me. But when you're working for me as a student, you're first going to learn how to draw. You're going to learn the basics of drawing things as they are." For years, his father made the young Andrew practice drawing very simple objects—cubes, spheres, pyramids—over and over again. This repetition drove the sensitive Andrew almost crazy. But that kind of training clearly shows in Andrew's paintings, in his beautiful sense of proportion and accuracy, says Nat. Of his brother, Nat says that as a result of the early attention to practice, Andrew "has an eye like an eagle. His pencil sketches of a rope or the limb of a tree are simply phenomenal. It didn't just come by saying he wanted to do it. He had to work at it." To "work at it" means repetitive practice and drill.

Benjamin Franklin, the American statesman and inventor, described in his autobiography how he learned to write in a clear and logical style. He said he would repeatedly read through a passage in a well-written book to understand it rather than memorizing it, and then he practiced reproducing its structure and content. He would then *compare* his writing with the original and identify the differences. By repeating this practice cycle of reading, reproducing, and *comparing* his writing with the well-structured original, Franklin maintained that he acquired his skill in organizing his thoughts.

## WHAT DO WE MEAN BY PRACTICE?

Practitioners and researchers are realizing that the failure to find transfer is often "because of conditions that prevail during the original learning."[3] The knowledge base that's required—and eventually transferred to the target problem—is often of poor quality. As Mark Singley and John Anderson point out, "Multiple trials are essential because many studies have probably underestimated transfer by failing to ensure that something was learned in the first place."[4] In other words, much of the failure to find transfer in the classroom and elsewhere is because the original material was not sufficiently practiced and thus mastered. It's often as simple as that. It has in fact been known for quite some time that there is no other learning variable that influences learning as much as the degree of mastery of the original material. We might think that the requirement of mastering material would be simple common sense. Apparently it's not.

As Henry Ellis the early transfer researcher concluded, "If it is assumed that transfer is a function of the amount learned, then more trials should be given in the early problems in order to maximize transfer."[5] More recently, in analyzing the elements of learning, Laura Resnick concludes that they "require sustained long term cultivation and do not emerge from short term quick-fix interventions."[6] Nathaniel Gage and David Berliner, two of the most respected educational psychologists and authors of perhaps the most widely used text book in educational psychology stress: "Provide lots of practice on the original task before you ask students to transfer their learning. . . . Experts get to be experts only after much experience."[7] But all practice is not created equal. Controversy has always surrounded the concept.

As early as the 1950s, renowned psychologist Jerome Bruner noted that "we are in the midst of a controversial area," for the wisdom of common sense and of most psychologists is divided sharply on the matter of practice and skill. Bruner says,

> 'Practice makes perfect' is a well-thumbed proverb and the darling of practically all S-R [stimulus–response] learning theory. To be sure, it is a moot point in these theories just what it is that practice makes one perfect at. Nobody denies that it enables one to be automatic at the thing being practiced, but there is still debate on whether it also improves one at things beyond what one has practiced.[8]

And therein lies the rub. What do we mean by practice, and under what conditions should a high level of practice be practiced, and is there some learning that does not require a great deal of practice? I'll address these issues below.

With exceptions that I'll address later, practice remains a general rule for learning and transfer. And, again, lots of it. John Anderson's extensive cognitive work on skill acquisition clearly shows the importance of practice. It requires, he says, at least 100 hours of learning and practice to acquire any significant cognitive skill to a reasonable degree of proficiency. For instance, after 100 hours a student learning to program a computer has achieved only a very modest facility in the skill. It has been well known for some years that skillful chess players have become skillful not merely because they are innately endowed, but because they have spent thousands of hours playing chess.[9]

How many learners do this? How many educational environments demand it? With the exception of areas requiring motor skills like sports or learning a musical instrument, the answer is: virtually none. For some reason we don't expect drill and practice for mental expertise. We should. Indeed, we must.

An interesting study of successful composers and painters of fine art, by John Hayes, reveals that very few composers and fine artists produced masterworks with less than 10 years of reflective experience. Hayes found that what composers need in order to write excellent musical scores "is not maturing but rather musical preparation. The results make it dramatically clear that no one composes outstanding music without first having about 10 years of intensive musical preparation." In short, 10 years of reflective practice. In analyzing how expertise is acquired, Hayes and others conclude that

the most obvious answer is practice, thousands of hours of practice. . . . There may be some as yet undiscovered basic abilities that underlie the attainment of truly exceptional performance . . . but for the most part practice and ability level are by far the best predictor of performance."[10]

Other studies have found similar results.[11]

All too often we think that great expertise in an area is largely due to innate talent. There is no shortage of anecdotal biographical accounts that seem to confirm this belief. The evidence, however, is to the contrary. Expertise is largely due to practice, practice, and then more practice. K. Anders Ericsson and Neil Charness, in what is considered a seminal research-based paper entitled, "Expert Performance: Its Structure and Acquisition,"[12] found that comprehensive reviews comparing the beginning ages and the amount of practice for international, national, and regional-level performers in many different areas, those who attained higher levels of performance tended to start practicing from 2 to 5 years earlier than did the less accomplished performers. Moreover, those who attained higher levels of performance spent more time on deliberate practice than did the less accomplished individuals—in fact they spent many more hours on practice. This was true even when there was no difference in the total amount of time both groups spent on other activities.

Some of the problems of achieving transfer in school and laboratory conditions show the importance of practice for adequately encoding information and knowledge. Carl Bereiter correctly notes that in the training phase of the majority of experiments on transfer, the learning mode and the time allotted (read: practice and encoding) is very brief, allowing little opportunity for the development of any true understanding that would mediate transfer. Still another is that transfer must be demonstrated by the participant in a specific way and at the whim of the experimenter: transfer now, or forever be seen as a nontransferrer.[13]

Similarly, others have lamented that often experimental findings are "generated during rather shallow understanding and problemsolving tasks."[14] Whether in the laboratory, in the classroom, or in natural settings, without sufficient practice enabling the adequate encoding of learning, transfer fails.

There is a direct and continuous correlation between the number of hours spent on practice and degree of expertise. For example, it has been found that by age 20, top-level violinists have practiced an average of 10,000 hours. Think about this statistic: it means that by age 20, these violinists have practiced the equivalent of nearly 40 full hours a week of practice for nearly five years, or for nearly one-quarter of their entire lifetime. By contrast, the next most accomplished violinists had practiced an average of 7,500 hours. The top-level violinists have practiced 5,000 more hours than the lowest level of expertise. These kinds of findings have implications for areas other than instruction; they have implications for student expectations as well. Findings such as these prompted John Hayes to suggest that since the mastery of a field requires many years, it's "an important item of metacognitive knowledge that we ought to teach to our students. Some students may be inappropriately discouraged by early setbacks because they believe that failure indicates lack of talent rather than lack of knowledge, and practice."[15]

New studies of the brain using magnetic resonance imaging (MRI)—a method that measures the amount of blood oxygen in various areas of the brain—have found that practiced, repetitive motor sequences can trigger changes in the areas of the brain that receive sensory information and control motor function. At the Laboratory of Neuropsychology at the National Institute of Mental Health and the National Institutes of Health, Avi Karni and colleagues measured brain activity once a week for 5 weeks in the primary motor cortex of six men performing two different but quite similar finger-tapping sequences at a set pace.[16] Each subject practiced one of the sequences 10 to 20 minutes a day but only performed the other sequence during testing sessions. Throughout these sessions, the researchers measured brain activity using MRI. After 5 weeks, it was found that tapping the practiced sequence activated a larger portion of the motor cortex than did tapping the other sequence. The changes endured a year later, with no practice in the intervening time, as did superior performance on the practiced sequence. It is interesting to note that *such performances don't transfer to learning other, similar sequences but only to the sequence that has been practiced.* The researchers think the brain sets up larger-than-normal *expert* circuits to handle specifically practiced sequences of movements.

In another study, Thomas Elbert and colleagues examined the brains of stringed-instrument players.[17] String players use their left-hand fingers much more than their right-hand fingers—and much more than the average person. Six violinists, two cellists, and a guitarist were subjects as well as six nonmusician control subjects. Using MRI, the researchers measured brain activity in their subjects' somatosensory cortex while applying a light touch to their fingers. They found that touching the string-player subjects' left fingers activated a larger area of the cortex than it did for the nonmusicians.

The effect was greatest for subjects who started playing a stringed instrument before 13 years of age, but the response was also quite significant for those who started later in life. People who start playing violin later in life can capture some extra space for their fingers, but not the same amount available to young people, he explained. There is every reason to assume that these findings regarding the practice of motor skills equally applies to learning in general.

In all types of learning situations, informal instructional situations, on-the-job instruction, as well as in classroom training situations in business, long-term practice is paramount! As the well-known educational practitioner and researcher, Wilbert McKeachie, has perhaps too bluntly put it, "There does not seem to be much support for the relatively short-term programs widely promoted for gullible business managers."[18] Certainly business managers have considerable time pressures and thus find promises of quick fixes irresistible. The fact is, there are no quick remedies for either simple learning or for productive transfer. We must get beyond the constant educational fads that have characterized the entire history of education.

Herbert Simon and associates conclude thusly:

> We have no reason to suppose, however, that one day people will be able to become painlessly and instantly expert. The extent of the knowledge an expert must be able to call upon is demonstrably large, and everything we know today about human learning processes suggest that even at their most efficient, those processes must be long exercised. Although we have a reasonable bias for hope that we may find ways to make learning processes more efficient, we should not expect to produce the miracle of effortless learning.[19]

So what is to be understood by the terms practice and drill?

## GOOD PRACTICE VERSUS BAD PRACTICE: WHAT THEY DO

I opened this chapter by saying, practice makes perfect, right? Wrong. Practice doesn't necessarily make perfect. Practice makes perfect only if done appropriately. The question is, then, what does appropriate practice mean? The short answer is: *reflective* practice, not the mindless rote drill that was often standard in the days of the one-room schoolhouse. The longer answer is more complex. For example, the nature of practice cannot be merely defined in terms of repetition. The purpose for which the repetitive practice takes place must be specified. Is it the job of rote drill to render the activity automatic, or is it the job of practice to create refinement of learning?

There are two basic approaches to processing information. First is controlled processing which is conscious, relatively deliberate, slow, and limited in terms of short-term memory capacity. Controlled processing is typically best for novel situations or in situations in which stimulus–response relations are inconsistent or changing. Far transfer is usually attained with this kind of processing. The second approach involves automatic processing that develops as a consequence of repetition. Automatic processing is performed on a nonconscious level, like driving a car; it is fast, inflexible, difficult to suppress, and relatively unlimited in terms of memory capacity. With repetitive practice, activities that once required active control become automatic, thus freeing the learner's limited attentional capacity for other tasks. Sheer repetition is typically better for situations in which consistent stimulus–response relations remain the same (e.g., typing). At best, near transfer is usually attained with this kind of processing.

Optimizing automatic processing requires a special kind of practice called reflective or deliberate practice. For example, playing golf every chance we get doesn't mean we are acquiring appropriate practice. Experience and surveys show that in popular everyday activities like playing golf and tennis, most people don't spend much time on reflective or deliberate practice. Once people attain a "good-enough" level of performance, their primary goal shifts to the inherent enjoyment of the activity, or to win, so most of their repeated performances are simply playful interactions. During such repetitions, even those who want to improve their game seldom encounter the same or similar situations needed to improve their game on a repeated and predictable basis. Tennis players, for example, who want to eliminate a weakness in their game like a poor backhand maneuver, may encounter a relevant situation only once during a game. By contrast, a tennis coach would give the person many deliberate opportunities to practice and improve their backhand performance. Similarly, in work situations where actions are repeated, the goal is typically to produce a product or to compete. In work situations, people tend to rely on previously well-established routines rather than exploring new methods with unknown results.

All in all, though, most people automatically and intuitively accept that for acquiring proficiency in motor skill activities like sports, practice, practice and more practice is a given. But for some reason we don't seem to accept that what is required for physical or motor skills or routines is equally required for achieving proficiency in most mental functions. This is true even for learning strategies. In discussing the teaching of problem-solving strategies, Wilbert McKeachie advises,

> To keep students from becoming lost in thought and overloading their cognitive capacity, they need to have lots of practice so that strategies are organized and auto-

mated. It is not enough to know that a strategy would be effective; the student must have a sense of competence in the skills involved.[20]

Simple repeated play, work, and learning performances are not adequate practice situations. Overlearning a task is frequently necessary. In overlearning, learners are presented with many extra practice opportunities after they have already demonstrated mastery. Overlearning a task is particularly important when the task is not likely to be engaged in often, or when it is necessary to maintain a given performance level during times when there may be few practice opportunities.

Deliberate or reflective practice does much more than make perfect. By automating an activity it frees up short-term memory and other mental resources for us to work with (e.g., talking to a friend or thinking about other things while we are driving down the highway). When lower-order components of an activity are so well learned that they can be carried out automatically, there is an increased capacity for higher-order task analysis, planning, and monitoring functions. Without automating, there may be insufficient processing capacity available for higher order skills. Learners become overloaded with processing demands, which results in poor performance. Not all tasks should be practiced to such a level, however. As Earl Butterfield and Gregory Nelson, two well-known researchers, point out,

> The educational implication of automatization is that drill should be reserved for skills for which little stimulus–response change is expected. For example, we should continue to drill spelling, grammatical rules, and arithmetic facts, because they rarely change. By automatizing such skills we enable more complex performances which depend on them. For example, writers for whom spelling, punctuation, and selecting verb forms have become automatized have more attention and memory capacity for their rhetorical goals and making their meaning clear.[21]

There are many other advantages to making certain tasks automatic.

Over 40 years ago, Jerome Bruner noted "We may take as a tentative conclusion that overtraining and mastery aids generic coding."[22] By *generic coding*, Bruner was referring to what are now called mental "schemas" as well as other abstract mental structures that lead to transfer. Current research has demonstrated, for example, that as people come in contact with problems or practice problem solving, a kind of grammar or abstract structure of the knowledge domain is stored in memory. In such a grammar or abstract schema transfer "slots" are created into which corresponding or similar information can be inserted. A useful analogy of abstract grammars or schemas is that of mathematics. For example, $1 + 1 = 2$ is an abstract structure into which apples, peaches, pears, or Buicks can be inserted.

Further benefits are derived from deliberate practice. Ericsson and Charness point out that practice to automatic levels can decrease the time it takes to respond to a stimulus. The consequences of practicing to an automatic level (along with the appropriate memory processes) often allows us to exceed the physical limits of our reaction time by a kind of inferential prediction or extrapolation. They note that the analysis of a perceived situation and its automatically evoked response is central to understanding skilled performance, but it is not sufficient to account for the speed of that response in many kinds of expert performances:

> The time it takes to respond to a stimulus even after extensive training is often between 0.5 and 1.0 seconds, which is too slow to account for a return of a hard tennis serve, a goalie's catching a hockey puck, and fluent motor activities in typing and music. . . . For example, elite athletes are able to react much faster and make better perceptual discriminations to representative situations in their respective domains, but their simple reaction times and perceptual acuity to simple stimuli during laboratory tests do not differ systematically from those of other athletes or control subjects.[23]

From the practice-makes-perfect perspective, deliberate practice can actually conjugate into more than a present-perfect activity, as it were, but into projected future-perfect activity as well.

No amount of practice, deliberate or otherwise, is perfect for all situations, however. Practice to an automatic level often results in negative transfer if the stimulus–response situation is different from the practice situation. Practice to automatic levels may also short-circuit the initiation of more conscious or controlled processes. It may also weld the learning to the concrete situation in which it was learned. Extensive practice to automatic levels tends to create what is called routine expertise, which is based on procedural or how-to knowledge—not adaptive expertise, which tends to be based on conscious or controlled processing of information.

Another type of practice not often recognized is mental practice. It is sometimes called mental rehearsal. This type of practice is not to be underestimated. Sports psychology has been utilizing what is called imagery conditioning for years. Imagery conditioning or mental practice involves repeatedly and systematically imagining or visualizing performances in your mind's eye. In our computer age, we might call it virtual practice (to transfer the concept of virtual reality from the artificial intelligence field). For example, professional golfers will carefully imagine themselves on the golf course going through all of the movements they want to practice. Virtual practice has proven quite successful in many sports programs. Conditioning oneself with mental imagery is not a "New Age" method. The study of imagery in psychological research has a long and reasonably successful history.[24] Mental practice has been a research interest of physical education for some time now with both positive and negative conclusions. Current research has demonstrated most of us typically employ imagery in our mind's eye when thinking about an activity.

As with many areas of learning and instruction, we have limited knowledge about many variables affecting practice. We have known for some time, for example, in some situations, massed practice is best and at other times spaced practice is best. We also know that feedback generally facilitates practice. But we don't know all we should. In fact, a little knowledge about practice or how to facilitate transfer is often counterproductive and counterintuitive. Richard Schmidt and Robert Bjork explain that they

> have repeatedly encountered research findings that seem to violate some basic assumptions about how to optimize learning in real-world settings. For example, increasing the frequency of information presented to learners about performance errors during practice improves performance during training, yet can degrade performance on a test of long-term retention or *transfer* [italics added]. Increasing the amount of task variability required during practice, in contrast, depresses performance during training, yet facilitates performance on later tests of the ability to *generalize* [italics added] training to altered conditions.[25]

Findings such as these challenge common views of practice and skill learning. More precise questions remain unanswered about when factors that enhance learning performance in the practice situation actually interfere with retention or transfer performance.

In sum, the question of mastery comes down to this, according to Bruner:

> Learning often cannot be translated into a generic form until there has been enough mastery of the specifics of the situation to permit the discovery of lower-order regularities which can then be recombined into higher-order, more generic coding systems.[26]

By mastery of specifics, Bruner is talking about both knowledge base and repetitive practice. Yet a final caveat: not only does unreflective practice not make perfect, but it appears that some people learn formal rules and acquire mental schemas and transfer-ability without a great deal of repeated practice, often with one example being sufficient. Now, in order to practice our learning, or more precisely, to transfer what is learned, a practice environment is beneficial.

## PTOLEMAIC PRACTICE AND PRACTICA

The second meaning of the term *practice* is to work at something as in a profession or vocation. There is a continuing and increasing trend of vocational majors in higher education, where students major in vocational programs that purport to prepare them for a specific profession. Many of these vocational programs were historically housed in vocational technical institutes or trade schools. As the consequence of political and social forces, they then moved to community colleges and finally to university campuses. The U.S. population wants children to be educated. The issue is, however, what is meant by education. For the vast majority of the population education means preparation for a job. So far so good, depending, of course, on what is meant by preparation for a job.

College and university campuses have increasingly instituted these vocational majors. As a part of those majors, there is a growing number of what are called practica or internship courses being offered. These are credit courses that provide students with what is called "real-world" experiences in work settings where "real" professionals *practice* their trade, and where students can practice their incipient skills. The implications for promoting transfer in these vocational practica and internships, though potentially profound, remain problematic in practice.

Unlike some of my colleagues, I am not against vocational or professional majors on college and university campuses (though I confess that at one time I was), at least not on intellectual grounds. To be against such majors is to engage in the most blatant kind of intellectual snobbism. In principle—and I stress, in principle—just about any vocational major can be made as intellectually rigorous as any traditional major like English, history, math, engineering, and so on. In principle, there is no reason why plumbing or auto mechanics are not valid majors in higher education (in fact we already have similar majors in higher education, e.g., hotel and restaurant management). Certainly, anyone who has had their houses plumbed or autos repaired would agree that something seems to be wrong with the *training* in these vocations. The physics, chemistry, and mathematics inherent in these vocations are at least at the level of most other traditional majors, and of a higher level than some. A vocational training orientation can be applied to any major. It is not the subject matter that makes a vocational major, but the pedagogical approach to it. A deep and serious approach to just about any subject area— vocational or otherwise—leads to seeing relationships with most all other areas, Plato included. There is no contradiction between vocational education and learning how to think well.

Stephen Norris insightfully points out that

> training thinking skills is not dissimilar from teaching diagnostic skills to a trainee physician. The skill involved is being able to "read" specific content as clues to an underlying process that is not directly observable but which holds the key to making correct inferences.[27]

Moreover, vocational practica experiences—at least ideally—are made to order for promoting transfer. Typically, however, they don't.

Again, Norris insightfully recognized that with both critical thinking and diagnosing

> the problem of transfer is that the same underlying principle may manifest itself in a bewildering array of symptoms. Skill will generalize only with adequate exposure to this range of symptoms; no amount of practice with the principles themselves will do the job.[28]

The problem is, many—if not most vocational majors—are not as rigorous as the more traditional majors. This has serious implications for transfer.

Unfortunately, most of these vocational programs *train* students instead of *educating* them. They teach simple cookbook skills—and as we have seen, such concrete training programs are not conducive to transfer. I will illustrate this section on practice both from my personal experience and from psychological research, the two areas that I know best and in which I have most knowledge base. It is important to note for purposes of transfer that although I present evidence from psychology, similar professions, such as clinical social work, psychodynamic psychiatry, and other clinical allied health professions, such as occupational therapy and the practice of general medicine, exhibit the same problems of transfer. I teach many of these students and have supervised practica, so I have considerable familiarity with vocational programs and their students, with how practica experiences work, and with what they do and don't do for the student.

Most of these vocational students (but not only vocational students) come into my abnormal psychology class and simply want the "facts" and a cookbook for recognizing schizophrenia or bipolar disorder (a form of depression), and a comparable receipt for methods of therapy. Now one could say that these are just undergraduate students who do not yet know any better. But the attitude of just wanting the "practical" facts is held not just by undergraduates but by the general public. Moreover, this professional practice attitude of just wanting "useful" facts is widespread in graduate professional schools as well. I have had occasion to deliver lectures to medical students. My colleagues in those settings complain about the same practitioner-oriented student attitudes as I do. For example, a typical required course for medical students is psychopharmacology. Psychopharmacology is the study of the actions and effects of psychoactive drugs and the action produced in organisms by chemical substances that are used to treat and diagnose disease, such as the biochemical mechanisms of drug action including drug-induced side effects. Psychopharmacology is a difficult course requiring knowledge of biology, chemistry, and physiology—clearly a necessary course for future physicians who will be prescribing drugs to patients. But many medical students do not want this course in the curriculum; what they want is a course in pharmacy. Relatively speaking pharmacy, is a "how-to" course on dispensing drugs. Now, I don't know about you, but I don't want a physician prescribing drugs who has not had a course in pharmacology, or a psychiatrist prescribing psychoactive drugs who has not had a course in psychopharmacology.

Now, as I pointed out in the last chapter, Ptolemy's model of the solar system was based on practical everyday empirical data and personal experience acquired in a "real-world" setting. In the everyday world, we still experience the "proof" of Ptolemy's model: We personally observe the sun revolving around the earth, first visible in the east, traveling across the sky above us, and disappearing in the west. Though it doesn't need to be, much of the everyday world of professional experience is Ptolemaic. Now, where would atomic or quantum physics be if they simply depended on everyday experience? One of the most difficult concepts to explain to students—and to many practicing professionals—is the profound limitations of personal experience and knowledge gained from practical settings. I should also point out that the validity of vocational practicum courses may vary, as some subject matters lend themselves more to gaining knowledge in everyday situations. Physical science and engineering practica, for example, may provide more valid knowledge than those in the social, behavioral, and allied health sciences. Typically, the physical and natural sciences operate under more "real" concrete restraints than do the social, behavioral, and allied health sciences. Whatever the case, the generalization regarding practice situations still holds.

A host of very basic scientific problems and forms of reasoning are responsible for this situation. I will only mention a few. The first problem is the nature of the everyday sample of subjects that practitioners typically work with. Such samples are not representative of the total population of people with the problem. It is a highly select sample. Thus whatever characteristics are found in that sample cannot be *transferred* beyond that sample. Nor can such findings be used to develop valid theory. Yet this kind of evidence and reasoning is done routinely. For example, take the current psychological assessment of depression. A number of people with symptoms of depression are seen in individual therapy, group therapy, or in a general clinic setting. If it's found that 80% of the depressed patients come from what are called dysfunctional families, it is concluded that growing up in a dysfunctional family caused the depression. This is exactly the kind of evidence and reasoning on which so many recent books, talk shows, and magazine articles on adult children of alcoholics, codependency, and other popular syndromes are based. The simple facts are simply otherwise.

In order to make this claim about dysfunctional family life "causing" depression, it's necessary to carry out studies in (a) the general population and (b) the population of depressed people. When such studies are carried out, we find that (a) there are many people in the general population who are not depressed but who grew up in dysfunctional families, and (b) that there are many others who are depressed who did not grow up in dysfunctional families. Therefore, coming from a dysfunctional family has no clear relationship to causing depression. Simple? Yes. Yet it's seldom adhere to in practice. Worse yet, such reasoning is passed on to practica students. I see the effects of this in my classes. The cult of personal and professional experience is pervasive.

For the most part, all we know about clinical subjects is what they are like when admitted into therapy. For example, we know from research with depressed people that they often recall their parents as being generally much more rejecting than are parents recalled by nondepressed people. As it turns out, however, such recall is specific to the time in which the depressed people are in fact depressed. Before they become depressed or after their depression is lifted, their recall of their parents' rejecting behavior tends to be no different from the recall of the subjects who have never been depressed. As most every first-year text in psychology points out, to generalize (to transfer) from a clinical sample (or any other selected experience) is inappropriate.

A further illustration of reasoning with clinical data is provided by Robyn Dawes.[29] Most sadly, he says, before Down's syndrome (which used to be known as "mongolism") was discovered to be due to the presence of a third 21st chromosome, it was noted that women with Down's syndrome children reported having had a high incidence of psychological "shocks" during early pregnancy; the practitioner who collected such reports concluded that the Down's syndrome might be caused by stress in pregnancy.

Imagine a student of space sciences on a practicum learning from a practicing NASA supervisor that based on his or her everyday experience, the sun revolves around the earth. Sound preposterous? Perhaps. But this is essentially occurring in many professional programs of study and their practica. Again, I should point out that the problem lies not with the data gathered under practical conditions, but with the minds and methods used to analyze it. I would also like to make it clear that despite the serious transfer problems with knowledge acquired in clinical/practitioner situations, they can be productive situations for generating hypotheses. Unfortunately, these hypotheses tend to be immediately transformed into "theory," or worse yet, "fact."

## TRANSFER IMPLICATIONS FOR PROFESSIONAL PRACTICA AND SUPERVISION

Popular and professional wisdom holds that providing students with the opportunity to practice their learning in a "real-world" work setting gives them the "practical" opportunity to transfer their learning. In terms of current practices, there is very little evidence that this is the case. For example, June Fotheringhame, in a study of field training published in the *Journal of Occupational Psychology*, concludes as follows:

> An even more diffuse educational notion, a received wisdom rather than a tested fact, is that practical methods rather than non-practical are more likely to promote transfer. This study has, again, equivocal findings here that suggest that actual practice is not salient over non-practical teaching in the transfer-effectiveness of a method of training.[30]

In fact, most evidence suggests—at least in a wide range of practice settings—that the so-called real world of practice is in fact the unreal world where students often learn the equivalent of the Ptolemaic model of the solar system.

Dawes's excellent research-based book documents the widespread and serious problems with clinical (read: practitioner) type training programs, so I won't detail his findings. As hard as it may be for the general public to believe, the facts are these: there is precious little evidence to suggest that "clinical" and other mental health practitioners are very competent at diagnosing, treating, and teaching effective clinical skills. This discouraging news is not new, however. In the early 1980s, what was then the premier professional association in psychology, the American Psychological Association, formed a task force on the evaluation of education, training, and service in psychology. The report of this task force concluded that *there is no evidence that professional training and experience are related to professional competence.* This is straight from the horse's mouth, as it were. Both before and since this report, others have reviewed and conducted research and repeatedly and consistently concluded similarly, or only slightly more optimistically.[31] Clinical judgment, training, and experience have consistently been found to be not strongly related to psychotherapy outcome, and professional diagnosis has been found to be not much better than those of graduate students in other fields—or of diagnoses done by secretaries.

In addition, the prediction of behavior by professionals has been found to be inferior to those based on simple actuarial tables. Moreover, practicing clinicians tend to maintain that having close face-to-face contact and one-on-one interview information from patients allows them to make better predictions and diagnoses. The evidence does not support this claim. In fact, the more information clinicians have, the worse their predictions and diagnoses tend to be. This is as true for most of the so-called hard diagnoses like neurological disorders as it is for the more softer psychological ones.[32] Why is this the case? The answer is clear: it is a direct consequence of the Ptolemaic nature of evidence gathered in everyday and clinical settings, evidence that gets taught to students in practica and internship courses by those who supervise and teach them. Accordingly, the limited database provided by professional practice situations creates Ptolemaic theories that professionals then attempt to put into practice and unfortunately pass on to students. This need not—indeed, should not—be the case, especially for professional programs that are offered from a college or university campus. College and university vocational programs, unlike similar programs offered at vocational schools, should be based on ongoing *applied* research just like any other major. Unfortunately, many programs are not based on rigorous research.

In order for us to learn and transfer appropriately from our experience—everyday, or clinical—we must receive valid feedback to correct distortions in the information (data) we receive. The problem with everyday nonresearch-based professional practice situations is that practitioners do not receive the feedback they need in order to validly assess the data they receive from their experience. Such feedback is important for people to learn anything from experience, whether it's learning a concept, how to deal effectively with people, or a motor skill. As Robyn Dawes points out,

> Even in learning to drive a car or sit in a chair, feedback must be immediate, systematic, and subject to a minimum of probabilistic distortion. But the feedback most professional clinicians receive about their judgments and decisions is neither immediate nor systematic . . . [and] learning can occur in the absence of feedback about actual negative instances only when it is based on a well-corroborated theory to make the transition from theory to fact (that is, when the expert has access to a specific model).[33]

Such models simply do not exist in the many areas in which practitioners most often make confident judgments. Consequently, supervisors often lack insight into their own judgment policies, and their descriptions about how they reach conclusions tend to mislead students. What students often are taught in such practica then, is not about the "real world" at all, but quite the opposite. Ptolemy is teaching interstellar navigation.

Finally, as indicated in the last chapter, sound practice depends on a good theoretical knowledge base. As indicated at the opening of this chapter, for adequate learning to occur, let alone transfer, students must practice, practice, practice. It will come as no surprise to teachers of any subject what Tan found in her research with science students: Most students, he says, skim "through the textbook without thinking about or trying to understand the material in any way. . . . Active processing was clearly not a matter of course for many students."[34] Tan further reminds us that "students who have not acquired 'the skills of learning' during their preclinical training and who have poor conceptual development will not, therefore, be capable of effectively integrating their physiological knowledge with their clinical experiences."[35] Appropriately then, I conclude this chapter with Tan's words:

> In the absence of high-level conceptual development students cannot apply theory to practice. It is argued that the early introduction of clinical experiences (in year-2) cannot promote effective integration between theory and practice and the development of an holistic attitude and heuristic thinking, when students lack prerequisite basic reasoning skills and do not know how to learn meaningfully.[36]

In short, transfer will not occur.

## CONCLUSION

These closing comments address not only what has been outlined in this chapter but for the last few chapters as well. Based on my reading of the transfer research and from my years of teaching experience, I have come to believe this: Unless schools create cultures of transfer, teach about transfer, and instill a spirit of transfer, requiring a well-learned knowledge base, and practice and drill of some systematic sort, teachers can adopt any instructional method they like in the classroom but, with few exceptions, neither significant learning nor significant transfer will take place.

### Notes

[1]Larkin, J., McDermott, J., Simon, D. P., & Simon, J. A. (1980). Expert and novice performance in solving physics problems. *Science*, 208, p. 1342.

[2]Brown, K. (1988). *Inventors at work: Interviews with sixteen notable American inventors*. Redmond, WA: Microsoft Press, p. 373.

[3]In Ericcson, K. A., & Charness, N. (1994). Expert performance. Its structure and acquisition. *American Psychologist*, 49(8), 725–747.

[4]Singley, M. K., & Anderson, J. R. (1989). *The transfer of cognitive skill*. Cambridge, MA: Harvard University Press, p. 35.

[5]Ellis, H. C. (1965). *The transfer of learning*. New York: MacMillan Company, p. 80.

[6]Resnick, L. B. (1987). Instruction and the cultivation of thinking. In E. De Corte, H. Lodewijks, R. Parmentier, & P. Span (Eds.), *Learning and instruction* (vol. I, pp. 415–441). Oxford: Pergamon Press, p. 433.

[7]Gage, N. L., & Berliner, D. C. (1992). *Educational psychology* (5th ed.). Boston, MA: Houghton Mifflin, pp. 332–324.

[8]Bruner, J. S. (1973). Going beyond the information given. In J. Anglin (Ed.), *Beyond the information given: Studies in the psychology of knowing* (pp. 218–238). New York: W. W. Norton, p. 230.

[9]Anderson, J. R. (1982). Acquisition of cognitive skills. *Psychological Review*, 89(4), 369–406, p. 369.

[10]Hayes, J. R. (1985). Three problems in teaching general skills. In S. F. Chipman, J. W. Segal, & R. Glaser (Eds.), *Thinking and learning skills: Vol. 2: Research and open questions* (pp. 391–406). Hillsdale, NJ: Lawrence Erlbaum Associates, p. 397.

[11]Frederiksen, N. (1984). Implications of cognitive theory for instruction in problem solving. *Review of Educational Research*, 54, 363–407, p. 370.

[12]Ericcson, K. A., & Charness, N. (1994). Expert performance: Its structure and acquisition. *American Psychologist*, 49(8), 725–747.

[13]Bereiter, C. (1995). A dispositional review of transfer. In A. McKeough, J. Lupart, & A. Marini (Eds.), *Teaching for transfer: Fostering generalization in learning* (pp. 21–34). Mahwah, NJ: Lawrence Erlbaum Associates, p. 38–39.

[14]Hammond, K. J., Seifert, C. M., & Gray, K. C. (1991). Functionality in analogical transfer: A hard match is good to find. *The Journal of the Learning Sciences*, 1(2), 111–152, p. 114.

[15]Hayes, J. R. (1985). Three problems in teaching general skills. In S. F. Chipman, J. W. Segal, & R. Glaser (Eds.), *Thinking and Learning Skills, Vol. 2: Research and Open Questions* (pp. 391–406). Hillsdale, NJ: Lawrence Erlbaum, p. 403.

[16]Karni, A., Meyer, G., Rey-Hippolito, C., Jezzard, P., Adams, M. M., Turner, R., & Ungerleider, L. G. (1998). The acquisition of skilled motor performance: Fast and slow experience-driven changes in primary motor cortex. *Proceedings of the National Academy of Science USA*, 95, 861–868.

[17]Elbert, T., Pantev, C., Wienbruch, C., Rockstroh, B., & Taub, E. (1995). Increased cortical representation of the fingers of the left hand in string players. *Science*, 270, 305–307.

[18]McKeachie, W. J. (1987). *The new look in instructional psychology: Teaching strategies for learning and thinking*. In E. De Corte, H. Lodewijks, R. Parmentier, & P. Span (Eds.), *Learning and instruction* (vol. I, pp. 443–456). Oxford: Pergamon Press, p. 447.

[19]Larkin, J., McDermott, J., Simon, D. P., & Simon, J. A. (1980). Expert and novice performance in solving physics problems. *Science*, 208, 1342.

[20]McKeachie, W. J. (1987). *The new look in instructional psychology: Teaching strategies for learning and thinking*. In E. De Corte, H. Lodewijks, R. Parmentier, & P. Span (Eds.), *Learning and instruction* (vol. I, pp. 443–456). Oxford: Pergamon Press, p. 450.

[21]Butterfield, E. C., & Nelson, G. D. (1989). Theory and practice of teaching for transfer. *Educational Technology Research & Development*, 37, 5–38, p. 12.

[22]Bruner, J. (1973). Going beyond the information given. In J. S. Bruner and J. Anglin (Eds.), *Beyond the information given: Studies in the psychology of knowing* (219–238). New York: W. W. Morton, p. 230.

[23]Ericcson, K. A., & Charness, N. (1994). Expert performance: Its structure and acquisition. *American Psychologist*, 49(8), 725–747, p. 730, 736.

[24]See for example, Adams, J. A. (1987). Historical review and appraisal of research on the learning, retention, and transfer of human motor skills. *Psychological Bulletin*, 101, 41–74; Ahsen, A. (1987). Image psychology and the empirical method. *Journal of Mental Imagery*, 11, 3 & 4, 1–38; Kosslyn, S. M. (1983). *Ghosts in the mind's machine: Creating and using images in the brain*. New York:

W. W. Norton; Kroger, W. S., & Fezler, W. D. (1976). *Hypnosis and behavior modification: Imagery conditioning.* Philadelphia, PA: J. B. Lippincott; Parker, J. F., Brownston, L., & Ruiz, I. (1993). Does imagery impede or facilitate transfer of learning? *Bulletin of the Psychonomic Society,* 31, 557–559.

[25]Schmidt, R. A., & Bjork, R. A. (1992). New conceptualizations of practice: Common principles in three paradigms suggest new concepts for training. *Psychological Science,* 3, 207–217, p. 207.

[26]Bruner, J. S. (1973). Going beyond the information given. In J. Anglin (Ed.), *Beyond the information given: Studies in the psychology of knowing* (pp. 218–238). New York: W. W. Norton, p. 232.

[27]Norris, S. P. (1992). Introduction: The generalizability question. In S. P. Norris (Ed.), *The generalizability of critical thinking: Multiple perspectives on an educational ideal* (pp. 1–15). New York: Columbia University, p. 64.

[28]Ibid, p. 64.

[29]Dawes, R. M. (1994). *House of cards: Psychology and psychotherapy built on myth.* New York: Free Press, p. 217.

[30]Fotheringhame, J. (1984). Transfer of training: A field study of some training methods. *Journal of Occupational Psychology,* 59, 59–71, p. 69.

[31]American Psychological Association. (1982). *Report of the Task Force on the Evaluation of Education, Training, and Service in Psychology.* Washington, DC: Author.

[32]See for example, Berman, J. S., & Norton, N. C. (1985). Does professional training make a therapist more effective? *Psychological Bulletin,* 98, 401–407; Dawes, R. M., Faust, D., & Meehl, P. E. (1989). Clinical versus actuarial judgment. *Science,* 243, 1668–1674; Faust, D., & Ziskin, J. (1988). The expert witness in psychology and psychiatry. *Science,* 241, 31–35; Faust, D., Guilmette, T. J., Hart, K. J., & Arkes, H. R. (1988). Neuropsychologists' training, experience and judgment accuracy. *Archives of Clinical Neuropsychology,* 3, 145–163; Garb, H. N. (1989). Clinical judgment, clinical training, and professional experience. *Psychological Bulletin,* 105, 387–396; Hayes, S. C. (1991). The emperor's clothes: Examining the 'delusions' of professional psychology: The healthy skepticism of David Faust. *Science,* 1, 22–25; Kutchins, H., & Kirk, S. A. (1986). The reliability of DSM-III: A critical review. *Social Work Research and Abstracts,* 22(4), 3–12; Kutchins, H., & Kirk, S. A. (1988). The business of misdiagnosis: DSM-III and clinical social work. *National Association of Social Workers,* 33, 215–220; Loring, M., & Powell, B. (1988). Gender, race, and DSM-III: A study of the objectivity of psychiatric diagnostic behavior. *Journal of Health and Social Behavior,* 29, 1–22; Roberts, A. H. (1985). Biofeedback: Research, training, and clinical roles. *American Psychologist,* 40(8), 938–941; Stein, D. M., & Lambert, M. J. (1984). On the relationship between therapist experience and psychotherapy outcome. *Clinical Psychology Review,* 4, 127–142; Wolfner, G., Faust, D., and Dawes, R. M. (1993). The use of anatomically detailed dolls in sexual abuse evaluations: The state of the science. *Applied and Preventive Psychology,* 2, 1–11.

[33]Dawes, R. M. (1994). *House of cards: Psychology and psychotherapy built on myth.* New York: Free Press, p. 119.

[34]Tan, C. M. (1992). An evaluation of the use of continuous assessment in the teaching of physiology. *Higher Education,* 23, 255–272, p. 259.

[35]Ibid, p. 264.

[36]Ibid, p. 255.

CHAPTER

11

# The Similarity-Based Brain: Evolutionary and Neurological Bases of Transfer

*Generalization of learning may well be a principal function of much of the initial struc-
ture of the brain.*

—HAPPEL & MURRE, *Design and Evolution of Modular
Neural Network Architectures*[1]

Any theory of transfer that attempts to explain how and why transfer works should be compatible with what we know about how the brain works. Otherwise, the theory may be sheer fantasy. In addition, this chapter is in keeping with what the research in chapter 9 clearly has shown: That understanding the theory underlying an area will help to promote transfer.

An explanation of transfer that is consistent with evolution and neurology would lend considerable support to both the theory and importance of transfer. In addition, supportive findings should help in further understanding transfer and to perhaps develop instructional methods specifically for transfer. For any instructional approach to be effective, it should be designed with an eye toward how the brain is structured and was "designed" to function.

In this chapter I present a provisional explanation of transfer based on the evolution and structure of the brain. I found the evidence to formulate this initial theory scattered widely throughout the brain research literature. I have tried to bring this evidence together in an informative and readable way. Although speculative and spotty, such findings are, nevertheless, suggestive for providing a neurological substrate undergirding transfer. Currently, no such theory exists, but there is a dire need for one.

How we are able to say that X is *similar* or the *same as* Y, or that this *is like* that, is a mystery, whether we are talking about transfer in general or about how we access analogies and metaphors that the transfer function creates. Cognitive scientist Keith Holyoak and philosopher Paul Thagard have been researching analogical reasoning for years. They remind us that we "know little about how analogy is performed by the human brain [and] we do not know in any precise way how analogical reasoning is performed at a neural level."[2] In a related vein, the philosopher Donald Verene, laments, "It is a scandal of logical thought that it cannot make clear the very basis upon which judgment itself is possible."[3] Although I don't presume to solve these neurological and philosophical problems, it is important to begin to explore their resolution.

Before examining neurological findings, it's important to note that neurologically based explanations typically bear no phenomenal or everyday relationship to commonsense images of the world we experience. For example, when seeing a "dog" there is no little picture or image of "Dog" in our brain. Instead, with brain-based explanations, Dog is represented with abstract symbols as in mathematics, by descriptions of idealized neural networks, or is represented in the language of electromagnetic frequencies. My purpose in applying evolutionary and neurological findings to transfer is fourfold. First, I want to show that what we know about brain processes—however abstractly explained—is consistent with my theory of transfer; second—and also consistent with my theory of transfer—this brain-based chapter will augment one's understanding of transfer; third, this information will enhance one's ability to engage in transfer; and fourth, the chapter will show the very essence or fundamental structure of transfer. Finally, I might note that as one of the two capstone chapters, this chapter is an absolute requirement for understanding deep transfer.

## EVOLUTIONARY ORIGINS OF TRANSFER

It is not uncommon for biologists of human behavior and ethologists who study animal behavior to trace current behavior patterns to evolutionary antecedents, to view current behaviors as higher level homologies or manifestations of more "primitive" (read: earlier) behavior patterns. Historically the philosophy of science has used physics as its model of understanding and doing science. Increasingly, however, there is a trend in psychology to derive a philosophy of science from biology. One of these trends is called evolutionary epistemology. From an evolutionary epistemology perspective, science philosopher Karl Popper and psychologist Donald Campbell suggest that[4] "the main task of the theory of human knowledge is to understand it as continuous with animal knowledge; and to understand also its discontinuity—if any—from animal knowledge."[5] Similarly, by extending Sir Francis Crick's principle of continuity,[6] (Crick shared a 1962 Nobel Prize with James Watson for the discovery of the structure of DNA), my theory of transfer is thus not only consistent with, but is buttressed by the evolutionary ascent of biological structures in our minds.

With an evolutionary decrease in genetic programming in the human species and the subsequent need for coping with an increasing amount of information from the environment, our brain must have evolved a mechanism for reducing and compressing this wealth of information to manageable proportions. I believe it was the philosopher Henri Bergson[7] who first introduced the idea of the brain as a reducing value. The idea that the brain filters out and compresses information is now commonplace in psychology. What I suggest here is that the neurological mechanisms undergirding transfer accomplish evolution's "goal" of reducing input to our nervous system.

Recall from chapter 2 that Nobel Laureate Frederick von Hayek[8] considered the perception of similarity relationships to be hard-wired in multiple ways into our brain: that our nervous system is a hard-wired instrument of classification, an activity that is dependent on transfer. The Nobel Laureate Gerald Edelman suggests that the brain has evolved so that it doesn't directly learn from the external world but instead—innately—"recognizes" the vast array of input from the world.[9] More on this radical pronouncement later. More recent research into the structure and function of the brain by the authors of the epigraph to this chapter suggests

> the structure of the brain has evolved to capture as many regularities of the human environment as possible and shows how neural structures not only allow for rapid and efficient learning, but also enable a system to *generalize its learned behavior to new instances* [italics added].[10]

Generalization, of course, is just another word for transfer. Indeed, it's beginning to appear that transfer is hard-wired into our brain.

To get a little more specific, let me begin with a familiar area: brain lateralization, more commonly known as "right brain and left brain" processes.

## BRAIN LATERALIZATION AND TRANSFER

In recent years hemispheric lateralization has gained widespread recognition by the general public. Lateralization refers to specific brain functions that have been attributed to either the right or left side of the brain's cerebral hemispheres. In fact, research shows a very complex and variable relationship between cognitive functions and brain lateralization, depending in large measure on the nature of the task to be carried out. Books about drawing on the right side of the brain and other so-called right brain—left brain techniques abound in the field of education. Unfortunately, most of these popular notions are grossly oversimplified distortions of the actual findings on brain lateralization, as Lauren Harris's critique, "Right brain training: Some reflections on the application of research on cerebral hemispheric specialization to education" shows,[11] and as documented by one of the foremost cognitive scientists, Robert Ornstein in his book, *The Right Mind: Making sense of the hemispheres*.[12] The rigorous research pertaining to education that does exist suggests that high achievers show more activation in their left hemisphere, whereas low achievers show more activation in their right hemisphere, and that contrary to popular conception, it's probably the left hemisphere that's underdeveloped. Furthermore, the right-hemisphere functions develop optimally only when interacting with the highly developed left hemisphere.[13] With this said, I will now proceed cautiously.

It does appear from neurological findings that transfer thinking as reflected in metaphor and other kinds of figurative language are all associated with hemisphere lateralization. More specifically, research from a broad spectrum of studies from different populations of subjects and using different methodologies all support the general consensus that metaphoric understanding is largely associated with (though not exclusively) the right hemisphere.[14] Much of this lateralization research has been conducted on patients with such severe epilepsy that their two hemispheres had to be surgically disconnected. This operation is called a commissurotomy, which involves severing the corpus callosum, the neural bridge between the two cerebral hemispheres that allows communication (bioelectrical transmission) between them. Thus, after a commisurotomy, information going to one hemisphere is physically no longer transmitted to the other.

We know that when we acquire new knowledge, it interacts with knowledge already stored in our long-term memory, and that this previous knowledge influences how we see and remember things. In part, it's this old knowledge that makes what we perceive meaningful to us. Although we don't know precisely what mechanisms are involved in the interaction between new and old information, Dahlia Zaidel's research suggests that "insights into these mechanisms may be gained by comparing meaning-systems in the left and right cerebral hemispheres."[15] She suggests—as others have—that there can be two complete meaning systems, one in the left and one in the right hemisphere, which can operate separately and simultaneously even in the normal brain. This is because each hemisphere appears to have a semantic memory system with some overlapping and nonoverlapping information between them. According to Zaidel, typically "these two systems interact in complex ways to achieve unified perception."[16] Although the dominant view is that the meaning of things in the physical world is processed only in the left hemisphere, which is specialized for language, not all events have a linguistic code or language-related meaning.

For example, under certain conditions memory for familiar faces, topography of a neighborhood, or musical melodies are functions that are largely associated with the right hemisphere. Therefore, the right hemisphere may also generate its own set of meanings that may be different from the left hemisphere's. According to Zaidel's research, facial features are recognized correctly by either hemisphere when a normal face is shown. But when face-like pictures with rearranged features are shown, recognition of features is accurate only by the left hemisphere. For the right hemisphere, systematic errors are made. In such cases, instead of pointing to the lips or the nose as actually shown, the right hemisphere points to features that typically occupy the position of the lips and the nose in a normal face. However, when pictures of individual geometric figures (e.g., circle, triangle) inside a non-face frame, such as a square, were presented, both hemispheres recognized the individual figures. Thus, the errors of the right hemisphere were specific to the face pictures, not to just any figures within the frame. Work on normal subjects has also confirmed this hemispheric bias in the intact brain.

Zaidel also worked in her laboratory with normal (intact) subjects who were asked to remember a series of paintings, half of which were surrealistic and half realistic. These paintings were then intermixed with an equal number of new paintings that were presented to the subject's left visual half-field (projecting to the right hemisphere) or right visual half-field (projecting to the left hemisphere). The subjects had to press one or two buttons to indicate if they remembered seeing the paintings earlier. The results showed better memory for surrealistic paintings when tested in the right visual half-field than in the left visual half-field, with no hemispheric difference for realistic paintings. Zaidel rightly concludes from her research that the right hemisphere specializes in processing standard or *stereotypical* concepts, whereas there is no effect of *typicality* in the left hemisphere. The left hemisphere is superior for processing unorganized scenes. She goes on to say that

> it is tempting to speculate that on those occasions when we do not see things as they are, when we are exposed to new information that appears to violate standard knowledge and we nevertheless apply conventional models, the conceptual system in the right hemisphere is dominant.[17]

Now, what all this means is that because seeing something as typical and applying old models to new situations requires *similarity judgments* of some kind, it therefore follows that the right hemisphere may be a primary neurological substrate for transfer.

Indeed, other research by G. Bottini and colleagues examined cerebral hemispheric activity in normal subjects using positron emission tomography (PET) scans to examine whether the right hemisphere plays a specific role in the interpretation of the figurative (or transfer) aspects of language.[18] A PET scan of the brain is a medical imaging technique that measures cellular activity by tracking the movement and concentration of a radioactive tracer. It produces cross-sectional x-rays of the brain's metabolic processes while at work. During regional cerebral blood flow measurement, subjects performed tasks involving both metaphorical and literal comprehension of sentences. After extensive PET testing, the researchers found "that the processing of metaphors gave rise to activation in a number of areas in the right hemisphere when compared with the processing of sentences at a literal level."[19] The authors go on to conclude that their study demonstrates that the neurophysiological correlates of complex cognitive processes involve a cluster of anatomical regions underlying episodic memory and mental imagery. Other studies, too, have suggested that the right hemisphere may be the seat of processing inferences.[20] As with judging typicality and applying old models to new situations, making inferences is more often than not based on *similarity judgments*. It therefore again follows that the right hemisphere seems to be strongly involved in some transfer functions. Thus research using literal language seems to most often show left hemisphere transfer, whereas research using metaphorical language and visual or imagery data seems to often show right hemisphere transfer.[21] Though all of the large-scale hemispheric evidence is reassuring, the question is, How might small-scale neural pathways in the brain work to generate transfer?

## NEUROLOGICAL NETWORKS, TRANSFERS, AND EVOLUTION

For transfer to be so fundamental and pervasive, it must have evolved a neurological substrate either through natural selection or as an accidental by-product of what was naturally selected. Bart Happel of the Leiden University Unit of Experimental and Theoretical Psychology and Jacob Murre at the MRC Applied Psychology Unit in Cambridge England suggest on the basis of their simulating neural networks that the very hardwired architecture of our brain is the result of a long evolutionary process during which a large set of specialized subsystems evolved interactively to carry out the tasks necessary for our survival. They also suggest

> that the evolutionary directives encoded in the structure of the brain may extend beyond merely an increased ability to learn stimuli necessary for survival. We propose that the initial architecture is not only important for rapid learning, but that it also induces the system to *generalize its learned behaviour to instances not previously encountered. Generalization of learning may well be a principal function of much of the initial structure of the brain* [italics added].[22]

Generalization of learning is, of course, just another way of describing transfer. These findings, too, would suggest that the foundation for transfer has apparently been laid by evolution and is directed at increasing the chances of survival for all species. I am reminded here of the famous dialogue found in Plato's *Phaedrus*, where he has Socrates say,

> I am myself a great lover of these processes of division and *generalization; they help me to speak and to think* [italics added]. And if I find any man who is able to see "a One and Many" in nature, him I follow, and "walk in his footsteps as if he were a god."[23]

These structures appear to have evolved on the basis of several neurological principles. Perhaps Plato knew something after all.

First, it's generally accepted that evolution designed our brain in an orderly fashion; second, that this order is layered in a hierarchical manner; third, there exists global and multiple parallel processing systems or pathways in our brain. Parallel distributed processing (PDP) systems are large networks of simple processing units, which communicate with each other by passing electrochemical messages back and fourth. In this model, the processing units all work in parallel (or simultaneously) without a specific controlling command structure. In a parallel distributed system, "Knowledge resides only in its connections, and all learning involves a modification of the connections."[24] In this kind of system, then, knowledge isn't located in any particular space. It's distributed throughout the entire brain. With each input added (i.e., knowledge), the connections are reinforced. Thus the process of recognition is the consequence of a statistical process, of assessing probabilities regarding the input as to what it is. More on this in a moment.

Fourth, in addition to hierarchical and global organizational systems, there are highly regular structures at a more microscopic level in the form of neural modules containing as little as a hundred cells, known as minicolumns. These minicolumns have been proposed as the basic functional units of the cerebral cortex, that part of the brain largely responsible for reasoning as we humans know it. Happel and Murre note that the structure of these pathways is *similar* (i.e., analogous) to the broad division of the primate visual system into two principal pathways: One pathway processes visual input in a coarse manner and has a fast response time, the other pathway carries out a much more detailed analysis and is much slower at processing input.[25] This, too, will become important in a moment.

According to Happel and Murre, their approach to understanding how our brain works offers advantages that other theories do not. For example, the PDP approach, involving many of the current connectionist models of how neurological pathways work, relies on very little initial built-in structures. Some of these networks even assume a total interconnectivity between all neural nodes in the network. Others assume a hierarchical, multilayered structure in which each node in a layer is connected to all other nodes in neighboring layers of neurons. The advantage of such fully connected, but low in built-in initial structures is that they are extremely flexible. Given enough resources (e.g., sufficient neural nodes and time), any input and output mapping can be appropriately encoded and processed. Although for many situations, having total connections among the nodes is a desirable characteristic, there is a downside to it: When learning large-scale tasks "from scratch," so to speak, such networks may require an incredible amount of time and resources, as the number of iterations necessary for a network to reach convergence increases with the size of the network. In addition, say Happel and Murre, implementation of such large systems becomes problematic. Thus a more *strategic* system must have therefore evolved. Herein lies the difference between Happel and Murre's neural modeling network and the other PDP models.

Typical models of neurological networks, including connectionist models, tend to be based on a learning "metaphor," whereas Happel and Murre's model is based on a biological evolution "metaphor" that works largely by neural natural *selection*, not by *learning*. This was an important and crucial difference. The use of biological metaphors in modeling and computing (called biocomputing) has increased in the past decade. Accordingly, Happel and Murre point out, "It is important to note that the modular architecture of these networks is not the result of a learning process. Instead, what is learned depends on the initial architecture"[26] or built-in structure of the brain. This initial architecture is the consequence of what are called genetic algorithms that are search procedures created by the mechanism of natural selection and by the subsequent genetically based programming.

The processes of evolution, then, are used as real-world models for solving practical and theoretical problems, not artificial or computer-programming-like models. They report that all models of neural simulations "that use *generalization* [italics added] to measure fitness arrived at modular configurations that were very similar, indicating that they form functionally advantageous architectures *that capture important regularities present* [italics added] in the input domain."[27] Learning in biological neural systems, they suggest only,

> serves as a mechanism for fine tuning these broadly laid out neural circuits . . . that were phylogenetically and ontogenetically established. Learning processes operate at an even smaller time scale of minutes or seconds. . . . Or to put it differently, learning is directed by the initial architecture of the brain. Although it is improbable that the genes code all structural information about the brain, they may be the ultimate determinant of what mental functions can and cannot be learned.[28]

Happel and Murre further suggest that learning from examples (which themselves, as we have seen, are the consequence of similarity transfer) can be viewed as a method to reduce the intrinsic entropy or disorder in the system by excluding nonrelevant connections that are incompatible with a learning set (entropy is the amount of disorder or randomness in a system; in information theory, entropy represents "noise" or random errors occurring in the transmission of signals or messages).

Effective extraction of rules from examples must be directed at locating mappings in the network that are compatible with the entire task domain rather than just with the encountered examples. Such mappings are said to *generalize* well from the learning situation to the task situation. In general, then, the extraction of effective rules is likely to occur if the summed probability of all internal network configuration connections is high. Thus, say the authors,

> If the architecture prohibits the formation of undesired mappings, learning is greatly facilitated and *the network will generalize well* [italics added]. . . . This would explain why for many vital learning tasks only a minimal exposure to relevant stimuli is necessary. Evolution coarsely programs the brain to function in specific task domains. Learning completes these neural programs by fine-tuning the connections and dynamics. The

combination of an initial architecture produced by evolution and experience-based additional fine-tuning prepares the organism to function in an entire domain, rather than just the limited part of the environment to which it was exposed.[29]

The authors go on to conclude that if the above is an important underlying principle of learning, then it must be concluded

that the hidden structure of the brain may capture many more regularities of the world around us than we have expected so far. . . . The main conclusion that can be drawn from the above two experiments is that an initial modular architecture can induce a system to better generalize its learned behaviour to instances never encountered before.[30]

It appears, then, that our brain has evolved to function largely on the basis of innate invariance—*or generalization/similarity*—relations, with the innate module designed for quick recognition of surface similarities that are then later processed by specific learnings. This mechanism may have evolved because of its survival characteristics. Certainly the method is simple enough that even the lowest of species can utilize to some degree (recall chapter 2 on the difference between rats, chimps, and humans).

The multiple connections allow much of the knowledge of the entire system to be applied to any given instance of an event or problem. Because no information resides in a specific place, individual units or brain cells may be destroyed, but memories or concepts can continue to exist. Furthermore, because of the massively distributed character of information in the system, decisions can be arrived at even if the relevant information turns out to be "noisy," incomplete, or approximate. As Howard Gardner notes, "These properties seem closer to the kinds of search and decision organisms must carry out in a complex and often chaotic natural world."[31] Applied to transfer of learning and to the importance of knowledge base (see chapter 6), this means that with each added piece of knowledge, the entire system is enhanced or made robust. Each added piece is not just stored as a single link or node representing a particular idea or concept from a particular field or context.

The reason for this is that most any piece of knowledge shares some information with other pieces and is thus stored distributively; there is considerable overlap, which creates mental associations and mappings of similarities of data. With the continued adding of knowledge, the "summation" strength of the overlaps in the system are increased, thereby increasing the probability that one piece of knowledge will retrieve or be recognized as like another. The main implication is that increased knowledge base increases the probability of transfer of learning.

## NEURAL MODULES

Another current explanation of how the brain works is the modularist view. In this view the mind is made up of a series of separate modules, with each specialized for a particular task. Howard Gardner's well-known book, *Frames of Mind*, essentially represents this view.[32] Gardner suggests that there are different modules for mathematics, language, arts, athletics, and other skills. Applied to transfer, the modular view of the mind would suggest that this is why most learning is context dependent or encapsulated in a particular field and tends not to transfer. It will probably turn out that both the modularists and the general processing models are correct, that the brain is made up of specialized modules operating largely by their own laws, and that a general processor operates in an integrative mode that requires a transfer function in order to abstract out the invariances among the modules. Applied to transfer of learning, these two different models—parallel and modular—could explain why narrow *training* leads only to very near transfer at best, and that the larger the knowledge base, the more likely the general processing properties of the brain are activated, eliciting action from the modules. Although somewhat simplistic, *training* probably conditions only the specialized modules, and *learning* largely conditions the brain's general processing capacity.

If this dual model of the brain is correct, the implications are clear for the importance of enlarging our knowledge base. Donald Rumelhart, one of the main theorists of the PDP model of the brain concludes, "I have become increasingly convinced that much of what we call reasoning can be better accounted for by processes such as pattern matching and *generalization* [italics added], which are all carried out by PDP models."[33] What this means is that with the increasing size of a knowledge base, there is an increase in mental patterns and an increase in the recognition and *matching* of mental patterns. In short, an increase in transfer of learning. An implication of this two-phase knowledge-base paradigm of transfer is that since we are dealing with mental patterns and probabilities, significant or far transfer cannot be taught by simple strategies and cookbook-type training methods. A few other researchers—working from different perspectives—have also noted this implication. For example, Johnson-Laird states that transfer "cannot be guaranteed by any computationally tractable algorithm,"[34] meaning that significant or far transfer cannot be engineered by traditional training methods of systematically breaking learning down into its component parts and then applying quick strategies; its much too modular and nondeterministic. In short, spontaneous far transfer can't be programmed—at least very easily.

Finally, this two-phase model of the brain perhaps explains the years of consistent finding of little to no transfer from one context, situation, discipline, or instructional setting to another (see chapter 8). The modular nature of the human mind tends to encapsulate experience and learning (e.g., rendering learning context specific). Encapsulated learning is not available to transfer to other modules—or at least it is available only with the greatest of effort and expense. A knowledge-base approach to learning tends to create permeability of the module boundaries. The implications for instruction are clear: Modular knowledge remains largely modular and does not transfer easily.

## THE SIMILARITY-BASED TRANSFER BRAIN

Throughout this book and culminating in this chapter and the next, we have seen that the concept of similarity has been fundamental to transfer and to reasoning in general. Despite all this we also saw that reasoning by similarity can be deceiving and dangerous, leading us astray, especially reasoning on the basis of superficial or surface similarities. We also saw that we often are oblivious to the most blatant similarities and fail to transfer the relationship. This is yet another paradox of transfer. There may be serious evolutionary reasons, however, for both our bias toward surface *similarity* as the access point into deep transfer, and for not perceiving similarities when they exist.

First, a reason for our propensity to focus on surface similarity is that there seems to be a positive correlation between surface similarity and deep important underlying structural similarity. That is, surface similarity is sometimes a good indicator of deeper kinds of transfer. First-glance similarities are fast evaluations that are often needed to avoid danger. In evolutionary terms, if it looks like a hungry tiger, prowls like a hungry tiger, and growls like a hungry tiger, not only is it probably a tiger, but in terms of the probabilities, we damn well better assume it's a hungry tiger. In short, it may have more survival value to assume that a surface similarity is meaningful than to assume it is not. Evolutionarily speaking, the consequences of an invalid surface similarity is typically not as serious as ignoring a valid one. If you don't recognize that an animal is a tiger your life may be lost. In such an environment, playing the surface-similarity probabilities, then, has survival value.

Second, a reason for us to be oblivious to many similarities is perhaps understandable given the large size of our everyday knowledge base. For an animal having a large knowledge base, seeing similarity everywhere, the costs of checking all events for their similarities would be prohibitive. Thus a conservative approach to seeing similarity may be reasonable. In any event, as we have seen above, based on the work of Happel and Murre, the very structure of our brain may have evolved to operate on the basis of feature of similarities in our environment, to generalize—in other words, to transfer. Indeed, according to Happel and Muree, the hidden structures of our brain may recognize many more regularities in the world around us than we have expected. Also according to Happel and Murre, the evolution of our brain has evolved so that it has two different basic modes of responding to the world. The first is a pathway for *rapid* analysis of stimuli, the second pathway is for conducting a slower and more detailed analysis.

This two-phase or double pathway has also been found in a brain structure known as the amygdala, an almond-shaped structure located at the base of our temporal lobe. Recent findings by Joseph LeDoux, professor of neural science and psychology at New York University, showed that the amygdala is one brain structure responsible for registering and responding to emotional stimuli, and it can do so independently of our higher brain centers (e.g., the cerebral cortex).[35] The amygdala appears to be responsible for a rapid processing of emotional stimuli (perhaps like sighting what appears to be a tiger). When the amygdala receives a sensory pattern, it may make an invalid inference as to what the pattern is. Thus in rapidly responding to stimuli, it may often respond inappropriately to memory traces of past stimuli, leading to psychological dysfunctions. LeDoux's research and Goleman's[36] excellent translation of LeDoux's findings exclusively focus ensuing psychopathology on this fast and invalid processing of similarities.

If we look at the research from the perspective of transfer, pathology is clearly the consequence of inappropriate transfers from memory. Goleman describes the functioning of the amygdala in metaphorical terms. He says that it functions "something like a neural *Name That Tune*, where . . . on the basis of just a few notes, a whole perception is grasped on the basis of the first few tentative parts."[37] The fine-tuning, or slower processing, may come later. LeDoux says that such rapid initial emotional perceptions have survival value. Again, if it looks like a hungry tiger, prowls like a hungry tiger, and growls like a hungry tiger, not only is it probably a tiger, but in terms of the probabilities, we damn well better emotionally respond as if it's a hungry tiger. So we have here yet another piece of the puzzle of transfer that's consistent with neurological findings. To this, we can add the following.

## INVARIANCE-BASED BRAIN
## CIRCUITS AND TRANSFER

A further possibility supporting the present theory of transfer and a similarity-based brain derives from the theoretical work of the neuroscientist Karl Pribram.[38] Similarity relations are also fundamental to Pribram's holonomic theory of the brain, which suggests that the brain functions as a spectral frequency analyzer. His research indicates that individual cells and ensembles of cells conform to certain mathematical functions called Fourier and Gabor transforms. Pertinent to transfer, these mathematical functions (I am told by those more knowledgeable than I) involve the application of *constants, identities, equalities,* and *associations,* not discrete on–off functions found in many computer programming languages.

Now—and this is where we really leave the familiarity of our personal experience of the world—according to Pribram, in a holonomic brain, percepts and properties are selected from a primitive matrix in which frequency or spectral conjunctions abound. Everyday categories and objects are constructed by operations performed on this primitive frequency matrix. Largely responsible for the operations that convert the spectral domain to the everyday space–time domain of our experience are dendritic microprocesses (dendrites are kind of like connectors at the end of neurons), which function as cross-correlational devices. "Cross-correlations," explains Pribram "are a measure of *similarity* [italics added] of two original images." More importantly he says, "a measure of *similarity* [italics added] is precisely what is required for recognition" of the world as we know it.[39] This is probably a good general description of how transfer is created on a fundamental level.

According to Pribram, a cell's response is defined by a manifold of frequency averages not by simple identical features (in our terms, surface similarity). The sum of the manifold is constituted by that which remains *invariant* across the various processing stages or levels involved in mental processing. The interesting and difficult problem, Pribram points out, is specifying the "transfer functions," the transformation codes involved in matching or correlating one code with another, or one level to another. Now, from a holonomic brain theory perspective, metaphorical and analogical transfer are not fundamentally apprehended by composing or mapping concrete identical features or elements, as most contemporary cognitive research indicates—though there is little doubt that they are experienced this way—but rather are generated by a featureless process of cross-correlational frequency *invariance* among or between events.

Thus our phenomenal or everyday experience of concrete features of similarity and transfer is the end-state or final product of this fundamental process. Inversely, concrete similarity becomes only an access point, a stimulus activating microneurological subprocess of frequency analysis and cross-correlations. One of the implications of such a theory of invariance for transfer seems to be that to improve the ability to apprehend *equivalence* or *invariant* transformations is to increase to the extent to which the primitive spectral matrix is provided with a wide-spectrum knowledge base (recall chapter 6). In my reading of this theory, such a neurological base would increase the ability of a system to more accurately disregard irrelevant information and superficial similarities, and/or to cancel them out in an averaging process based on probabilities. Such a process would tend to generate *equivalences* or *invariants* in our learning that are increasingly complex and which are more sensitive to small but significant nuances. Hence, making possible spontaneous and significant transfer.

Further, says Pribram, during frequency analysis and cross-correlations, neural cells respond to successive *harmonics* to a given base frequency. What this means is that a sound with a fundamental frequency of, say, 440 Hz (that is, the vibrations of an instrument repeat themselves 440 times each second) is actually a complicated oscillation that also contains a *harmonic* of 880 Hz, another *harmonics* of 1,320 Hz, and so on. This harmonic analysis capacity of cellular functioning, as Pribram—engaging in some transfer thinking himself—points out, is *isomorphic* (i.e., something being structurally *the same as*) abstract transformation groups in mathematics. I would like to add that it also probably reflects the neurological basis of higher order transfer thinking.

## CONCLUSION

We have seen that the transformations of invariance, the transforming of apparent *differences* into "sameness," or *similarity* undergirds transfer of learning. But its importance goes beyond its typically recognized instances. Indeed, Ernest Nagel in his classic book, *The Structure of Science*, makes clear that

> recognizing the great theoretical and practical importance of invariance formulations, many writers have therefore identified *invariance* with *objectivity* |italics added|, so that according to these thinkers only what is expressible in such invariant form merits the title of 'genuine reality.'[40]

In the next chapter, we will see the significance of transfer in some of its basic forms like metaphor, analogical reasoning, mathematics, and harmonic structure.

## Notes

[1]Happel, B. L. M., & Murre, J. M. J. (1994). Design and evolution of modular neural network architectures. *Neural Networks*, 7, 985–1004, p. 985.

[2]Holyoak, K., & Thagard, P. (1995). *Mental leaps: Analogy in creative thought.* Cambridge, MA: MIT Press, pp. 264–265.

[3]Verene, D. P. (1981). *Vico's science of the imagination.* Ithaca, NY: Cornell University Press, p. 174.

[4]Popper, K. R. (1987b). Natural selection and the emergence of mind. IN G. Radnitzky & W. W. Bartley (Eds.), *Evolutionary epistemology, rationality, and the sociology of knowledge* (pp. 139–155). La Salle, IL: Open Court Press; Campbell, D. T. (1987). Evolutionary Epistemology. In G. Radnitzky & W. W. Bartley (Eds.), *Evolutionary epistemology, rationality, and the sociology of knowledge* (pp. 47–89). La Salle, IL: Open Court Press.

[5]Popper, K. R. (1987). *Natural selection and the emergence of mind.* In G. Radnitzky & W. W. Bartley (Eds.), *Evolutionary epistemology, rationality, and the sociology of knowledge* (pp. 139–155). La Salle, IL: Open Court Press, p. 117.

[6]Crick, F. H. C. (1968). The origin of the genetic code. *Journal of Molecular Biology*, 38, 367; See also Crick, F., & Mitchison, G. (1986). REM sleep and neural nets. In R. E. Haskel (Ed.), *Cognition and dream research.* New York: Institute of Mind and Behavior. |Also published as a special double issue of *The Journal of Mind and Behavior*, 7(2&3).|

[7]Bergson, H. (1923). *Creative evolution.* New York: Henry Holt.

[8]Hayek, F. A. (1952). *The sensory order: An inquiry into the foundations of theoretical psychology.* Chicago: University of Chicago Press.

[9]Edelman, G. (1992). *Bright air, brilliant fire: On the matter of mind.* New York: Basic Books.

[10]Happel, B. L. M., & Murre, J. M. J. (1994). Design and evolution of modular neural network architectures. *Neural Networks*, 7, 985–1004, p. 985.

[11]Harris, L. J. (1988). Right brain training: Some reflections on the application of research on cerebral hemispheric specialization to education. In D. L. Molfese & S. J. Segalowitz (Eds.), *Brain lateralization in children: Developmental implications* (pp. 207–35). New York: Guilford Press.

[12]Ornstein, R. (1997). *The right mind: Making sense of the hemispheres.* New York: Harcourt Brace.

[13]Lay, L. Y. V. (1989). Hemisphericity and student achievement. *International Journal of Neuroscience*, 48(3–4), 225–232.

[14]Anaki, D., Faust, M., & Kravetz, S. (1998). Cerebral hemispheric asymmetries in processing lexical metaphors. Neuropsychologia, 36, 691–700; Bottini, G., Corcoran, R., Sterzi, R., Paulesu, E., et al. (1994). The role of the right hemisphere in the interpretation of figurative aspects of language: A positron emission tomography activation study. Brain, 117(6), 1241–1253; Chernigovskaya, T. V. (1994). Cerebral lateralization for cognitive and linguistic abilities: Neuropsychological and cultural aspects. Studies in Language Origins, 3, 55–76; Chiarello, C. (1991). Interpretation of word meanings by the cerebral hemispheres: One is not enough. In P. J. Schwanenflugel (Ed.), The psychology of word meanings. Hillsdale, NJ: Lawrence Erlbaum; Kosslyn, S. M., & Koenig, O. (1995). Wet mind: The new cognitive neuroscience. New York: The Free Press; McIntyre R. C., Pritchard, P. B., & Lombroso, C. T. (1976). Left and right temporal lobe epileptics: A controlled investigation of some psychological differences. Epileseia, 17, 377–386; Winner, E., & Gardner, H. (1977). The comprehension of metaphor in brain-damaged patients. Brain, 100, 717–729.

[15]Zaidel, D. W. (1994). Worlds apart: Pictorial semantics in the left and right cerebral hemispheres. Current Directions in Psychological Science, 3, 5–8, p. 5.

[16]Ibid, p. 5.

[17]Ibid, p. 6.

[18]Bottini, G., Corcoran, R., Sterzi, R., Paulesu, E., Schenone, P., Scarpa, P., Frackowiak, R. S. J., & Frith, C. D. (1994). The role of the right hemisphere in the interpretation of figurative aspects of language: A positron emission tomography activation study. Brain, 117(6), 1241–1253.

[19]Ibid, p. 1250.

[20]Beeman, M. (1991). Semantic processing in the right hemisphere may contribute to drawing inferences from discourse. Brain and Language, 44, 80–120.

[21]See also Danesi, M. (1989). The neurological coordinates of metaphor. Communication & Cognition, 22, 73–86, for a review of right hemispheric lateralization and metaphoric language.

[22]Happel, B. L. M., & Murre, J. M. J. (1994). Design and evolution of modular neural network architectures. Neural Networks, 7, 985–1004, p. 1000.

[23]Plato. (1956). Phaedrus (W. E. Helmbold & W. G. Rabinowitz, Trans.) New York: Bobbs-Merrill.

[24]Rumelhart, D. E. (1989). Toward a microstructural account of human reasoning. In S. Vosniadou & A. Ortony (Eds.), Similarity and analogical reasoning (pp. 298–312). New York: Cambridge University Press, p. 299.

[25]Happel, B. L. M., & Murre, J. M. J. (1994). Design and evolution of modular neural network architectures. Neural Networks, 7, 985–1004.

[26]Ibid, p. 995.

[27]Ibid, p. 1000.

[28]Ibid, p. 987.

[29]Ibid, pp. 987, 1000.

[30]Ibid, pp. 987, 1000.

[31]Gardner, H. (1985). The mind's new science: A history of the cognitive revolution. New York: Basic Books, p. 133.

[32]Gardner, H. (1983). Frames of mind: The theory of multiple intelligences. New York: Basic Books.

[33]Rumelhart, D. E. (1989). Toward a microstructural account of human reasoning. In S. Vosniadou & A. Ortony (Eds.), Similarity and analogical reasoning (pp. 298–312). New York: Cambridge University Press, p. 299.

[34]Johnson-Laird, P. N. (1989). Analogy and the exercise of creativity. In S. Vosniadou & A. Ortony (Eds.), Similarity and analogical reasoning. New York: Cambridge University Press, p. 313.

[35]LeDoux, J. E. (1994). Emotion, memory and the brain. Scientific American, (June), 50–57; LeDoux, J. E. (1993). Emotional memory systems in the brain. Behavioural Brain Research, 58, 69–79; LeDoux, J. E. (1991). Emotion and the limbic system concept. Concepts in Neuroscience, 2, 169–199.

[36]Goleman, D. (1995). Emotional intelligence: Why it can matter more than I.Q. New York: Bantam Books, pp. 17–29.

[37]Ibid, p. 24.

[38]See Pribram, K. (1991). *Brain and perception.* Hillsdale, NJ: Lawrence Erlbaum; Pribram, K., Newer, M., & Baron, R. (1974). *the holographic hypothesis of memory structure in brain function and perception.* In D. Krantz, R. Atkinson, R. Luce, & P. Suppes (Eds.), *Measurement, psychophysics and neural information processing* (pp. 416–457). San Francisco: W. H. Freeman; Pribram, K. H. (1988). *Brain organization and perception: Holonomic and structural determinants of figural processing.* Unpublished manuscript, Stanford University; Pribram, K. (1971). *Languages and the brain: Experimental paradoxes and principles in neuropsychology.* Englewood Cliffs, NJ: Prentice-Hall; Pribram, K. (1986). The cognitive revolution and mind brain issues. *American Psychologist, 41,* 507–520.

[39]Pribram, K., Newer, M., & Baron, R. (1974). *The holographic hypothesis of memory structure in brain function and perception.* In D. Krantz, R. Atkinson, R. Luce, & P. Suppes (Eds.), *Measurement, psychophysics and neural information processing* (pp. 416–457). San Francisco: W. H. Freeman, p. 429.

[40]Nagel, E. (1961). *The structure of science.* New York: Harcourt, Brace & World, p. 275. Perhaps in no other subject have I found these assumed deep implications running rampant in the background of teaching than the subjects of race and gender.

# CHAPTER 12

# The Harmonic Structure
# of Mind: Higher Level
# Everyday Transfer Thinking

*Much, if not all, of what we call intelligence may be the ability to perceive successive analogies at higher and higher levels of abstraction, a multiple repetition of a single basic neural process of organization.*

—JOHN PLATT, *Yearbook of the Society for General Systems Research*[1]

Although most people may not know what the harmonic mind is, everybody has one, and they likely use it from time to time. In fact, those who have had formal music lessons or who are fairly skilled in mathematics may quickly recognize what I call the harmonic structure of mind (henceforth shortened to just harmonic mind). I say that those familiar with music and math may recognize the harmonic mind because certain aspects of both music and math evolve from it. In this chapter I will explain what a harmonic mind is, what its structure looks like, and why it's important in everyday transfer thinking.

Initially think of this basic harmonic structure as being like the animal classification system learned in biology, where we have successive levels beginning with species, genus, family, order, class, phylum, and kingdom. In chapter 2, I suggested that the basic structure of transfer was exemplified by proportional and progressive reasoning, as in this arithmetical series: 2, 4, 8, 16, 32. Stated in analogical form *2 is to 4 as 4 is to 8 as 8 is to 16 as 16 is to 32* (or more concisely notated, $2:4::4:8::8:16::16:32$); this elegant analogical structure is probably hardwired into our brain.

The biological classification system can be put into this analogical form thusly: species *is to* genus *as* genus *is to* family *as* family *is to* order *as* order *is to* class, and so on. This is basically the entire story of the harmonic mind. The rest of the examples are simply variations on this fundamental structure that we see expressed in many different areas of life. For example, recall from the last chapter that a sound with a fundamental frequency of, say, 440 Hz is actually a complicated oscillation that also contains the *harmonic* overtones of 880 Hz, 1320 Hz, and so on, to higher levels. We can see that the latter two frequencies are reciprocals of the base frequency.

It is important to understand the harmonic mind because without it, we engage in only the simplest of transfer. Not understanding this harmonic structure is like only knowing or recognizing the relationship that 1 stands in relation to 10 but not seeing that 10 stands in same relationship to 100, and 100 in same relationship to 1000, and so on. Again, in analogical form: 1:10::10:100::100:1000. With this progression, we have the basic harmonic form of higher level transfer thinking. We will also see in this chapter that this progressive and harmonic form can be expressed as a spiral (see Figure 4). Let me illustrate this using words instead of numbers.

In chapter 2, I pointed out that the concepts of *adaptation* in biology (the alteration in an organism resulting from natural selection enabling the organism to survive), *learning* in psychology (an individual's acquiring knowledge

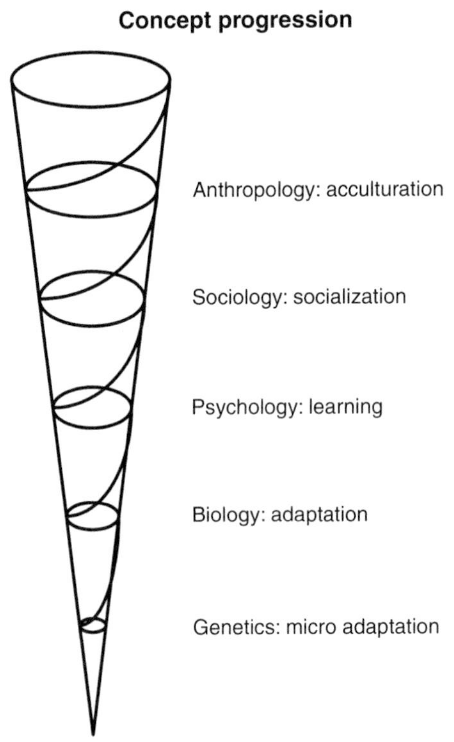

**Concept progression**

Anthropology: acculturation

Sociology: socialization

Psychology: learning

Biology: adaptation

Genetics: micro adaptation

**FIGURE 4**
Harmonic levels of transfer: Concept progression

through practice, training, or experience), *socialization* in sociology (individuals assimilating the values and behavior patterns of their culture), and *acculturation* in anthropology (adopting cultural traits or social patterns of another culture) are essentially the same concept. Now, each succeeding concept is a higher order form of the other. Thus, in analogical form, we have adaptation *is to* biology *as* learning *is to* psychology *as* socialization *is to* sociology *as* acculturation *is to* anthropology. This is the same progressive *form* as the above: species *is to* genus *as* genus *is to* family *as* family *is to* order *as* order *is to* class, and $2:4::4:8::8:16$. This isn't just an esoteric exercise. It's the harmonic structure of higher level transfer thinking that helps us to efficiently store, integrate, remember, process, and retrieve information. Such a structure becomes a memory or mnemonic device for learning (see Figures 4 and 5).

As I unpack this concept of a harmonic mind, I show its pervasive form. This progressive form of analogical transfer is also seen in the basic structure of higher level mathematical thinking. Now, before those who consider themselves not to be very good at math begin to panic, I should point out that just

## Levels of organization

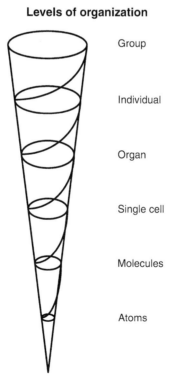

Group

Individual

Organ

Single cell

Molecules

Atoms

**FIGURE 5**
Harmonic levels of transfer: Levels of organization.

because someone doesn't seem to possess high mathematical technical ability, doesn't necessarily mean that they won't be good at transfer. Although all A's are Bs, not all Bs may be A's. What this logical formula simply means is that although all those good at math (A's) are also good at transfer (Bs), all those good at transfer (Bs) may not be good at math (A's). Therefore, someone not good at math may still be good at transfer in nonmathematical domains. I will explain this further below. But first I look closer at different examples of this progressive and harmonic form of transfer thinking.

## OCTAVES AND HARMONICS IN MIND

Anyone who has had music lessons will recall that an octave is the interval in our system of eight degrees between two full tones, one of which has twice the vibrations per second as the other. The number *eight* implicit in the term *octave* stems from the musical major scale (*do, re, me, fa, sol, la, ti, do'*) in which *do'* the octave above *do*, is the eighth step along the scale. The similarity between tones an octave apart is variously called octave equivalence or octave generalization.

The ancient Greeks thought octave equivalency reflected something cosmic about the simplest of mathematical ratios (e.g., $2:1$), because the pitch of a vibrating string will rise by an octave if a string is vibrated at half its length. Since then, such simple ratios have been understood in terms of the physical laws governing the periodicity of vibrating objects. Such objects tend to vibrate at frequencies that are roughly integer multiples of the lowest or fundamental frequency. These frequency components are called harmonics.

The capability to perceive "different" melodies, or the transposition of different octaves into the *same* musical experience, appears to be built into both single brain cells and hardwired into our neurological pathways. In music, transposition refers to writing or performing a composition in a key other than the original. In mathematics it can refer to moving a term or sign from one side of an algebraic equation to the other side. Though the sign has been reversed, it is said to have maintained its equality. As noted in chapter 2, the capacity for transposition is related to one's place on the evolutionary scale. If a rat is trained to go toward a light of intensity $L_1$ and to avoid intensity $L_2$ which is twice the intensity of $L_1$ and is then presented with intensity $L_3$ and $L_4$, where $L_4$ is twice the intensity of $L_3$, the rat will not respond. Chimpanzees, and young children, however, will make this transposition. They will consider intensity $L_1$ in the first situation as the *same* as intensity $T_3$ in the second situation. Put in analogical terms, $L_1:L_2$ as $L3:L_4$ (see Figure 2 chapter 2). This is the same process as hearing a melody played in one key as being the *same* melody played in a different key, even though not a single note in the new octave is the same as the notes in the old octave.

Years ago while writing my undergraduate senior thesis on analogical reasoning, I read a book on the subcortical mechanisms of behavior.[2] The authors of the book cited an experiment with cats that consisted of teaching the animals to respond to a particular tone, after which they were subjected to ablation of their auditory cortex. Naturally enough, after having their auditory cortex disconnected, the cats no longer responded to the tone to which they were originally taught to respond. They did, however, respond to a tone that was an *octave* removed from the original training tone. I was both struck and delighted, for I saw in this experiment a possible neurological basis for a theory of transfer that I was just beginning to think about. We have now known for some time that certain cells of the auditory cortex have more than one "best frequency," and that in most cases, the additional best frequencies are approximately octave multiples of the "fundamental" best frequency. Early experiments found that conditioned responses to specific tones were elicited up to five octave levels of generalizations. But the presence of octave generalization in the auditory cortex doesn't necessarily mean that it's related to behavior and learning in the everyday world (though I believe it does). I continued to look for similar findings.

I then read a book on stimulus generalization in learning that indicated that the brain might be hardwired to respond to harmonic frequencies, itself a kind of octave phenomenon.[3] This "octave generalization" effect in learning was first noted by Lloyd Humphreys[4] and subsequently studied by Blackwell and Schlosberg.[5] For example, rats trained to a 10,000-cps tone were tested for generalization at other frequencies. The percentage of responses to the octave tone of 5,000 cps was some 13% higher than that expected on the basis of a smooth decreasing curve drawn through the other points. Typically, a conditioned response to a tone decreases as the frequency stimulus diverges from the original tone. But as a new tone approximates an octave or harmonic of the original tone, the conditioned response is nearly as strong as with the original tone. In other words, though quantitatively divergent, the response is greater when a new frequency stimulus is qualitatively closer (i.e., an octave or harmonic). Similar results have been observed to a color spectrum.[6] Here, then, we seem to have a neurological or hardwired instance of proportional transfer, or what I refer to as analogical transfer progression (e.g., 2:4::4:8::8:16::32, etc.). Although others have noted this octave structure for some time, it has not been related to the cognitive or neural structure of transfer.

Recently, the neurological research of Jamshed Bharucha and W. Einar Menci on the neurological mechanisms behind the recognition of octaves suggests that although octave equivalence is widely believed to be universal, it may not be octave recognition, *qua octave*, that's innate, but a particular learning mechanism that is responsible for it and other invariance transformations. They suggest that the first question can be addressed in terms of the perceptual learning of categories through neural self-organization. A general-purpose perceptual learning mechanism coupled with the acoustic regularities of the environment would not only enable octave equivalence to be learned but would compel such learning.[7]

The authors suggest that if such phenomena can be shown to be the result of perceptual learning, via mechanisms that are not specific to music or even auditory cognition, then they may have widespread application for explaining other cognitive domains, such as our ability to recognize general pattern invariancies in the world. Thus the universal perception of octave and harmonic phenomena may be either directly or indirectly based on innate neurological structures.

## MOLLUSK SHELLS AND THE HARMONICS OF TRANSFER THINKING

The great Swiss psychologist, Jean Piaget (1896–1980), although known mostly for his developmental theory of children's cognitive development, thought of himself as a genetic epistemologist, that is, as one who studies the biological basis of how we acquire and develop logic and thought. Piaget was a master at transfer thinking. One has only to look at his book, *Biology and Knowledge: An Essay on the Relations between Organic Regulations and Cognitive Processes*, to recognize his ability at transfer.[8] Terms and phrases like *it's like . . . it's analogous to . . . compare . . . invariance . . . transfer . . . it's comparable to . . . it's the same law . . . it's parallel to . . . it's equal to*, and *it's isomorphic to . . .* dot almost every page of his book. Piaget was a child prodigy, publishing in professional journals when he was around fourteen years old. His first love was biology. More particularly, he was fascinated by the mollusk shell. A mollusk is a marine species characterized by shells with whorls overlapping each other taking on a logarithmic spiral shape. (Essentially a logarithm is a mathematical power or exponent or an arithmetical constant applied to a base number that is then raised to a higher order.) The well-known nautilus shell is a prime example of a logarithmic spiral.

Each successive level of a harmonic-like spiral grows out of and is a higher order exponent of its base level. Piaget considered cognitive development as a kind of octave or harmonic-like spiral structure. He referred to this structure as *epigenetic*. An epigenetic cognitive structure is a kind of harmonic-like spiral where each new turn is a higher order manifestation of learning below it, just as by analogy 4 is to 2 and 8 is to 4, or 16 is to 8. It is interesting to note that in biology, epigenesis refers to the theory that individuals develop by *successive differentiation* of an unstructured egg. Even more interesting, it has always seemed to me that Piaget's conception of the development of our cognitive structure as epigenetic was transferred (consciously or nonconsciously) from his early study of the mollusk shell with its spiral structure.

Great scientists and thinkers often think in epigenetic or at least in simpler octave-type forms of thought. We have only to look at the history of chemistry. One such example is Dmitri Ivanovich Mendeleev (1834–1907), the Russian chemist who discovered the periodic law and constructed the period table of the elements in 1869. He took the 63 elements that were known at that time, wrote the names and properties of the 63 elements on 63 separate cards, and stuck the cards on the wall of his laboratory. By carefully re-examining the data, sorting out the *similar* elements and pinning their cards next to each other on the wall, a discovery was revealed: he discovered that the properties "were periodic functions of their atomic weights" that repeated themselves periodically after each seven elements—a kind of analogy to the musical octave (do, re, me, fa, sol, la, ti, do'). From his "transfer" table or structure, he was able by interpolation and extrapolation to then correct previous erroneous atomic weights of some elements and to successfully predict three new elements from gaps in his octave-like periodic table.

John A. R. Newlands (1838–1898), an English chemist, anticipated by about three years Mendeleev's basic idea of the periodic law. The analogy with the musical octave was clear to him. In 1866, Newlands read a paper at the English Chemical Society in which he compared the arrangement of the elements to the keyboard of a piano with its 88 notes divided into periods or octaves of eight. He said that the elements should be divided into octaves because each eighth element starting from a given one is a kind of repetition of the first, *like* the eighth note of an octave in music. He in fact called this the *Law of Octaves*. At the time, his use of the octave analogy was met with ridicule. The Law of Octaves was only accepted after Mendeleev completed his work five years later. Progressive higher order transfer thinking at work.

Now at the risk of being perceived as mystical, this octave or harmonic-like transfer structure is found throughout the biological world. Early in my thinking about the harmonic, octave, or spiral transfer structure of mind, a colleague sent me an article written by a classical scholar living in a mud-floor hut somewhere in the hills of Italy. It seemed the scholar was obsessed by the spiral structure of sea shells. Like Piaget, he, too, saw the transfer in the spiral of mollusk shells. He used them as a model to explain the structure of the continuous analogy—what I refer to as analogical progression—more specifically, comparing the spiral structure with Aristotle's idea of the continuous analogy. Recall the form: 2:4::4:8::8:6::32, and so on. He published his comparisons in an obscure journal in an article entitled, "The Continuous Analogy: The Uses of Continuous Proportions in Plato and Aristotle."[9]

Preus cited the great Scottish biologist d'Arcy W. Thompson's book, *On Growth and Form*.[10] Thompson discovered that the multiple body shapes of animals belonging to the same biological family could be represented by a systematic *proportional* distortion of a single basic shape or structure, somewhat like the stretching of a figure drawn on a rubber balloon that's then inflated. For example, with primates, Thompson found that the differing skull shapes of gorillas, chimpanzees, baboons, and humans, if drawn on a rubber sheet, are simply different proportional distortions of the same basic skull. These distortions, or transformations, can be expressed by mathematical formulas. Thompson also showed that other biological forms are susceptible to analysis in terms of continuous proportions. One marvelous example is Thompson's analysis of phyllotaxis or leaf arrangement, in which the sequences of the Italian mathematician, Leonardo da Pisa Fibonacci (1170–1240), play a central role. The Fibonacci sequence, 0,1,1,2,3,5,8,13,21, etc., is one in which each term is the sum of the two preceding terms. Fibonacci sequences frequently occur in higher mathematics. In the structure of the pine cone, for example, there are a number of spirals, one set going in one direction around the cone, the other set going in the other direction. If one counts these spirals, one finds that the numbers of the spirals are three and five, or five and eight. In a daisy, the florets also form spirals.

Further, there is a harmonic-like spiral form manifested in many other phenomena, for example, the logarithmic spiral. This spiral was perhaps first recognized and analyzed in 1638 by the French philosopher Rene Descartes (1596–1650, better known for his premise, "I think, therefore I am."). Described in mathematical terminology, the logarithmic spiral is one where a |plane| curve proceeding from a fixed point such that the arc intercepted between any two radii at a given angle to one another will always *be similar* to itself. This definition is

> the most fundamental and intrinsic property of the curve, namely the property of *continual similarity* |italics added|, and the very property by reason of which it is associated with organic growth in such structures as the horn or the shell. For it is peculiarly characteristics, of the spiral shell, for instance, that it does not alter as it grows; each increment is *similar* |italics added| to its predecessor.[11]

Again, the form of the logarithmic spiral is perhaps best exemplified by the nautilus shell, which is also Piaget's epigenetic spiral. Piaget employs the term "reflective abstraction" to describe a cognitive process in which an operation that organizes one cognitive level is rediscovered at a second more general level and, in organizing this new level, enriches and integrates the previous level by combining it with newer elements, thus maintaining a continuity and coherence in development while allowing for the generation of novelty.

Marshal McLuhan, the prophet of the current personal computer age, recognized the everyday importance of the logarithmic spiral in thinking and reasoning. He noted that the Hebrew and Eastern modes of thought approach problems in a spiral fashion, where the entire message can be traced and retraced on the rounds of a concentric spiral with seeming redundancy. He says,

> One can stop anywhere after the first few sentences and have the full message, if one is prepared to "dig" it. This kind of plan seems to have inspired Frank Lloyd Wright in designing the Guggenheim Art Gallery on a spiral, concentric basis. It is a redundant

form inevitable to the electric age, in which the concentric pattern is imposed by the instant quality, and overlay in depth of electric speed. But the concentric with its endless intersection of planes is necessary for insight. In fact, it is the technique of insight.[12]

What is called the Archimedean screw is based on a spiral. Archimedes (287–212 B.C.) was the famous Greek mathematician and physicist who invented a spiral apparatus for carrying water to higher levels. It is said to have consisted of either a spiral tube around an inclined axis or an inclined tube containing a large broadly threaded screw. One has only to read any of the great mathematicians to see that they think in epigenetic harmonic-like transfer structures. Jacques Bernoulli (1654–1705), the Swiss mathematician, for example, was so enamored of the logarithmic spiral that like Archimedes, he had it inscribed on his tombstone. Indeed, much of mathematical thinking is in fact higher order transfer as we will now see.

As I cautioned in the opening of this chapter, before those who consider themselves not to be very good at math begin to panic, just because someone doesn't seem to possess high ability at mathematics, it doesn't necessarily mean that they won't be good at higher order transfer thinking.

## MATHEMATICAL STRUCTURE AND TRANSFER

German philosopher and historian Oswald Spengler (1880–1936) understood that transfer ability and mathematics were related, though independent. He believed that "a high mathematical endowment may without any mathematical science whatsoever, come to fruition and full self knowledge in technical spheres."[13] He believed that the primary cognitive operation that reflected mathematical structure was the ability to systematically use analogical reasoning. Indeed, mathematical structures and cognitive structures may simply be different forms of the same neurological process.

Piaget describes attending a conference outside Paris on mental and mathematical structures. The conference brought together psychologists and mathematicians. Present was the renowned mathematician Jean Alexandre Dieudonne, who represented the Bourbaki group of mathematicians. He was known for mistrusting anything that had to do with psychology. Dieudonne's talk described the three mother structures of mathematical thought. Piaget then gave his talk in which he described the structures that he had found in children's thinking. To the great astonishment of Piaget and Dieudonne, both saw that there was a direct relationship, a *similarity*, between these three mathematical structures and the three structures of children's operational thinking. Piaget said,

We were, of course, impressed with each other, and Dieudonne went so far as to say to me: "This is the first time that I have taken psychology seriously. It may also be the last, but at any rate it's the first."[14]

The point is that both men recognized the analogous structure between the three master structures of mathematical thought and the three basic stages of cognitive development in children's thinking. The significance of the parallel of mathematical development and cognitive development is that it can be seen as lending added support to the theory of transfer presented here.

On a very rudimentary level, every external application of mathematics rests on the analogical transfer between the particular mathematical operations and the physical fact to which it applies. In order for $1 + 1 = 2$ to be useful it must be put into correspondence or applied to something: apples, oranges, or trees. This is almost trivial. The important aspect involves the internal structure of mathematics. According to the noted French mathematician and physicist, Henri Poincaré (1854–1912),

> If mathematics had no other instrument, it would immediately be arrested in its development; but it has recourse anew to the same process—i.e., to *reasoning by recurrence* [italics added] . . . It is therefore mathematical reasoning par excellence.[15]

Reasoning by recurrence, of course, involves transfer because in order to see something as a recurrence of something, it must be recognized as the *same* thing.

In chapter 2 I suggested that to explain transfer is to repeat the *same* thing. However, that is not to say that it's *simply* repeating the *exact* same thing; rather it's repeating the *same thing* with its variations. In mathematics such repetition is called the *differentiation of an invariant* through its various mathematical forms. Sir Arthur Eddington (1882–1944), noted English astronomer and physicist at Cambridge University who also made major contributions to the study of evolution, believed that analogical transfer is similar to the mathematical process of a Hamiltonian differentiation of an invariant, named after its creator the Irish mathematician, William Hamilton (1805–1865).[16] This mathematical function has great generality and can be used to generate any number of equations, including the equations of motion for dynamic systems.

If I may speculate further, this differentiation of an invariant may be related to the research findings on teaching for transfer. This research shows that for transfer to occur, the original learning must be repeatedly reinforced with multiple examples or similar concepts in multiple contexts (differentiation?); and I would add, on different levels and orders of magnitude. Teaching for transfer, then, involves returning again and again to an idea or procedure but on different levels and in different contexts (see chapter 9), with what appears to be different examples. But from a transfer perspective, "different" examples are but variations on a single idea or concept.

French mathematician and physicist Jean Joseph Fourier (1768–1830) formulated a mathematical method for analyzing periodic functions of phenomena. Fourier analysis is an infinite series of numbers that involves the application of *constants*. What apparently characterizes Fourier mathematical logic is that its basic operations function on the basis of *identity, equality, inclusion*, and *association*, not on the basis of computational, on–off functions found in many computer programming languages, which are based on the work of George Boole (1815–1864), the renowned English mathematician (who was self-taught and did not hold any higher academic degree). Karl Pribram's research indicates that individual cells and ensembles of cells conform to certain harmonic and Fourier transforms. This harmonic analysis capacity of cellular functioning, as Pribram has pointed out, is *isomorphic* (i.e., analogous) to abstract transformation groups in mathematics. French mathematician Poincaré believed that the selective criterion of the mathematician has an aesthetic character in the sense that only *"harmonic combinations of ideas"* [Italics added] have the possibility of proving detailed mathematical analysis as valid mathematical truths.[17]

In an early study of perception entitled, "Functional Geometry and the Determination of Pattern in Mosaic Receptors," John Platt concludes with the quote that opens and presages the entire thesis of this chapter: "Much, if not all, of what we call intelligence may be the ability to perceive successive analogies at higher and higher levels of abstraction, a multiple repetition of a single basic neural process of organization."[18] It does appear that transfer ability and mathematical ability are integrally related on some fundamental neurological level.

## TRANSFER ABILITY

My relating transfer to mathematics should not discourage many who see themselves as not being good at higher mathematics (myself included). To reiterate, although analogical transfer ability, which is manifested mathematically in abstract proportional forms, is characteristic of all good mathematicians, those not skilled in higher mathematics may nevertheless be good at transfer. Again, although all those good at math are also good at transfer, all those good at transfer may not be good at math.

But, as it turns out, many who are good at transfer are also good at math. A *Journal of Educational Psychology* article found added support for past recognition of the relationship between transfer and math ability. The authors reported that the skills of students who were identified as superior at problem solving

> was most evident when they correctly categorized isomorphic problems that had the same structural features but differed in surface features. Differences in expertise therefore become evident in analogical transfer when experts show spontaneous positive transfer to problems that share only structural features, and notices show spontaneous negative transfer to problems that share only surface features. This analysis is also supported by the finding *that students who were majoring in mathematics did better than did the students in the introductory psychology course in correctly selecting isomorphic word problems as analogous problems* [italics added].[19]

This does not come as a surprise, however. We have known for some time that those who perform well on the Miller Analogies Test (MAT) tend to have higher mathematical ability as well as score higher on I.Q. tests than those who score low on the MAT.[20] As Aristotle suggested: "The greatest thing by far is to be a master of metaphor. It is the one thing that cannot be learned from others. It is the mark of genius."[21] We also know that the MAT predicts success in graduate studies (or it used to before grade inflation).

It has also been known for some time that those in different disciplines or professions score higher than others on the MAT. Unfortunately, education students tend to score on the low end of the MAT. Why this is the case I am not certain, but one explanation is that there are two basic metaphorical or transfer abilities, one content oriented and one very abstract. The latter would be more conducive to mathematical transfer. To put it in Howard Gardner's terms, multiple intelligence theory provides some ways for looking at the issue of metaphoric ability. He says that it may be the "particular hallmark of logical-mathematical intelligence" to be able to perceive patterns in the environment and thus individuals with this ability may be predisposed to see analogical and metaphoric relationships. Gardner says,

> Some modest support for this speculation comes from the fact that scores on the widely used Miller Analogies Test (MAT) correlate highly with other measures of logical power. It is also possible—in fact, highly likely—that the capacity to discern metaphors and analogies exists within particular domains. As I noted earlier, the capacity to contrive spatial images or metaphors has been of great usefulness to scientists who are trying to discover new relationships or to convey to a wider audience those relationships that they have uncovered.[22]

Moreover, he says, it is quite probable that those who become skilled at discovering relationships within their chosen areas can become good at transfer. Thus, he says that

> within the language domain, the poet will discern many analogies and metaphors across semantic categories, even as the painter, the architect, or the engineer may discover numerous metaphors and analogies within the particular symbol systems favored in their respective domains. Thus, at least within particular domains, individuals with well-honed skills may well be the prime candidates to become effective metaphorizers.[23]

In a wonderful little book entitled, *Poetry and Mathematics*,[24] Scott Buchanan suggests that the underlying structure of poetry and mathematics are very similar. Once again, we see that the basic structure of transfer is hardwired. It appears that mathematical transfer is a manifestation, *par excellence*, of our wiring for some kind of invariance transfer function.

I would like to conclude with a quote from the poet William Blake (1757–1827), who intuitively exemplified transfer thinking in the harmonic-like structure of his poem, *Songs of Innocence*.

See the world in a grain of sand
And heaven in a wild flower,
Hold infinity in the palm of your hand,
And eternity in an hour.[25]

Transfer thinking, then, is a kind of poetry, as well as a kind of mathematics. Although mathematicians think in abstract bare-bones structures and their equivalence transformations, poets think in voluptuous metaphorical flesh tones. To achieve expertise in transfer thinking, then, is to apprentice oneself to mathematicians and poets.

# Notes

[1]Platt, J. (1962). Functional geometry and the determination of pattern in mosaic receptors. *Yearbook of the Society for General Systems Research*, 7, 103–119, p. 115.

[2]McClearly, R., & Moore, R. Y. (1965). *Subcortical mechanisms of behavior.* New York: Basic Books.

[3]Mostofsky, D. (Ed.). (1965). *Stimulus generalization.* Palo Alto, CA: Stanford University Press.

[4]Humphreys, L. G. (1939). Generalization as a function of method of reinforcement. *Journal of Experimental Psychology*, 25, 361–372; see also Humphreys, L. G. (1951). Transfer of training in general education. *The Journal of General Education*, 5, 210–216.

[5]Blackwell, H. R., & Schlosberg, H. (1943). Octave generalization, pitch discrimination, and loudness thresholds in the white rat. *Journal of Experimental Psychology*, 33, 407–419.

[6]Thompson, R. F. (1965). The neural basis of stimulus generalization. In D. I. Mostofsky (Ed.), *Stimulus generalization* (pp. 178–155). Stanford, CA: Stanford University Press; Kalish, H. (1969). Alternative explanations. In M. H. Mark (Ed.), *Learning: Processes* (pp. 276–297). New York: Macmillan.

[7]Bharucha, J. J., & Menci, W. E. (1996). Two issues in auditory cognition: Self-organization of octave categories and pitch-invariant pattern recognition. *Psychological Science*, 7, 142–149, p. 142.

[8]Piaget, J. (1971). *Biology and knowledge: An essay on the relations between organic regulations and cognitive processes.* Chicago, IL: University of Chicago Press.

[9]Preus, A. (1970). The continuous analogy: The uses of continuous proportions in Plato and Aristotle. *Agora*, 1, 21–41.

[10]D'Arcy, T. (1968). *On growth and form.* Cambridge, UK: Cambridge University Press.

[11]D'Arcy, T. (1968). *On growth and form.* Cambridge, UK: Cambridge University Press, p. 757.

[12]McLuhan, M. (1964). *Understanding media.* London: Routledge & Kegan Paul, p. 26.

[13]Spengler, O. (1932). *Decline of the West.* (Volume I) New York: Knopf, p. 58.

[14]Piaget, J. (1970). *Genetic epistemology.* New York: W. W. Norton, p. 26.

[15]Poincaré, H. (1952). *Science and hypothesis.* New York: Dover, p. 9.

[16]In Korzybski, A. (1933). *Science and sanity: An introduction to non-Aristotelian systems and general semantics.* Lakefield, CT: International Non-Aristotelian library, p. 565.

[17]In Somenzi, V. (1981). Scientific discovery from the viewpoint of evolutionary epistemology. In M. D. Grmek, R. S. Cohen, & G. Cimino (Eds.), *On scientific discovery: The Erice lectures*, 1977 (pp. 167–177). London: D. Reidel Publishing Company, p. 172.

[18]Platt, J. (1962). Functional geometry and the determination of pattern in mosaic receptors. *Yearbook of the Society for General Systems Research*, 7, 103–119, p. 115.

[19]Reed, S. K., Willis, D., & Guarino, J. (1994). Selecting examples for solving word problems. *Journal of Educational Psychology*, 86(3), 380–388, p. 386.

[20]De Cato, C. M. (1982). Admissions criteria and later performance Graduate Record Exam, Miller's analogies, and GPA as predictors of professional competency. *Psychological Reports*, 51, 1149–1150.

[21]Cooper, L. (1960). *The rhetoric of Aristotle.* New York: Appleton-Century-Crofts, p. 101.

[22]Gardner, H. (1983). *Frames of mind: The theory of multiple intelligences.* New York: Basic Books, p. 290.
[23]Ibid, p. 290.
[24]Buchanan, S. (1929). *Poetry and mathematics.* New York: John Day.
[25]Blake, W. (1991). *Songs of innocence and experience.* Princeton, NJ: William Blake Trust/Princeton University Press.

# Deep-Context Teaching
# for Transfer

*Indeed, few of those who now loudly proclaim that cognition and learning are context-bound have followed the implications of this assertion through to its inevitable conclusion.*

—DAVID LOHMAN, *"Encouraging The Development of Fluid Abilities in Gifted Students"*[1]

The research on transfer and on education that I have presented in this book, along with my experience teaching, have forced me to no longer do "business as usual" in the classroom. Indeed this research and my experience has led to a paradigm shift in my educational philosophy and practice. For lack of a better term, I call this shift deep-context teaching. In brief, deep-context teaching involves addressing the conditions surrounding a subject matter, in general, and students' expectations, beliefs, and values relating to learning, in specific. These deep contexts function as "filters" through which students "hear" and evaluate information. Deep-context teaching is directly related to motivating and readying students for deep learning (see chapter 7). Though this concept may have a familiar ring to it, the sound of deep-context teaching is played in a different key and is arranged differently from the concept of context as typically discussed in the literature. Certainly, as teachers, we include a certain amount of contextual and motivational issues in our teaching. Deep-context teaching, however, is more programmatic, deep, and far-reaching.

One of the most pervading themes throughout this book has been the importance and effects of context on transfer, beginning with the long established fact that learning is all too often welded to the context or situation in which it is learned (see chapter 1) and that transfer is conditional upon culture and other contexts surrounding it (see chapter 8). The importance of context on learning, then, is certainly not novel. Nor is the term *deep* scarce in the educational literature. We frequently find the phrases *deep processing*, and *deep learning*.[2] In contrast, we seldom find the phrases *deep context*, or more infrequently, *deep instruction*. Unwrapping and integrating these latter two concepts leads to deep-context teaching.

Once again, in explaining and applying this concept, I will be doing so from the educational context I know best: the college classroom, more specifically the first-year introductory psychology classroom. This educational context is not all that different, however, from the later years of high school and from other adult educational contexts. The difference is one of degree, not a qualitative one. Deep-context teaching, then, refers to addressing the counterproductive erroneous (a) knowledge, (b) beliefs, (c) expectations, (d) values, and (e) assumed implications, (f) about a subject matter, or (g) about learning; these are directed at changing (h) awareness, (i) motivation levels, and (j) students' reception of instructional material, whether written or verbal. If these contexts are not addressed, learning may, at best, be shallow and not lead to significant transfer. In addition, there is an important aspect of deep-context teaching that pertains to teachers. Let's look at deep context a little more closely.

## DEEP-CONTEXT SUBJECT MATTER

I first began thinking about deep context years ago when it became clear to me that something was interfering with students' learning and understanding (presuming that they studied the material). It took me a while by listening carefully to students' questions and by seeing how they incorrectly answered test questions despite my having spent considerable time on the test material. It finally dawned on me that students were coming into my psychology courses with all manner of erroneous pop-culture beliefs about psychology (see chapter 9) propagated by the mass media. They wouldn't often volunteer these beliefs, however, so I had to ferret them out. I found that I had to address these erroneous notions that students had in their heads about psychology before I could teach, and before they could learn scientific psychology.

Then I came across the research in science teaching showing that the erroneous theories that students come into the science classroom with block their understanding of science concepts. Studies have consistently demonstrated that naive or beginning physics and biology students hold fundamentally erroneous theories about these subjects that interfere with their learning and transfer (see chapter 9).[3] This is the essence of what is termed *negative transfer*. The everyday theories students possess act like the antibodies in the immune system, which function to neutralize and eject foreign material. Deep-context teaching thus involves ferreting out and teaching to this deep context. On the basis of these two realizations, it became clear that there were other deep-context issues that I had to confront in order for me to teach effectively, and for students to learn (effective teaching doesn't necessarily result in student learning).

Whether discussion or lecture, teaching remains largely centered on the subject matter, with an eye to contexts of its application. This is the traditional approach that most of us inherited from a different time and place, a time and place where college students came to the classroom (a) with a different educational background, and (b) with different contexts in their heads. Comparatively speaking, prior to the middle 1960s, students came into the high school and college classroom with their minds a *tabula rasa*. Since then— in many ways—the generations of students raised on TV come into the classroom with much more contextual awareness than the generations prior to the middle 1960s.

Today's student is much more aware of political, ideological, and other pop culture issues (however distorted). In addition, prior to the middle 1960s teachers—and especially college professors—were seen as "objective" sources of information. The subsequent TV generations "know better." The TV and postmodern student is acutely aware of identity politics, gender issues, and of the situated nature of knowledge—though they may not know these labels. Yet, most of us still teach in a relatively traditional mode as if their minds were a blank slate; as if these deep contexts didn't exist. The lecture/discussion mode directed almost exclusively at the subject matter is still the predominant method of teaching, at least in the college classroom. Yes, questions and discussion in class may automatically address some of this deep context, but, by and large, even discussion of an issue leaves most deep context untouched (see below).

Let me offer an initial paradigmatic example of the distorting filtering effects of deep context, expectations, and values that students often bring into the classroom. On several occasions I have asked students to complete a voluntary and anonymous questionnaire. I pass this out prior to any lectures and typically to first-year students who have not had much opportunity to inquire of other students about me. The final two True/False questions I ask are (1) Your instructor is probably a Republican, and (2) Your instructor is probably pro-life on the issue of abortion. I do explain to them that I know they don't have any information about me, but to make a choice, anyway. Many students—sometimes a majority—answer true to both these questions; others answer true to one of them and false to the other (in fact, both are false). Without the benefit of specific information about me, students are, of course, left with reasoning on the basis of their deep-context beliefs about what I represent as (a) a tweed sport coat-wearing, (b) older male. The point is, unless I address this deep context, it will influence or filter the instructional material that I present in class.

One other example. Often what the students assume is implied in what is said can function as deep context. Sometimes students are not directly aware of these assumed implications; sometimes they are. I was talking about the decrease of American students majoring in hard subject areas such as physics, math, and engineering and the increase in these areas of international students, especially Asians and East Indians. I started to transition to another topic when a student raised her hand and said, "I don't think this is because they are more intelligent than we are!" The student assumed that this was an implication of what I had said. It wasn't, of course. In any case, somewhere as deep context, she either had heard the idea before or had somehow (erroneously) deduced that this was the implication of what I had been saying. In teaching today I have found few other issues involving such deep-context teaching implications as race and gender. Deep erroneous implications of a subject, then, may function as deep-context interference with learning and transfer. These make excellent models of understanding deep contexts.

Though I can't address every possible implication of what may function as deep context, one can be aware and directly address some of the more "pop" notions of a subject that students may have in their heads. Deep erroneous implications of a subject, then, may function as deep-context interfering with learning and transfer. If instructors don't know what's in students' heads, they are not providing the contextual conditions necessary for them to effectively learn. I should note, too, that students may be only peripherally aware of the deep contexts that are operating in the background; for other deep-context material they are only too aware.

## POP CULTURE AS DEEP CONTEXT

In chapter 8 I presented some of the research showing that cultural and other specifically situated contexts differentially impact learning and transfer. The research on cultural influences on learning mostly addresses the different ways cultures conceptualize phenomena that may interfere with learning. But I am not just talking about different cultural understandings of phenomena, I am talking about cultural norms and beliefs that interfere with deep learning; indeed, I am talking about a pervasive contextual atmosphere of counter-learning. In chapter 8 I mentioned the long recognized norms in the United States of an (a) anti-intellectual cultural climate, and (b) an overly "pragmatic" or instrumental approach to learning; to these I now add (c) certain religious beliefs.

It's no secret that the U.S. culture is at the very least ambivalent about deep learning and thinking. In our current pop culture, to call someone an "intellectual" is meant as an insult. Then, of course, we have other insulting terms for people who learn and think: We call them eggheads, nerds, geeks, etc., who are out of contact with the "real" world. Tell Microsoft's billionaire-geek, Bill Gates, that he is not in contact with the "real" world. We glorify sports and entertainment figures, but not people who think. Oh, we throw around Einstein's name every now and then, but even these references are short-lived because they are (rightly) seen as so anomalous and unreachable that they are not meaningful to the average person. Our culture also discourages deep learning and thinking by defining "useful" as that which can immediately be used (recall in chapter 6, the section entitled, "The Usefulness of Useless Knowledge"). These cultural antilearning contexts aren't lost on students; they hear, see, and incorporate them only too readily.

Moreover, students come into our classrooms with certain religious beliefs that interfere with learning and transfer. For example, in terms of holding a Christian belief in the literal biblical account of Genesis and Creationism, how is it possible for a teacher to teach, and for a student to engage in deep learning, about Darwinian evolution? The answer is, that though it may be possible, it's highly unlikely for most people. Galileo (1564–1642) and others have apparently been able to separate their religious beliefs and their science. And in terms of the so-called New Age spiritual beliefs which many students have in their heads, believing that crystals under their pillow will cure their illness, how is it possible to teach scientific concepts and principles about physical health and the findings of scientific psychology? Again, it's possible, but unlikely.

Without at least addressing these deep contexts, any learning that may occur will be superficial and nonmeaningful. The learning that does occur will be either by rote, or be so similar to sheer rote learning we won't be able to tell the difference. As a result, it will not be integrated into the students' knowledge base and cognitive apparatus and thus will not transfer very far. Without addressing these cultural deep contexts, we are, in effect, reducing education to a form of training where the learning is merely "tacked on" to the student, and is, at best, tucked away in some restricted mental module and rarely seen again.

## INDIVIDUAL EXPECTATIONS AS DEEP CONTEXT

In addition to cultural norms, there are other deep-context expectations about learning that students carry around in their heads that inhibit learning. Somewhat arbitrarily, I have separated cultural norms and individual expectation about learning. Strictly speaking, these expectations also come from culture and they get massively reinforced every day. Another reason for addressing deep-context expectations is that thwarted expectations lead to negative reactions. So we must head them off at the pass, so to speak.

Many students expect that if they are majoring in, say, physical therapy, that they shouldn't have to suffer through a lot of courses like history or psychology. So, implicit in many classrooms are students silently asking themselves, "Why do I have to learn this stuff?" Deep-context teaching suggests that we have to answer this unasked (sometime even asked) question. We have to show students that deep learning takes discipline and lots of hard practice (see chapter 10). Another expectation among many students is a sense of entitlement that learning should be easy and instant, like a video game. It isn't, of course.

There are other deep-context issues, but this Coda is not the place to detail them. However, there is one that I must note. Students often expect that the information and views that they hear in classes are "just your opinion." Students are bombarded with multiple views of issues and ideas on TV. Many have no notion of how to evaluate what they are hearing. For example, students sometimes say to me that Professor X disagrees with what I might be saying about a psychological issue. As it turns our Professor X is from the humanities department. In other words, students often don't know or appreciate the difference between what their English teacher says about human behavior and what biologists and psychologists may say.

This deep-context expectation about assessing information (i.e., belief) has to be addressed. I typically speak to this issue in my introductory material on scientific methods, pointing out the difference between literature, philosophy, and science. Certainly I wouldn't presume to tell students something contrary to Professor X's analysis of Lawrence Durrell's novels from his Alexandria Quartet (though it's one of my favorite pieces of literature).

There are other deep-context issues and conditions that impinge upon learning in the classroom that teachers can't do very much about. These contexts include the effects of TV on attention span, personal problems, having to work (perhaps full-time) while taking classes, squeezing in night classes until nine or ten o'clock. Then there are still others like the campus culture and the antilearning dorm life that we may possibly have some minimal influence on.

Deep context is crucially important because it filters how students encode the information they receive, which in turn influences how they are able to store it, retrieve it, and apply it; all of which influences transfer (see chapter 7). If information is inappropriately filtered, it doesn't lead to the encoding of a valid knowledge base. And as we have seen (chapter 6), without a valid knowledge base valid transfer is not possible.

## DEEP CONTEXT AS DEFAULT POSITION

I mentioned in chapter 1 that when students are given different forms of the *same* question on an exam that has been constantly reinforced with multiple examples throughout the entire course, they frequently fail to transfer their knowledge to virtually identical questions. From a transfer perspective, this is not surprising, as we have known for some time that learning tends to be welded to a particular context. Now, just as new learning is welded to a context, deep contexts—or old learning—tends to operate as a default position when thinking and reasoning and when answering test questions if the new learning hasn't been encoded (read: learned) appropriately. From pilot research in my classes, it seems that (a) when new learning about psychology contradicts deep-context pop psychology, questions are answered from the default position of pop psychology knowledge; and (b) when new learning about psychology is not encoded appropriately, the default position is used to answer virtually identical questions in which either the wording has been changed slightly, or for transfer questions where the subject or content has been changed. Here's an example.

When I teach about the various problems with sampling procedures used in research, I use particular examples to illustrate these problems. If this knowledge about sampling problems is learned, questions that are based on these particular examples will tend to be answered correctly. But when "transfer" questions about sampling use other examples, especially from pop psychology, the questions tend to be answered from student's deep-context pop psychology default position. In other words, new learning *is to* being welded to a particular context as old learning *is to* being a default position.

## APPLYING DEEP-CONTEXT TEACHING

The degree to which deep context needs to be addressed, and how it is to be applied, depends on a number of factors. One obvious factor is the grade level of the student. A second is the individual level of awareness and motivation for learning. Although I first began to recognize the need for deep-context teaching in the context of increasingly inadequately prepared students, these are not the only students who benefit. Even many students who seem to be motivated and who exhibit a high ability for learning the subject material can benefit as well. I have found that these two kinds of students, however, benefit differentially. For the underprepared student, the benefit of deep-context teaching is largely an increase in motivation and readiness to learn, whereas for the higher-ability student the increase seems to be the integration and transfer of the learning.

A third factor is the degree to which deep context needs to be addressed. A fourth is how it is to be addressed in a specific subject matter. For example, there probably are not as many interfering pop cultural influences in the mathematics classroom or in courses specifically designed for a professional major as there are in general education courses, or in learning psychology. Thus, to what degree and how deep-context teaching is applied is variable.

I mentioned above that in student questions and discussion, either as part of a lecture format or as a student-centered discussion, some deep context will automatically be addressed. Some of the more important deep context won't, however, for three reasons. First, students may not be entirely conscious of their deep context. Second, they may not be aware of its pertinence to the subject. The third and most problematic reason has to do with student norms against examining deep context. The findings of a recent study comes as no surprise to many of us.[4] A survey of 200 students found (a) that many felt they had a right not to have their views challenged in class, (b) 84% of first-year students chose the statement "It is important for the college community to make sure all of its members feel comfortable" over the statement "People have to learn to deal with being uncomfortable," and (c) only 5 of 200 students indicated that they would talk about multicultural issues because they thought it might open their minds.[5] So even in a teaching environment of student-centered discussion, or a values clarification approach where some of this deep context is directly examined, some deep context may be largely unreachable.

I recently reorganized a large part of my social psychology course around the issue of ethnic prejudice where I integrated many concepts not typically discussed in the text as specifically related to prejudice. Many in the class were older nontraditional students who lived off campus, so the fear of having to deal with any possible "fallout" of the discussion was not a large factor. In addition, the class had no ethnic minorities in it, so this aspect of potential conflict was not a fear. Moreover, because the majority of the class was female, I made a concerted effort to draw parallels between racism and sexism. I have been teaching for many years and I am well acquainted with how to foster discussion. This class was the worst class I ever experienced. I simply could not get them to discuss this topic. I recall, too, a research-based class on hypnosis where an older student informed me that this was the "work of the devil," and walked out.

There is a downside to deep-context teaching: It has a price. The price is that the time spent dealing with deep contexts reduces the traditional time committed to directly teaching the subject matter itself. So teachers must make a decision about whether the priority is effectively teaching to all students in a class, or to reduce the amount of deep-context teaching by directing it to only a certain proportion of students. This downside has obvious implications for setting and maintaining a given academic standard in a subject area. This decision is, of course, either a personal or an institutional one.

Two final points. First, because deep-context teaching typically involves countering various contexts, in effect, it can be seen as counter-context teaching. Second, as we have seen, deep-context teaching often requires being in conflict with prevailing student, institutional, and cultural norms and values. But what choice do we have if we are to still call what we do in the classroom "education," as opposed to "training," and if our goal is transfer?

# CONCLUSION

There is a "kicker" involved in deep-context teaching that I haven't yet mentioned. The kicker is us teachers. To one degree or another, many of us are afflicted with the same erroneous knowledge base, expectations, and cultural values that impact upon subject matter and learning. We are a part of, and subject to, many of the same forces that impact our students. Thus, trying to change the deep context of teaching and learning is somewhat like trying to build a boat in midocean. Somehow we need to create a dry dock in this ocean of countercontexts. The problem is that many of the educational institutions, as well as the culture at large, mitigate against change. We need to deal with this context on both a personal and a professional level.

Finally, I often make the following analogy from my experience conducting T-groups: In order for a group to be productive, leaders often have to "unfreeze" the group. What this means is forcing some conflict and awareness of problems and issues that the group doesn't want to deal with. Like unfreezing a group, deep-context teaching is unfreezing students' minds. All of these deep contexts tend to create a certain state of mind in students. Our job as deep-context teachers is to drive students *out of their minds*.

## Notes

[1]Lohman, D. F. (1992). Encouraging the development of fluid abilities in gifted students. In N. Colangelo, S. G. Assouline, & D. L. Ambrosen (Eds.). *Talent development: Proceedings from the 1991 Henry B. and Jocelyn Wallace National Research Symposium on talent development* (pp. 143–162). New York: Trillium Press, p. 154.

[2]See, for example, McKeachie, W. J. (1987). The new look in instructional psychology: Teaching strategies for learning and thinking. In E. De Corte, H. Lodewijks, R. Parmentier, & P. Span (Eds.), *Learning and instruction* (vol. I, pp. 443–456). Oxford: Pergamon Press, p. 447; Mittelholtz, D. J. (1988). *The effects of essay tests on long-term retention of course material*. Unpublished doctoral dissertation, Educational Psychology, University of Iowa, Ames.

[3]See Galili, I., & Kaplan, D. (1996). Students' operations with the weight concept. *Science Education*, 80(4), 457–487; Howe, A. C. (1996). Development of science concepts within a Vygotskian framework. *Science Education*, 80(1), 35–51; Wittrock, M. C. (1985). Learning science by generating new conceptions from old ideas. In L. H. T. West & A. L. Pines (Eds.), *Cognitive structure and conceptual change* (pp. 259–266). New York: Academic Press; Wollman, W. (1984). Models and procedures: Teaching for transfer of pendulum knowledge. *Journal of Research in Science Teaching*, 21(4), 399–415; Sutton, C. (1993). Figuring out a scientific understanding. *Journal of Research in Science Teaching*, 30, 1215–1227.

[4]Trosset, C. (1998). Obstacles to open discussion and critical thinking. *Change*, September/October, 44–49.

[5]Ibid, p. 49.

# Index